Tina Modotti

Tina Modotti

IMAGE, TEXTURE, PHOTOGRAPHY

Andrea Noble

University of New Mexico Press

Albuquerque

Library of Congress Cataloging-in-Publication Data:

Noble, Andrea
    Tina Modotti: image, texture, photography/Andrea Noble—1st ed.

    p.   cm.
    Includes bibliographical references and index.
ISBN 0-8263-2254-9 (cloth)
    1. Photographic criticism.   2. Photography, Artistic.   3. Modotti, Tina,
1896–1942—Criticism and interpretation.   4. Feminist criticism.
I. Title: Image, texture, photography. II. Title.
TR187   .N63 2000   770.92—dc21
                                                    00-009607

For my mother, Joyce, and my grandmother, Phyllis

Contents

List of Illustrations

Acknowledgments

This book began as my doctoral dissertation, which was researched and written in the main during a busy period of my life when I started my first academic post at the University of Aberdeen and my daughter was born. My acknowledgments are therefore not wholly academic, for I owe a debt also to a number of people who supported me in the daily balancing of the personal and the professional. Special thanks first off to my colleague and friend Alex Hughes for her stimulating criticism and insightful comments throughout all stages of the writing of the book. I am also immensely grateful to Ian Macdonald not only for reading and commenting on drafts of the manuscript but also for his exceptional democracy and warm generosity. I am grateful to the students in my Modotti course at Aberdeen, whose enthusiasm and inquisitiveness got me thinking in all sorts of different ways. Thanks to two special friends from the Aberdeen years, Meg Bateman and Liz Weir, whose support and friendship saw me through. I thank Paul Julian Smith for his commitment to and enthusiastic support for this project, Dawn Ades and Nick Griffiths for their challenging comments and suggestions, Julia Biggane for reading and commenting on the manuscript, and Maurice Biriotti for help in the early days. Thanks also to Anne R. Gibbons for her meticulous copyediting and to Dana Asbury at University of New Mexico Press. Finally, as always, extra special thanks to Lalo and Alma who share in the ongoing juggling act and who gave me the opportunity to disappear at crucial moments.

I am grateful for financial assistance from the University of Birmingham Faculty of Arts Postgraduate Scholarship, the Carnegie Trust for a travel award that allowed me to carry out research at the University of Texas, Austin, and the University of Aberdeen Faculty of Arts for a semester's research leave that made finishing this project possible.

Introduction

Photographs, which package the world, seem to invite packaging.
Susan Sontag, *On Photography*

Donation

A 1993 article in the British edition of *Vogue* magazine tells the story of how the Museum of Modern Art in New York came to be in receipt of a series of prints by the Italian American photographer Tina Modotti: "In the early fifties . . . a man appeared at the front desk, put a large brown paper parcel on it, declared that he wished to give this 'anonymous gift' to the institution—and rushed out of the building." The brown paper parcel that envelops the photographic prints raises a number of intriguing questions. Why was the donation made in the 1950s? Why was it made at this particular historical juncture? Why was it anonymous? What exactly did the prints represent? Who was the donor? What happened to the prints once entrusted to the safe-keeping of the museum? Besides some of these more pragmatic questions, which are concerned with the circumstances and consequences of the donation itself, the image is also shot through with metaphorical resonances. The brown paper parcel conjures up an image of concealment, containment, and mystery.

This image is a critical metaphor in my study, which aims to "unwrap" a number of Modotti's photographic prints and to offer readings of them. Reading, however, is always a form of re-wrapping, and in this case the critical methodologies that enfold the study are specifically theories of feminism and visual culture that rose to prominence in the late twentieth century. In the introduction to a special issue of the journal *Differences*, the feminist art historian Griselda Pollock offers a useful suggestion of what "reading" visual culture might involve:

> Despite being concerned with the visual arts, . . . the discipline of art history can never be exclusively defined by visuality. The making of art objects, monuments, buildings, sculptures, prints, and all the range of materials which are the topic of art histories involves a complex of historical, institutional, sociological, economic, as well as aesthetic factors. Feminists working in and

against this field need to deal as much with issues of training, patronage, access to exhibiting facilities, languages of art criticism, and mechanisms of the market, as with the semiotic and ideological productivity of the "image" itself.[2]

Arguably one of the leading international feminist art historians, Griselda Pollock's work has been extremely influential in my own development as a "reader" of visual culture. Taking my cue from Pollock then, I adopt her notion of the "productivity of the image," combined with the more broadly institutional factors that surround it, as a working definition for the project of photographic reading on which I am embarked. My own readings involve taking selected photographs through a series of theoretical and cultural contexts in order to explore how the prints might be seen to signify specifically as photographic images. Despite the growing body of work on Modotti, this kind of detailed contextual analysis of the photographic images she produced still remains to be done. However, before it is possible to make such readings, a number of important issues need to be worked through. As a starting point, therefore, I return to my opening metaphor, to focus on one particular feature of this image: the packaging itself that envelops the prints. I am interested in the packaging because, in contradistinction to the aura of secrecy and mystery surrounding the donation, it also symbolically suggests that from the outset Modotti comes to us prepackaged. And to come prepackaged implies that the product contained within the packaging is already known to the consumer. Now, to a certain extent, we *do* know a considerable amount about one particular aspect pertaining to the product in the package, namely Modotti's biography. Since the anonymous donation of the photographic prints in the 1950s, Modotti's life has been the subject of considerable critical attention.

There is no shortage of material that, in one form or another, purports to document Modotti's life.[3] The following biographies all appeared within ten years of one another: Mildred Constantine's *Tina Modotti: A Fragile Life* (originally published in 1983 but reissued and revamped in 1993 by Bloomsbury to coincide with Hooks's biography, which appeared the same year); Christiane Barckhausen-Canale's *Verdad y Leyenda de Tina Modotti* (1992); Pino Cacucci's *Tina Modotti* (1992); Margaret Hooks's *Tina Modotti: Photographer and Revolutionary* (1993); and Patricia Albers's *Shadows, Fire, Snow: The Life of Tina*

Modotti (1999). All these texts, with varying degrees of success, seek to chart Modotti's life (and loves). In addition to these conventional "factual" biographical accounts, Modotti's life has been the subject of Elena Poniatowska's best-selling novel *Tinísima* (1992); a play, *Tina Modotti* (1986), by the Mexican Víctor Hugo Rascón; and an award-winning series of poems by the North American Margaret Gibson entitled *Memories of the Future: The Daybooks of Tina Modotti* (1986). Modotti's letters to Edward Weston were also collected together from Weston's papers and published in 1986 in English by Amy Stark, and in 1992 in Spanish by Antonio Saborit. There have also been a number of exhibitions of Modotti's work, accompanied by catalogs. Most notable among these was the 1982 Whitechapel exhibition in London curated by Laura Mulvey and Peter Wollen. In 1995 the Philadelphia Museum of Modern Art hosted a major retrospective of Modotti's work, guest-curated by Sarah M. Lowe. Both exhibition catalogs in different ways focused quite overtly on biographical details. What is the allure of Modotti's life for those scholars of a biographical bent?

Biography

Assunta Adelaide Liugia (Tina) Modotti was born on 16 August 1896 into a working-class, socialist family in Udine, Italy.[4] In 1898 the entire family immigrated to Austria where Modotti's father, Giuseppe, found work in a bicycle factory. The family returned to Italy in 1905, the same year in which Giuseppe immigrated to the United States, joining his brother in Pennsylvania before proceeding to San Francisco where the whole family was eventually to settle. Tina Modotti remained in Italy with her mother, Assunta, and her siblings, until gradually, the family was reunited with the father in California. In 1913 Modotti joined her father and her sister Mercedes, who had moved to the United States two years earlier. On arrival, she worked as a seamstress and doll maker; she was also active in amateur dramatics within San Francisco's Italian community.

It is believed Modotti met the painter and poet Roubaix de l'Abrie Richey (known as "Robo") in 1915 at the Pan Pacific International Exposition and married him in 1917. A romantic and bohemian figure, born Ruby Richey in Oregon to a pioneer family, Richey embellished his French Canadian heritage (his maternal grandfather was French Canadian), reinventing himself as the exotic-sounding Roubaix de l'Abrie Richey. The couple moved to Los Angeles, where Modotti found work as an actress in silent movies in Hollywood.[5] In 1920 Modotti starred in the film *The Tiger's Coat*, then had supporting roles in *Riding with Death* (1920) and *I Can Explain* (1922). It is at this time that Modotti met and began an affair with the North American photographer Edward Weston (1886–1958), who was to become a formative influence in her life. Weston was a frequent visitor to de l'Abrie Richey's studio, which had become a gathering point for a bohemian circle of artists and writers. A number of Mexicans formed part of the gatherings at the studio. Among them figured the poet and translator Ricardo Gómez Robelo, who was soon to be called out of exile and summoned back to Mexico by José Vasconcelos, a key figure in the revolutionary government, with the promise of a post in the Public Education Ministry. At the invitation of Gómez Robelo, Robo traveled to Mexico in 1921, sending letters back to Modotti that enthused about the cultural renaissance taking place in Mexico in the aftermath of the 1910–20 revolution. Modotti began planning a trip to join Robo in Mexico, possibly in the company of Weston. However, her journey was precipitated by the news of the sudden illness of Robo, who died while Modotti was on her way to join him in 1922. A year later Modotti and Weston traveled to Mexico City, together with Weston's son Chandler, and they set up a studio there.

While in Mexico, Modotti took up photography. She and Weston agreed on some kind of informal "contract," whereby he would teach her photography in exchange for her running the household and acting as an interpreter. Mexico was also the place where she became involved in radical politics and where she struggled to reconcile her photography with her politics. As she explains in a letter to Weston, "I cannot—as you once proposed to me 'solve the problem of life by losing myself in the problem of art'—Not only I cannot do that but I even feel that the problem of life hinders my problem of art." Weston viewed the apprenticeship as something that offered Modotti the possibility of increased autonomy. He notes in his *Daybooks*, "she wants to learn photography and is doing well. She has no wish to return to the stage and photography would make her to some extent independent."[6]

Both Modotti and Weston soon became established in Mexico, socializing and working alongside members of the Mexican cultural elite, including such key figures in the cultural renaissance as the muralists Diego Rivera, José Clemente Orozco, and David Alfaro Siqueiros; the government minister for public education José Vasconcelos; the painters Gerardo Murillo (known as Dr. Atl), Jean Charlot, Roberto Montenegro, Nahui Olín, Miguel and Rosa Covarrubias, and possibly for a brief time Frida Kahlo. Over the next two years, Modotti and Weston undertook a number of key collaborative projects. In 1924 they both exhibited prints at a group show at the Palacio de Minería in Mexico City. In 1925, at the state museum in Guadalajara, they held their first joint exhibition, which was favorably reviewed by Siqueiros, and a number of their prints were purchased for the Jalisco state museum. They also worked with the North American Anita Brenner, who was compiling a book on Mexican arts and crafts entitled *Idols behind Altars*. Commissioned to provide photographic illustrations for the project, they traveled extensively in Mexico with Weston's other son Brett, taking more than four hundred photographs. The *Idols behind Altars* project has become the subject of intense debate as critics vie to establish the authorship of the series of prints that Weston, Modotti, and even Brett Weston made during their travels. If we are to believe Weston, Modotti went along simply as an assistant: "As I review our travel and adventure from the vantage ground of my comfortable desk I think this: that if a woman had not been in our party, especially Tina, with her tact and sympathy for the Indians, a woman which made the group seem less aggressive, Brett and I would never have finished the work."[7]

Whoever was ultimately responsible for the bulk of photographic prints generated by the project, Modotti and Weston had started to receive positive reviews from influential critics. In 1926 Diego Rivera wrote an exuberant review of the photography of Modotti and Weston for the magazine *Mexican Folkways*:

> Edward Weston realiza ya EL ARTISTA DE AMERICA; es decir aquel cuya sensibilidad contiene la modernidad extrema de la PLASTICA DEL NORTE y la VIVIENTE TRADICION NACIDA EN LA TIERRA DEL SUR. Tina Modotti, la discípula, ha hecho maravillas de sensibilidad en un plano quizá más abstracto, más aéreo, tal vez más intelectual, como era natural para un temperamento italiano, cuyo trabajo florece perfectamente en México y se acuerda justamente con nuestra pasión.
>
> [Edward Weston is THE AMERICAN ARTIST; that is to say, one whose sensibility contains the extreme modernity of

the PLASTICITY OF THE NORTH AND THE LIVING TRA-
DITION OF THE LAND OF THE SOUTH. Tina Modotti, his
pupil, has done marvels in sensibility on a plane, perhaps, more
abstract, more aerial, even more intellectual, as is natural for an
Italian temperament. Her work flowers perfectly in Mexico
and harmonizes exactly with our passion.][8]

Both photographers were also involved at this time in separate projects. Modotti had begun to photograph the frescoes of Rivera and
Siqueiros and to publish photographs in the journal *Mexican Folkways*,
while Weston was busy evolving into a mythical artist figure and pho-
tographing his famous series of nudes of Modotti, his muse and model.

Although Modotti and Weston were involved in a sexual relationship on their arrival in Mexico in 1923, it broke down during their
stay, and both took other lovers while continuing to live and work
together. The relationship came to an end in 1926 when Weston
returned to California, while Modotti stayed on in Mexico. They
were to correspond, however, until 1931.

In 1927 Modotti made a firm commitment to politics and became
a member of the Partido Comunista Mexicano. Modotti's biographers
tend to assert that her political awareness developed at an early age,
during her childhood in Italy and Austria. Given that a number of her
siblings also became politically active as adults, this conjecture about
their upbringing seems plausible. Sarah M. Lowe cites Modotti's
experience as a factory worker in both Europe and the United States
as the determining factor in her later political activity. She also men-
tions that de l'Abrie Richey was possibly an anarchist and certainly
contributed satirical political cartoons to the left-wing magazine
Gale's. Whatever the roots of Modotti's activism, it became increasingly defined during her stay in Mexico as she involved herself in campaigns such as "Manos Fuera de Nicaragua" and the committee in
support of the Italians Sacco and Vanzetti. Her photographs started to
appear in international political journals, magazines, and newspapers,
including the paper of the Partido Comunista Mexicano, *El Machete*.[9]

It would be wrong to overlook the fact that Modotti's choice of
partners (with the exception of Edward Weston) was influenced by
her political beliefs. After Weston's departure, Modotti began an affair
with the artist and political activist Xavier Guerrero, whom she had
met in the United States in 1922 while he was on a trip to promote an

exhibition of Mexican art. In the same year, Guerrero was sent to the Soviet Union, where he received a letter from Modotti breaking off the relationship. Through her collaboration on *El Machete*, she had met and begun an affair with the Cuban political activist Julio Antonio Mella. For many of Modotti's biographers, 1929 marks a key moment in Modotti's life, for it was in this year that she witnessed Mella's assassination at the supposed hands of the Cuban government.[10] This event was followed by fierce and defamatory press coverage of Modotti within Mexico and beyond.

But 1929 not only was a significant year in terms of her personal life but also marked an important point in Modotti's professional career. First, she embarked on what was to become her final photographic project in Mexico, in the late summer of that year. She traveled to the Isthmus of Tehuantepec, where she made a series of photographs of the women and children of the region. Then, in December, she held her first solo photographic exhibition at the Universidad Autónoma in Mexico City. Billed as "La primera exposición fotográfica revolucionaria de México," it was preceded by lectures on her photography presented by the critic Baltasar Dromundo and the muralist David Alfaro Siqueiros. The exhibition coincided with the publication of the only article on photography Modotti ever wrote. In it she articulates her belief in the social value of photography:

> La fotografía, por el hecho mismo de que sólo puede ser producida en el presente y basándose en lo que existe objetivamente frente a la cámara, se impone como el medio más satisfactorio de registrar la vida objetiva en todas sus manifestaciones, de allí su valor documental, y si a esto se añade sensibilidad y comprensión de asunto, y sobre todo, una clara orientación del lugar que debe tomar en el campo del desenvolvimiento histórico, creo que el resultado es algo digno de ocupar un puesto en la producción social a la cual todos debemos contribuir.
>
> [Photography, precisely because it can only be produced in the present and because it is based on what exists objectively before the camera, takes its place as the most satisfactory medium for registering objective life in all its aspects, and from this comes its documental value. If to this is added sensibility and understanding and, above all, a clear orientation as to the place it should have in the field of historical development, I believe

that the result is something worthy of a place in social production, to which we should all contribute.][11]

By 1929 Modotti had indeed achieved that "certain degree of independence" that Weston had predicted. A testimony to her success is the fact that she was offered the position of official photographer of the Museo Nacional in Mexico City. However, she turned the post down. As she explains in a letter to Weston: "Many have criticized me for the refusal but both as a member of the party and as companion to [Julio Antonio] Mella it would have been impossible, the government here did nothing absolutely to bring about justice, when they had all the opportunity in the world, they had the most responsible one of the guilty in their hands and they let him go free."[12]

Despite the respect that she clearly commanded in cultural circles, Modotti's radical political activities had become increasingly threatening to the Mexican government. Following an assassination attempt against the newly elected president Pascual Ortiz Rubio in 1930, she was falsely accused of participation and deported from Mexico under Article 33 of the Mexican constitution, which provided grounds for expelling "pernicious foreigners."[13] She was deported aboard the *Edam*. Bound ultimately for Europe, the ship was also carrying a fellow Italian passenger and political activist, Vitorrio Vidali, who was later to become Modotti's lover. This partnership has attracted a considerable amount of controversy, as Vidali, by some accounts, was responsible for the murder of Julio Antonio Mella.[14] The ship docked briefly in the United States, but Modotti was refused entry because she would not renounce her political views. Modotti therefore continued on to Europe, settling briefly in Berlin. On arrival in Berlin, she quickly became disillusioned with photography, having encountered technical problems and a saturated market. In a letter to Weston dated 23 May 1930, she expresses her frustration at not knowing which path to take:

I feel there must be something for me but I have not found it yet. And in the meantime the days go by and I spend sleepless nights wondering which way to turn and where to begin. I have begun to go out with the camera but, *nada*. Everybody here been telling me the graflex is too conspicuous and bulky. . . . Besides a smaller camera would only be useful if I intended to work on the streets, and I am not so sure that I will. I know the material found on the streets is rich and wonderful, but my experience is that the way I am accustomed to work, slowly planning my composition etc. is not suited for such work. By the time I have the composition or expression right, the picture is gone. I guess I want to do the impossible and therefore I do nothing.[15]

Aside from the letters that Modotti continued to send to Weston, and a meeting with Anita Brenner, this period of Modotti's life lacks documentation.[16] It appears that while maintaining a studiously low profile, she stepped up her political activity, taking part in secret missions in the name of the fight against fascism.

Vitorrio Vidali, who had last seen Modotti at their port of arrival in Europe, joined her in Berlin toward the end of 1930. A staunch Stalinist, Vidali persuaded Modotti to accompany him to Moscow. From Moscow, she wrote Weston a final letter dated 12 January 1931, in which she seems once more to have found a sense of direction and to have emerged from the delusion of Berlin: "I have been living in a regular whirlpool ever since I came here in October, so much so that I cannot even remember whether I have written to you or not since my arrival. . . . I have never had less time for myself than right now. . . . There would be so much to write about life here, but no hay tiempo—I am living a completely new life, so much so that I almost feel like a different person, but very interesting."[17]

In this final letter, Modotti asks Weston if he knows anyone who would buy her Graflex camera from her, as she wishes to sell it in order to buy a Leica. However, by most accounts, the period in Moscow spells the end of Modotti's career as a photographer. She declined an invitation to become the official photographer of the Soviet Communist Party in order to devote herself entirely to working for International Red Aid, an organization with which Modotti had become involved in Mexico. According to Margaret Hooks, International Red Aid (often referred to by its Russian acronym MOPR) was ostensibly a non-Party organization that provided aid to political prisoners and their families. Modotti initially worked as a translator and reader of foreign newspapers at the headquarters of Red Aid, under Stalin's former personal secretary, Yelena Stassova. However, in time, she undertook clandestine missions in fascist Europe, carrying funds for the defense of political prisoners. In 1933 Modotti was elevated onto the Red Aid Executive

Committee; she was later sent to run a Red Aid center in Paris with Vitorrio Vidali. Once Vidali was forced to return to Moscow, his false identity having been discovered, Modotti was left in sole charge. Under Modotti's direction, the Paris office organized the International Women's Congress against War and Fascism before she returned to Moscow. Her stay in Moscow was brief; she and Vidali were dispatched to Spain on the eve of the Civil War, amid the purges that were taking place in the Communist Party at this time.

In Spain, under the pseudonym María del Carmen Ruíz, Modotti worked on the Spanish Red Aid Newspaper *Ayuda*, gathering information on political prisoners. At the outbreak of the civil war, she was sent to work in a tuberculosis clinic in Madrid, in order to care for the Republican soldiers wounded in the fighting. In the meantime, Vidali adopted the name Carlos Contreras, becoming Comandante Carlos, founder of the Fifth Regiment. Hooks states that by this time, Modotti occupied a high position in the Red Aid and was charged with a number of important tasks including the medical care of the Communist leader Dolores Ibarruri, or "La Pasionaria."

On the defeat of the Republicans in 1939, Modotti and Vidali were forced to return to Mexico, where they set up house together. Modotti dedicated herself to helping Republican exiles in Mexico and to small-scale political activity. Initially she lived under a false identity; however, in 1939 with the help of influential friends, she was able to get the deportation decree of 1930 annulled by President Lázaro Cárdenas. Modotti nevertheless continued to maintain a low profile until her death on 5 January 1942. She died, according to her death certificate, of a heart attack, in the back of a taxi.

Beyond Biography

There are, undoubtedly, many good reasons for writing and reading the story of Tina Modotti's life. First, Modotti's life has the basic ingredients of adventure, sex, and danger that make of it a "good read." For a UK/U.S. reading public, it has the added advantage of being acted out, in part, against an exotic Mexican backdrop. Second, there is the question of Modotti's sex. Biography has long been devoted to the telling of exceptional men's lives, at the expense of women's. It has, therefore, come under the scrutiny of feminist scholars keen to make good the erasure of the stories of women's lives and to reinsert them into the history of culture. According to the Personal Narratives Group: "Women's personal narratives are, among other things, stories of how women negotiate their 'exceptional' gender status both in their daily lives and over the course of a lifetime. They assume that one can understand the life only if one takes into account gender roles and gender expectations. Whether she has accepted the norms, or defied them, a woman's life can never be written taking gender for granted."[18]

The fleet of biographies that appeared on Modotti in the 1980s and 1990s are all directly or indirectly involved in the process of negotiating Modotti's "exceptional" gender status. In the words of Margaret Hooks, each is inflected to a greater or lesser extent by a desire to "demythologize Modotti *the legend*, extricate her from the shadows of her lovers and locate the woman and the artist at the center of her own history."[19] The value of so doing is beyond dispute. The problem with reading Modotti biographically, however, is that her photographic images are read reductively, if indeed they are read at all. It is ironic that although the relationship between the author and the text has been radically challenged in the light of post-1968 developments in critical theory, Modotti's biography continues to be inextricably linked to her photographs.[20] This does not always entail biographical readings of the photographs. In Sarah M. Lowe's study, for example, the reverse is the case—the photographs are used to illustrate Modotti's life:

> Modotti's life story is the stuff of legends: it has inspired poets and novelists who use her biography as a point of departure. Yet the very elements that lend themselves to legend and too easily to caricature . . . also distort perception of her, and we lose sight of both her humanity and the material reality of her life. One remedy for this is . . . to read Modotti's photographs using biography and thus to normalize Modotti's life and work. To acknowledge those biographical dimensions allows us to retrieve Modotti from the margins of artmaking, to dislodge her from the center of her legend, and to place both her art and her experience within a social and photographic context.[21]

Lowe's study is certainly an important contribution to Modotti scholarship, and I draw upon the insights it offers. However, it exemplifies the almost inevitable union of photographs and biography that has characterized this scholarship to date.

Despite the wealth of material that is now available on Modotti's life, her photographic prints remain effectively sealed in the brown paper parcel in which they were handed over to the Museum of Modern Art. Whereas Modotti the *woman* comes biographically "prepackaged"—albeit in a variety of different kinds of packaging—the photographs themselves remain largely unread. Their status as unread entities, I suggest, is attributable to two principal and interrelated factors. Both these factors must inform any study of Modotti's photographic output. First, Modotti's images remain unread because, until feminist interventions into visual studies, her status as a woman photographer has precluded their reading. That is, as a woman photographer, Modotti worked from within a tradition of visual representation where women have conventionally figured as passive objects of the gaze.[22] Feminist scholars have pointed out that there is a correlation between visual culture and the social and psychic construction of sexual difference. This correlation has had limiting consequences for women, whose role as cultural producers has been problematized by their representation as passive objects within the visual realm. Second, Modotti's images remain largely unread precisely because they are photographic images. Despite the sophisticated and groundbreaking work of theorists such as Abigail Solomon-Godeau, Victor Burgin, John Tagg, and Roland Barthes, the academic study of photography is still in its infancy. Unlike the sister discipline of art history "proper," within photography studies there is no extensive body of readings of seminal photographs, in the same way that, say, there exist multiple readings of Edouard Manet's *A Bar at the Folies Bergère*, to name but one example.[23]

Thus if Modotti is an unread woman photographer, her images, as photographic images, require specific ways of reading that at present hardly exist. Photography is beset by a series of considerations that specifically pertain to photographic representation and have concerned photography from its very inception in 1839. I sketch out here a notion of what these considerations might be, drawing on an essay by Martin Jay, "Photo-unrealism: The Contribution of the Camera to the Crisis of Ocularcentrism." Jay describes three issues that emerged soon after photography was invented and that continue to spark debate even today: "The first concerned the relation between photographs and optical truth or illusion. The second introduced the vexed question, is photography an art? It had as its corollary, what is the impact of photography on painting and vice versa? And the third addressed the impact on society of the new invention."[24]

Jay's notion of the "relation between photographs and optical truth or illusion" figures prominently in my argument and is concerned with what we might term the bottom line of photographic representation: photography's status as a "message without a code."[25] When we think about photographs, there is no avoiding the fact that, unlike any other form of representation, photography enjoys a special relationship with reality, which, it is purported, photography is able to represent unproblematically.

Jay further highlights a basic irony that concerns the impact of photographic representation on the field of vision. Photographic representation not only registers reality, it also has the power to see a "reality" that exists beyond the capacity of human vision. According to Jay, the invention of photography was to have far-reaching consequences for debates about representation. If, following Roland Barthes, the concept of representation is based upon the classic subject who "casts his gaze toward a horizon on which he cuts out the base of a triangle, his eye (or his mind) forming the apex," then the subject at the apex of the triangle is presumed to have mastery over that which is viewed. Jay's point is that, far from reaffirming the authority of the disembodied gaze at the apex of the cone of vision, photography in fact called its very authority into question and revealed it as absolutely contingent. Jay demonstrates how the invention of photography radically destabilized the authority and mastery of Barthes's viewing subject at the apex of the triangle because progress in photographic technology meant that the ambit of vision was suddenly extended. Objects and phenomena that had previously been invisible to the "naked" eye suddenly came into the field of vision.[26] This had a dual effect. As well as expanding what could potentially be seen with the aid of technology, photography also highlighted the limits of human vision. Once the limits became visible, the power and authority derived from scopic mastery of the field of vision were dramatically called into question. This was to impact in important ways on society in general, and specifically on painting. But what particularly interests me about Jay's argument is his notion that "in grappling with these fundamental issues, nineteenth-century thinkers helped prepare the way for the twentieth-century interrogation of vision in its wider sense."[27]

Jay's notion of the involvement of photography in the interrogation of vision is, I suggest, the point of convergence of the two factors to which the unread status of Modotti's photographs can be attributed. If photography has prepared the way for an interrogation of vision, then theories of feminism have a serious stake in that project because feminist scholarship has identified a pressing need not only to reinsert women as cultural producers into the framework of visual representation but also to call into question the dominant structure of looking in Western society, whereby woman is framed as the passive object of the gaze. In other words, feminist scholarship is precisely concerned with interrogating vision, with revealing its structures as historically and culturally contingent, and most important, with challenging that contingency. In plotting out readings of a selection of Modotti's photographs, therefore, I privilege and affirm two notions of specificity: Modotti's sexual specificity as a woman photographer and the specificity of photographic representation as a signifying practice.

One further form of specificity merits mention at this point. Modotti lived in a number of different countries both in the Americas and in Europe. Yet despite her almost nomadic life, Modotti scholarship tends to focus on the seven-year period she spent in Mexico. This study is no exception. However, as the study marks a break with the biographical and a shift to the photographic, and given that the bulk of Modotti's images were produced in Mexico and depicted Mexican subjects, this study engages with the specificity of the Mexican context as the site of production of the photographs. This is not to suggest, however, that the Modotti-Mexico nexus is without tension and conflict. At a number of points throughout the book, therefore, I problematize and thereby raise questions around the wholesale "Mexicanization" of Modotti.

In chapter 1 I examine Laura Mulvey and Peter Wollen's essay that accompanied the 1982 Whitechapel exhibition of Tina Modotti's photographs and Frida Kahlo's paintings. This exhibition, part of a wider project of feminist excavation of women artists overlooked and neglected by the male-dominated art-historical institution, arguably triggered the critical attention that both Modotti and Kahlo received in feminist circles and beyond. It is still one of the most important frameworks within which to understand Modotti, and I return to it on a number of occasions throughout the book. My examination of the catalog essay locates it within a history of developments in feminist interventions into the visual realm and offers an account of its seminal status. Nonetheless, while the essay was of undeniable strategic importance at the time of its publication, it throws up a number of problematic issues. In particular, I focus on Mulvey and Wollen's claim that Modotti, herself the object of (male) others' gaze, was able to avoid objectifying others when she herself became subject of the gaze. The second section of chapter 1 locates Modotti as a photographer within the context of the discourses of the body politic that emerged as the nation sought to reconsolidate in the 1920s after the violent phase of the Mexican Revolution and, more particularly, the work of the muralist Diego Rivera, who rose to prominence in this period. Drawing on what Mulvey, in a later essay, terms a "feminist aesthetics of curiosity," I offer a comparative reading of Modotti's photograph *Open Doors* and Rivera's early murals, which calls for a more complex approach to questions of bodies and frames that, in a number of ways, come into focus in the ensuing chapters.[28]

Chapter 2 examines the sale in 1991 of Modotti's 1924 photograph *Roses*, at Sotheby's, New York. The first section in this chapter explores the factors that influenced the record-breaking sum that *Roses* fetched at auction. Focusing in turn on the publicity and literature surrounding the sale, and the cultural conditions in which the image was produced, I offer an account of why the signature "Tina Modotti" fetched such a high sum on the market. I argue that there were two key selling points in the sale: namely, the fact that Modotti was a woman photographer and that she worked within the exotic and distant context of 1920s Mexico, wherein women and exotic locations represent attractive commodities. In the second section, I make a reading of Roses in the light of Roland Barthes's concepts of *studium* and *punctum*. I take the photograph through a series of theoretical and cultural contexts in order to read *Roses*, against the grain of commodification, as a contestatory image.

I develop the theme of photographic signature in chapter 3 by looking at the way in which the commodification of Modotti and biographical accounts of her life exist alongside more traditional art-historical analyses of her photographs. Drawing on the work of the photography critic Abigail Solomon-Godeau, I make a reading of two images, *Hands Resting on Tool* (1927) and *Mella's Typewriter* (1928). I argue that when discussing photographic images, it is necessary to discard more conventional forms of art-historical criticism, for they tend to treat photographs as if they were paintings. In this way, conventional forms of art-historical criticism run the risk of eliding an account of photography's particular purchase on reality. Toward the end of this chapter I signal a shift in focus in my reading of Modotti's photographs. This shift, which emerges from my reading of *Mella's Typewriter*, advocates a move toward contextual reading.

In chapter 4 I examine one photograph, *Workers Parade* (1926), placing it in increasingly nuanced notions of context. The readings of this photograph, which depicts a sea of sombreros traversing the photographic frame, deals with issues of gender and marginality. I then trace the development of the sombrero as a specifically Mexican cultural icon back to its representation in photographs from the Casasola archive where it becomes imbued with revolutionary connotations and, crucially, becomes racially inscribed. By bringing into focus the racially inscribed body below the sombrero, I argue that *Workers Parade* raises questions not only about gender and marginality but also about Modotti's status as a cultural tourist in Mexico.

I pursue my reading of *Workers Parade* in chapter 5, in order to establish the cultural magazine *Mexican Folkways* as a material context in which to read Modotti's photographs. By taking a detour through both the discourses of *indigenismo* and theories of abjection broadly inflected by Kristeva's work, I read *Workers Parade* against the grain of context as a photograph that dramatizes the abject body. Chapter 5 takes a further psychoanalytic turn and marks a return to origins, namely to the maternal body. Having established *Mexican Folkways* as a viable context for reading Modotti's photographs, I reflect on Modotti's representation of the female body. In the light of the work of the Israeli artist and psychoanalyst Bracha Ettinger Lichtenberg, I set Modotti's *Aztec Baby* (ca. 1926–27) to work against its context and read its inscriptions of a matrixial dimension.

1

Opening Doors
Feminism's Beyond

Hollywood

In a much-cited letter to Edward Weston, after her expulsion from Mexico in 1930 while en route to Europe, Tina Modotti complained of her treatment by the U.S. journalists who were pursuing her in their quest for a "scoop." Clearly angered by her erasure in the press as a political subject, Modotti wrote:

> The newspapers have followed me, and at times preceded me, with wolf-like greediness—here in the U.S. everything is seen from the "beauty" angle—a daily here spoke of my trip and referred to me "as a woman of striking beauty"—other reporters to whom I refused an interview tried to convince me by saying they would just speak of "how pretty I was"—to which I answered that I could not possibly see what "prettiness" had to do with the expulsion of Communists—evidently women here are measured by a motion picture standard.[1]

Much later, in an essay accompanying an important feminist exhibition of two overlooked women artists, Tina Modotti and Frida Kahlo, held at London's Whitechapel Gallery, the British curators and critics Laura Mulvey and Peter Wollen pick up on this letter, commenting that it was "ironic, in a way, that it should have gone to Weston who did more than anyone else to promote and perpetuate the legend of Tina Modotti's beauty, both through his daybooks and through the photographs for which she was model, culminating with the famous series of her lying nude on the *azotea* in 1924."[2]

Modotti's letter is doubly ironic when read in tandem with a film-still from a 1920 Hollywood movie *The Tiger's Coat*, in which Modotti appeared in the starring role. In terms both of the place of its making and what it depicts, this film-still is a richly suggestive image that, among other things, casts Modotti in precisely the kind of iconic role that her letter to Weston denounces. Within the clip itself, the traditional role of woman as spectacle is graphically portrayed in the form of the painted canvas, on which we see a female figure in a classic pose of eroticized display. The painted female figure on the artist's canvas representing Modotti-the-actress is ironically symbolic of Modotti's "real-life" status as muse and model, and is echoed in the "motion picture standard" of which she complains and in images such as Edward Weston's famous series *Tina on the Azotea*. These photographs, as Mulvey and Wollen noted, promote just such a notion of Modotti as object for the desiring male gaze and systematically deny her status as a photographer and, therefore, producer of culture and meaning.

Despite the place of its making, however, the still lends itself to another kind of reading, one that—equally ironically—contests this kind of traditional representation of woman insofar as it encapsulates in a very straightforward manner a notion of what we might term feminist iconoclasm. That is, the still is graphically emblematic of a late twentieth-century feminist challenge—of which Mulvey's work, in particular, is exemplary—to the tradition of visual representation in which the female body is circumscribed as erotic spectacle. In the foreground, to the right of the still, are a palette and paintbrushes. Modotti-the-actress-model stands between them and a canvas. At her side stands the artist, his hands outstretched in exaggerated shock and disbelief. He looks on in horror at the knife in his model's hand, poised to slash the canvas in an act of defiant iconoclasm. What is so striking about this image is that it evokes a specifically feminist desire to shred the limiting visual documents that, in Mulvey's famous phrase, have confined women to the position of "bearer, not maker, of meaning."[4] In short, the still visually encapsulates a desire to wipe the slate clean of the limiting images of women that have predominated in Western visual culture and to replace them with something altogether different.

Although the first of Mulvey's essays, "Visual Pleasure and Narrative Cinema," has been superseded by more complex psych-

Figure 1.
Film-still from *The Tiger's Coat*, Hollywood, 1920. BFI Films.

oanalytic modes of analysis and the argument has well-recognized lim-
itations, I invoke it within the context of the current chapter for a
number of important reasons.[5] This essay on cinema spectatorship
represents a key moment within the history of feminist interventions
into the realm of visual representation: it identified the gaze and its
position within a phallic regime of sexual difference as a key issue for
feminist theories of vision, thus giving rise to a whole body of work on
gender and the gaze. Or to pursue the metaphor of the film-still,
Mulvey's essay first provided the theoretical tool/knife with which to
critique/slash the canvas of representation. The second essay, the
Whitechapel catalog essay "Frida Kahlo and Tina Modotti," not only
brought the work of the two women to international attention but also,
informed precisely by feminist cultural theory, has become a key text
in Modotti scholarship. In the late 1990s, then, Modotti came to us as
the product of specific feminist discourses of the 1970s and 1980s,

most notably as the product of the work of Laura Mulvey. The opening to this chapter, then, establishes two things. It signals the complex and charged relationship that Modotti enjoys within the visual realm, which is a key focus of this book. It also demonstrates that when we read Modotti as the dual subject-object of representation, we do so through the paradigm provided by a specific phase of feminist visual theory.

Feminism, by definition, is a critical and contestatory practice, which is driven by the political need to interrogate the structures around which sexual difference is organized. It is neither static nor univocal. Instead, it is a dynamic and evolving process. In recognition of this, I elaborate a critique of Mulvey and Wollen's essay, particularly its approach to Modotti. In my discussion of the Modotti-Mulvey connection I develop two strategies. The first locates the Mulvey and Wollen Whitechapel essay within the context of developments in feminist visual theory that emerged in the 1970s and 1980s. Although the exhibition marks a key moment in Modotti scholarship, in the light of advances in feminist theory, it now raises questions that require urgent attention. My second strategy is to work toward a reading of the Modotti photograph *Open Doors* via a contextualizing detour through Mexican cultural history, specifically the role of muralism in postrevolutionary Mexico. Picking up on and critiquing Mulvey and Wollen's notion of an "exemplary" female gaze, the aim of my reading is to shift the debate beyond the Mulvey moment of the 1980s and in so doing, to see beyond it, by looking at the "gaps" in the critical practice associated with the Mulvey moment.

Feminist Iconoclasm

When Modotti traveled to Mexico City in 1923, drawn particularly by the renaissance in visual culture that was happening there, her role was that of model and muse in the images of Edward Weston and the muralist Diego Rivera. In time she became established as an image-maker in her own right, but even up to the present day her status as model and muse tends to overshadow her status as a photographer. This phenomenon was underscored by a 1996 exhibition held in Mexico City to celebrate the centenary of Modotti's birth. Designed, in the words of its curator, Andrés Siegel, to: "Recrear algunos de los espacios y en tener una ambientación tanto sonora, a lo mejor holográfica, y recrear a Tina en el contexto, Tina en la Condesa, Tina en la Ciudad de México, Tina en su época." ["re-create some of the spaces [in which Modotti lived], with sound as well as holographic effects, and to re-create Tina in context, in La Condesa, Tina in Mexico City, Tina in her epoch,"] this exhibition welcomed its visitors not with a photograph made by Modotti but with a "spectacular" nude photograph of Tina on the *azotea* made by Edward Weston in 1924.[6] This photograph and, more generally, Weston's collection of nude images of Modotti belong to a long tradition of visual representation that ascribes a certain place to woman within culture: as lover, model, and muse, as body for limitless consumption.[7]

Given the enduring construction and discursification of Modotti-as-nude that is effected, among other things, by the *azotea* photographs, and given the way in which this construction has eclipsed her status as image-maker, it is not surprising that Mulvey and Wollen chose to read her in the Whitechapel essay as they did, that is, through the prism of feminist theory. The reading they provide of Modotti has gaps. It must, nonetheless, be understood as a seminal piece that issued from a specific historical/theoretical context. In the next section, I provide an overview of the Whitechapel exhibition and essay that seeks both to contextualize and also to offer an account of the exhibition and essay's seminal status. Once I have done so, I will go on to outline the gaps that have now, in the late 1990s, opened up in the essay.

The Whitechapel exhibition was not the first of its kind to show-case Modotti's photographs after the period of virtual anonymity through which the photographer passed after her death in 1942. As Mariana Figarella Mota notes, a number of exhibitions and biographies appeared before 1982, originating with the 1972 Italian exhibition *Tina Modotti, garibaldina e artista* to commemorate the thirtieth anniversary of Modotti's death. However, what distinguishes Mulvey and Wollen's approach to Modotti from those that preceded it is that the exhibition and essay worked from within debates around feminist aesthetics and was informed by a concern with the politics of representation. The essay belonged to a specifically feminist project of excavation—ushered in by Linda Nochlin's "Why Have There Been No Great Women Artists?"—which sought to "rescue" women cultural producers who had been overlooked and relegated to the cultural margins by male-dominated criticism. The essay thus sought to re-present the work of Modotti and Kahlo and, at the same time, to rework their significance from within a framework of a specifically feminist aesthetics and to politicize Modotti and Kahlo as subjects relegated to the cultural margins. The catalog comprised not only Mulvey and Wollen's essay—the section inspired by feminist research and theory—but also reviews and memoirs of Modotti and Kahlo by contemporary commentators, gathered from a range of sources. Those texts that focused primarily on Modotti include reviews of her photography by the muralist Diego Rivera and the critic Carlton Beals; a poem written by the Chilean poet Pablo Neruda, on the occasion of Modotti's death; and an abridged version of Modotti's article "On Photography" ["Sobre la fotografía"] that originally appeared in *Mexican Folkways*.[8] Just over half the catalog was given over to reproductions of images by the two women.

The overarching critical concern that informed Mulvey and Wollen's approach to Modotti and Kahlo relates to the question of marginality. Divided into eight sections, the catalog's first section is appropriately entitled "On the Margins," at the end of which the authors state: "An exhibition of work by Frida Kahlo and Tina Modotti automatically invites questions about 'marginality'—the status, in terms of mainstream art history as presented in books and museum displays, assigned to Mexican art and to women's art and (in Modotti's case) to photography."[9] In other words, the essay sets Modotti and Kahlo up as inevitably marginalized subjects insofar as they exist on the margins of what is an already peripheral cultural space. For Mulvey and Wollen, researching and writing in the early 1980s, the privileging of marginality was undoubtedly an essential strategic move. By playing up the issue of marginality, their essay posed an important challenge to the institution of art history by revealing its exclusions and omissions. At the same time, it placed questions of sexual difference firmly on the critical agenda:

> An exhibition of either artist alone would have asserted her individual importance, her specific contribution to an artistic practice—painting or photography—and to woman's cultural traditions. But the decision to bring the work of Frida Kahlo and Tina Modotti together is based on something more than the fact that they have been unjustly neglected and that their art and their lives are of great intrinsic interest. The juxtaposition is designed to raise a series of ideas

and arguments that are relevant to questions about women's art and feminist aesthetics.[10]

The essay also reflects the growing interest at the time in the representation of the body. The notion of the "discourse of the body"—the title of the final section—derives from the work of Michel Foucault, whose theoretical insights into the way in which power relations operate on and through the human body, conceived as a cultural rather than natural entity, was of critical significance at the time to the development of feminist thought. Mulvey and Wollen establish the representation of the female body within the visual domain as a particular concern for an understanding of women's art and feminist aesthetics: "Feminism has always been deeply concerned with questions about representation, with the politics of images. This concern is with the way that 'woman' has been used in male representation, and (the necessary other side of the coin) with women's relegation to a marginal area of culture, specifically the 'high arts.'"[11]

More specifically, Mulvey and Wollen have the following to say about Modotti and her representation in the photographs of Edward Weston: "Weston became famous as a photographer of the female nude. He claimed that it was the formal quality of the shape of the female body which interested him and that any erotic motive . . . was suspended in the photographic work. His particular form of voyeurism, of taking woman as an object of gaze, was justified in terms of pure aesthetic form. . . . The fact remains, however, that his nude photographs of Tina Modotti are often taken from above, looking down on her as she lies passively, sun-bathing or asleep, on the ground, in a conventional pose."[12]

Although it uses less academic language, the analysis of Modotti as erotic spectacle offered in the Whitechapel essay is consonant with the critical insights of Mulvey's earlier essay "Visual Pleasure, Narrative Cinema." With its focus on the configuration of gaze, body, and marginality, the Whitechapel essay functions as a barometer of precisely the kinds of critical concerns of its moment. Indeed, attesting to the historical importance of the Whitechapel exhibition within the context of British feminist theory Griselda Pollock and Rozsika Parker state that it "did not seek only to add to our knowledge about women artists but to change the way we see them and comprehend their work. It was an exhibition which demonstrated the enormous gains to be obtained if a show is not simply inspired by feminist research but shaped by feminist theory."[13]

The Whitechapel exhibition was not only shaped by but was also to shape feminist theory, going on to be reproduced in three critical anthologies: Rosemary Betterton's *Looking On: Images of Femininity in the Visual Arts and Media*; Laura Mulvey's own *Visual and Other Pleasures*; and *Art in Modern Culture: An Anthology of Critical Texts*, edited by Francis Frascina and Jonathan Harris for an Open University course entitled "Modern Art: Practices and Debates."[14] The enduring influence of the Whitechapel essay is particularly striking when we consider that as a catalog essay designed to accompany a temporary, traveling exhibition, its impact was more likely to have been short-lived.

Given the privileged status of the Whitechapel essay in other anthologies—especially in the Frascina and Harris volume, where the essay is preceded by an excerpt from Edward Said's *Orientalism*—it is, at first sight at least, strange to discover how elliptically Mulvey introduces the essay in her own book. Mulvey merely states in her introduction, "'Frida Kahlo and Tina Modotti' recorded and documented the Whitechapel exhibition and catalog, quite simply"; she allots her essay no further comment within the collection.[15] Mulvey does state, however, that the essays in the collection are the product of a particular moment, suggesting, therefore, that they are historically contingent:

> The articles [in the collection] were written between 1971 and 1986, a fifteen-year period that saw the Women's Movement broaden out from a political organisation into a more general framework of feminism. They were written to articulate rather than to originate, to catch something of the interests and ideas that were already around in the air. . . . Because context and moment were important in their inception, these articles have retained a link with their historical moment and context that, I hope, gives them a documentary quality.[16]

It is fairly clear that on writing the introduction to *Visual and Other Pleasures*, Mulvey herself, by this stage, was sensitive to the status of her essays as belonging to earlier moments in the development of feminist cultural theory. And it is Mulvey's own sense of the historical contingency of the Whitechapel essay that I now address in order to raise briefly a cluster of problems associated with its analysis of Modotti.

First, I suggest that the emphasis on Modotti's triple marginalization—as a woman, as a "Mexican," and as a photographer—is no longer politically tenable. Undoubtedly in the early 1980s the conflation of gender and marginality was a crucial category for analysis, and reading its manifestations represented an important contestatory gesture. To continue to pursue such a line of analysis, however, can lead us nowhere other than to confirm and therefore reinforce Modotti's peripheral status. When read with the benefit of hindsight, this is ultimately what the Whitechapel essay ends up doing, where Mulvey and Wollen argue, for example, that Modotti and Kahlo "were able to produce work quite as innovative and explosive in its implications as the mammoth productions of their confreres."[17] If Modotti and Kahlo as women were marginal to mainstream, masculine culture, to argue that they were able to produce work that was just as "innovative" as the mainstream does nothing to displace the fundamental binary opposition governing what is classified as marginal and what is central. Furthermore, despite the emphasis on marginality, it is arguable that the essay unwittingly marginalizes Modotti to Kahlo, and photography to painting. Amelia Jones suggests that Mulvey and Wollen force their comparison of Modotti and Kahlo: "Modotti was not Mexican-born like Kahlo but an Italian who immigrated to Mexico through the United States, and . . . the two artists employed different media (Modotti was a photographer, Kahlo a painter) and focused on radically different subject matter (Modotti's photographs feature external political events while Kahlo produced highly charged and extremely personal painting exploring the politics of female subjectivity)."[18]

I am not sure I fully endorse Jones's critique. There are good reasons for re-presenting Modotti and Kahlo together related to the need to critique the existing canon that has marginalized women and that privileges the individual mythic artist figure. One thing, however, is clear. When it comes down to analysis of individual images, the terms of reference employed in the essay—for example, "interior and exterior"—tend to generate more readings around Kahlo's paintings than they do around Modotti's photographs. This becomes apparent from even a cursory glimpse at the essay, where Kahlo's paintings are named, whereas Modotti's are referred to indirectly by description alone. This failure to name reflects, in turn, a failure to read Modotti's photographs.[19]

Second, we need to acknowledge the problems attendant on the continued practice of reading the female body as object of the male heterosexual gaze. Such a practice dominated critical discourse in the 1970s and 1980s. It was at that stage a matter of political exigency to examine and thereby lay bare the psychic investments that permeate the production and consumption of visual images. The danger with a practice of this kind, nevertheless, is that women end up as powerless victims, their docile bodies the site of male inscription. Modes of analysis that depend exclusively upon it allow little room for a more progressive notion of female agency. At points, the Whitechapel essay alarmingly denies its subjects' agency: "Looking at Frida Kahlo and Tina Modotti's work in relation to their lives and experience as women it is clear that conscious decisions about artistic stance are only to a limited extent the result of conscious controllable choice."[20]

Third, Mulvey and Wollen's text posits the possibility of a non-objectifying, "exemplary" female gaze. In the final section of the essay, they state: "Tina Modotti, whose career had begun as a film-actress and a model, redirected the look which had focused on her outwards when she herself became a photographer. . . . Modotti's [art became] one of depiction of others—predominantly women, but seen with an eye quite different from the one that had looked at her."[21]

Mulvey and Wollen are referring to the series of photographs Modotti made in 1926–27 of women and children and to the 1929 series of women from the Isthmus of Tehuantepec. They go on to claim that "Tina Modotti's photographs were not of 'beauties' but of peasant and proletarian women, marked by the conditions of their life. Often they are mothers with small children, their bodies framed to emphasize not their own form but that of their interaction with the children."[22] Mulvey and Wollen suggest that when Modotti, who as a woman photographer lived and worked in spaces that constituted her image as passive object, came to photograph others—indigenous women—she was somehow able to avoid subjecting the objects of her images to the same kind of reductive treatment to which she herself was subjected. Mulvey and Wollen's claim concerning the female gaze invokes that frozen moment of iconoclasm depicted in the film-still of *The Tiger's Coat*. That is to say, Modotti is object of the gaze who becomes subject; at the same time, as a photographer she is somehow able to place another kind of representation alongside the painted canvas, one that has the potential to challenge the authority and hegemony of the male gaze. I have a problem with this position (and these days, as her introduction to *Visual and Other Pleasures* suggests, Mulvey undoubtedly would too). What exactly is the difference between, say, *An Aztec Mother* (ca. 1926–27) and any other representation of indigenous subjects in circulation at the same time? I do not rule out the possibility of a different kind of female gaze, but I do suggest that this gaze would have to be more complex than the simple positing of a reductive "good" female gaze, as opposed to the "bad" male gaze.[23]

This might seem an obvious point to make. After all, feminist visual theory, including Mulvey's own work, has moved on radically since the Whitechapel essay. However, the same cannot be said of Modotti scholarship. After a period of critical neglect, without doubt Modotti currently receives more attention than ever before. But this renewed critical attention has tended to reproduce a kind of analysis that has patently not managed to part company with 1980s feminist visual theory. So, for example, in "Women, Images, and Visual Representation," Anne Higonnet claims that Modotti "provides the paradigmatic example" of the kind of women artists who "passed through men's orbits on the way to their own destinations." And she continues, "when [Modotti] went on to create her own work, she too often depicted women, but as active subjects rather than as passive objects; her photograph of a mother and child concentrates on the mother's powerful arm grasping and supporting a child whose sturdy physical presence as well as the mother's swelling abdomen attest unsentimentally to her fertility."[24]

Griselda Pollock has summarized the historical moment out of which the Whitechapel essay emerged in the following terms: "For a period during the 1970s, [feminist interventions in the visual arts] produced a 'negative aesthetics' amongst certain feminists in the cultural field, a radical distanciation from any aspect of the spectacle and visual pleasure, a distrust of the visual image, of the iconicity especially of women. The necessary work of ground clearing has been done and those artists associated most strongly with such moves, such as Mary Kelly and Laura Mulvey, have themselves reclaimed the territories of desire in the field of vision."[25]

The pertinence of Pollock's formulation of the state of play in feminist cultural theory does not simply reside in its cogent marshaling of the issues. First, by definition, the existence of a "negative aesthetics" is predicated on the possibility of a "positive aesthetics." This is arguably what, on one level, Mulvey and Wollen, followed later by Higonnet, suggest in their analysis: Modotti made "good," or "positive," images of women. The absolute terms in which the visual domain can be understood in what can be loosely termed "images-of-women" analysis has been thoroughly debunked.[26] It simply cannot account for the complexity of the relationship between visual representation and "reality" that is itself a product of representation. Second, Pollock's liberal use of spatial metaphors—distinction, ground clearing, territories, fields of vision, and culture—provides a potential key to how debates around the relationship of femininity to visual representation, and of Modotti's relationship to the realm of the visual, can be shifted beyond the Mulvey-Modotti moment. This key, I suggest, can also be found in the polysemous film-still.

The still from *The Tiger's Coat* does not merely lend itself to a reading based upon a notion of feminist iconoclasm, which I read ironically as a metaphor for Mulvey and Wollen's work on Modotti. It also raises questions about spatiality and framing. As such, it provides a clue toward a feminist aesthetics of vision that has the potential to take us beyond the Mulvey-Modotti paradigm. A number of different spaces are either framed within or implied by the still.

1. There is the space of the canvas on which the model is represented;
2. in the space behind it there is another painting, this time of a river estuary flanked on the right by sailing boats and on the left by a cityscape;
3. to the left of the represented space in which the action takes place, a window looks out on to what appears to be a garden that exists offscreen;
4. by implication the fictional, frozen space in which the action of the film takes place is also represented, existing as it does in relationship to the moving image, of which it is just one frame.

In the film-still, space is boldly construed as representation. That is to say, beyond the inclusion of the paintings and the window that gives off onto another, offscreen space, the clip is presented here as photograph. It is a commonplace of photography theory to state that on some level photographs enjoy a special ontological relationship with reality.[27] This photograph-cum-clip, however, disavows the existence of a straightforward relationship between image and "reality" insofar as reality here is film-text and is therefore unashamedly fiction. My aim in this brief return to the still from *The Tiger's Coat* is to underscore two elements that are visual tropes in the development of my argument: the poised hand ready to slash the canvas and the framing of space as representation. I now leave these tropes momentarily frozen in the narrative of this chapter and detour through Mexican urban space of the early 1920s, a place where I reanimate them in my discussion of the city, the nation-space, and the feminine gaze.

Mexico (City)

Having established Modotti's position within the context of the Whitechapel exhibition and essay, I now relocate her within a discussion of the topographies of cultural nationalism in postrevolutionary Mexico.[28] There is no space, in the context of the current discussion, to address the complexity of the events that led to the revolution.[29] It is important, however, to establish a number of points by way of introduction to the cultural issues that emerged during the postrevolutionary phase, which form the backdrop to my discussion of space and spatiality. In the period leading up to the revolution, Mexico had experienced a phase of unprecedented peace and stability after the turmoil of the postindependence years, when the presidency changed hands no fewer than thirty-six times. But peace and stability came in the form of the dictatorship of Porfirio Díaz, whose presidency lasted more or less continuously from 1874 to 1910. During the Porfiriato, as the period was called, the country underwent a process of rapid and dramatic modernization and urbanization, which in turn brought about economic and material progress. Despite the economic progress—or maybe because of it—the territory demarcated by the national boundaries still lacked a coherent identity. According to Alan Knight, Mexico at this time "was less a nation than a geographical expression, a mosaic of regions and communities, introverted and jealous, ethnically and physically fragmented, and lacking common national sentiments."[30] Largely unconcerned with the means by which these fragments were to cohere, Díaz was, nevertheless, concerned that they should adhere to the center.

Ensconced in Mexico City, Díaz allowed political abuse and endemic corruption to go unchecked—or even encouraged it—in the provinces in the name of tightening central control. Wealth in the form of land remained in the hands of a few privileged families, while great pockets of the population subsisted in abject poverty. French culture was a la mode among the Mexican aristocracy; French cuisine, de rigueur in the capital. Moreover, the city was made over in imitation of Paris, with the Paseo de la Reforma redecorated to look like the Champs Elysées. Yet sanitation and diet among the masses was so poor that average life expectancy was about thirty years. Despite the serious grievances many Mexicans suffered, revolutionary stirrings were first couched in political terms—"no reelección y sufragio efectivo." In time, however, as the fragmented and feuding factions gained momentum, what started out as a struggle waged at the level of constitutional change was to be hailed as Latin America's first major social revolution. Sweeping aside the dictatorship, the revolution put in its place a nationalist and capitalist state, which according to Knight, with "its contradictory blend of conservative and revolutionary elements, [has] created headaches for historians (especially those who want to segregate Mexicans neatly into revolutionary sheep and conservative goats)."[31]

As Knight suggests, Mexico in 1910 was more a fragmented mosaic than a nation, and the remapping of national space became a high priority in the aftermath of the revolution. With illiteracy estimated at approximately 80 percent and with a severely tarnished reputation abroad, most notably and importantly in the United States, the possibility of Mexico's accession to modernity was problematic. One of the principal tasks confronting the revolutionary state in 1920 was the invention and promotion of a new notion of national identity, one that would embrace the diverse peoples and regions that coexisted within the national territory. In particular, one segment of the population had hitherto remained outside the space of the nation, namely the myriad indigenous communities that lived in a state of cultural and economic dereliction. In opposition to criollo domination of Mexican society, which had at best denied and at worst despised its Indian heritage, an attempt was launched to "revalue" the Indians and to reinstate them within a reconfigured nation-space. The postrevolutionary project aimed to move toward a homogenous national identity, one that embraced and celebrated (certain aspects of) Mexico's hybrid ethnic makeup, which was officially recognized as stemming from dual Indian-Spanish roots. Official recognition of modern Mexico's roots was to give rise to the cult of the mestizo in a process that aimed to "mestizo-ize the Indians and at the same time, to Indianize the mestizos, to create a national synthesis on the basis of reciprocal contributions."[32]

At this time, despite the rapid urbanization that had taken place during the Porfiriato, Mexico's population as a whole, especially its Indian population, was predominantly concentrated in the rural zones of the country.[33] These Indian communities that existed on the periphery of the nation were seen at one and the same time as an obstacle to the coherence of the nation that was being forged in the metropolis and as a key to its formation and the country's subsequent accession to modernity. In the 1920s, therefore, the state set in motion a series of measures designed, if not to blur distinctions between urban and rural environments, then at least to build bridges between them. Bridges, by implication, potentially permit two-way traffic, even if the power relations between the two directions are unequal. And within the context of the current argument, the traffic that interests me is what we might term "body traffic."

On a pragmatic level, the city-state reached out beyond its boundaries, implementing a series of educational programs, sending teachers and other kinds of educators to rural Mexico on a classic cultural crusade. As Knight explains: "While presenting themselves as men of the people, many revolutionary leaders often entertained a dim view of the 'people.' Like their English revolutionary counterparts, they were torn between the competing goals of emancipating and enlightening people: the first implied trust; the second seemed to require strong-arming. And like their nineteenth-century predecessors, they saw the Mexicans as prey to drink, dirt, and disease. Indians, especially, languished in ignorance and sought consolation in drink."[34]

At the same time, as the city-state sent educators out, the regions were invited in. Ricardo Pérez Montfort describes the way in which the city-state cast its gaze out onto the regions, in an undeniably exoticizing gesture: "Durante los años veinte se convocó a las diversas regiones para presentarse con sus atuendos locales en la capital—los jarochos, los huastecos, los yucatecos, los de tierra caliente, los norteños etc.—con el fin de comprender y promover la variedad de lo 'típico mexicano'" [During the twenties the diverse regions were summoned to parade their local dress in the capital—people from Veracruz, people from Huasteca, people from the Yucatan, people from Guerrero, people from the north—the aim being to understand and promote the variety of what was "typically Mexican"].[35]

At the same time, as real bodies flowed into and out of the city, the nation's modernizing project also took place across the symbolic spaces of the capital and orbital cities in the form of the muralist project. Any discussion of visual culture in postrevolutionary Mexico in general— and the role that Modotti played within that postrevolutionary visual space in particular—cannot avoid the pivotal importance of mural painting. Initiated during the first postrevolutionary government of Alvaro Obregón—1920–24), the muralist project was engineered by the Minister for Education José Vasconcelos. Muralism constituted the expression and consolidation of Mexican culture and identity based on a nationalistic and populist ideology. Integral to the institutionalization of "mexicanidad," muralism was dominated by "los tres grandes," Diego Rivera, David Alfaro Siqueiros, and José Clemente Orozco. Of the "grandes," Diego Rivera has arguably become the most prominent of the three and his re-visioning of Mexican historical and contemporary identity occupies a number of prime urban positions, including the Escuela Nacional Preparatoria, the Secretaría de Educación Pública, and the Palacio Nacional. Indeed, the muralist project was an overwhelmingly urban project with most of the major murals situated in Mexico City and its orbital cities. All three buildings, located at the heart of Mexico City, are central to the institution of nation, the Palacio Nacional being doubly imbued with national and cultural significance, as the seat of contemporary government and positioned adjacent to the Aztec ceremonial precinct of Tenochtitlán. Beyond Mexico City itself, Rivera also painted murals in other urban centers: the Palacio de Cortés in Cuernavaca and the former chapel of the new agricultural college in Chapingo.

Muralism posits a constitutive relationship between the city-as-state and the body. Only this time, instead of being "Frenchified" the postrevolutionary city is "Mexicanized." Elizabeth Grosz has formulated this city/body interaction in the following terms:

> The city is . . . the site for the body's cultural saturation, its takeover and transformation by images, representational systems, the mass media, and the arts—the place where the body is representationally reexplored, transformed, contested, reinscribed. In turn, the body (as cultural product) transforms, reinscribes the urban landscape according to its changing (demographic) needs, extending the limits of the city ever

toward the countryside that borders it. As a hinge between the population and the individual, the body, its distribution, habits, alignments, pleasures, norms, and ideals are the ostensive object of governmental regulation, and the city is both a mode for the regulation and administration of subjects but also an urban space in turn reinscribed by the particularities of its occupation.[36]

Grosz's argument is useful here, for, on the one hand, it becomes possible to theorize the relationship between the indigenous body, visual representation, and the state in postrevolutionary Mexico; on the other, it provides a stepping stone toward a reconceptualization of the relationship between space and the body that is the focus of the following section. If the rural, regional bodies described earlier by Pérez Montfort started to flow into the city, images of these same bodies also began to occupy the symbolic spaces of the nation, such as the murals that were soon to cover the walls of the Palacio Nacional. Thus in a visualizing gesture that sought to break down the urban/rural dichotomy, to rehabilitate the indigenous past, and at the same time to reconcile it with the mestizo present, urban walls started to fill up with images of rural, indigenous bodies. These bodies, cast in essentially reifying and romanticizing terms, represent the drive to incorporate the rural and racial other into the space of the city-state, or in Grosz's words, to "citify" (read "civilize") the indigenous body. The city becomes at once a utopian visual space onto which revolutionary notions of Mexican identity become mapped, an entity actively involved in the construction of that new national identity. Furthermore, within the context of my argument, it is important to recognize questions of space and sexual difference are invariably played out in the dynamic relationship between the city and the body. As Grosz points out earlier in the same essay: "The city is one of the crucial factors in the social production of (sexed) corporeality: the built environment provides the context and coordinates for contemporary forms of the body. The city provides the order and organization that automatically links otherwise unrelated bodies: it is the condition and milieu in which corporeality is socially, sexually, and discursively produced."[37] To understand Modotti's intervention as a photographer into postrevolutionary space—a space actively engaged in the cultural mapping of its subjects—we must bring into focus issues of space, sexual difference, and framing.

Chapingo

Modotti's residence in Mexico coincided with the initiation of the muralist project to transform urban visual space into the space of the nation. Her involvement was twofold. First, she was commissioned to make photographs of the muralists at work and of their finished murals. Modotti's work as a photographer was bound up in the process of dissemination of the muralists' message beyond the physical spaces of the static metropolitan centers in which the murals were located. Second, Modotti is also said to have modeled for a fresco in the Chapingo murals that Diego Rivera carried out between 1924 and 1927, in which she is represented as Virgin Earth. It is important to qualify Modotti's role as model for Rivera, for Edward Weston's biographer, Ben Maddow, casts some doubt over the issue: "Tina took Weston to see Rivera's earlier work. Rivera wanted to use her as a model, but Weston, jealous, furnished him with nude photographs of her instead. Using these photographs, Rivera painted a gigantic figure, which lies prone in one of the murals at the National School of Agriculture."[38] Beyond the close link between artistic practice and sexuality that Maddow's anecdote underlines, Modotti's position within the Chapingo murals is worthy of further comment.

Chapingo crystallizes the whole rural-urban dynamic that was to come so sharply into relief in the aftermath of the revolution. Based in the State of Mexico and built originally as a Jesuit foundation at the end of the seventeenth century, Chapingo was transformed into a private hacienda at the end of the eighteenth century, before becoming the seat of the Escuela Nacional de Agricultura.[39] It is appropriate that an institution that came under attack during the revolution should become the site for rural policy and technology. Moreover, the "prone" female figure represents precisely one of the issues that lay at the center of the revolution: land reform. In these murals a parallel is established between the distribution and social transformation of the land and the natural evolution of the earth. Organized around strictly binary principles, the murals play out the time-honored themes of man as representing culture and as active participant in the revolution, as opposed to woman, who represents nature and the passive recipient of male action. But more than the fact that the murals conform to patterns of crude gender stereotypes, it is important to note that the representation of Virgin Earth embodies space: a "natural," untouched space that is to be tamed and controlled by revolutionary man. Moreover, the body as space is conceived according to what Elizabeth Grosz terms "the logic of penetration, colonization and domination." Both within the narrative scheme of the murals and in terms of their status as visual products to be viewed, the female body is represented as mappable terrain to be controlled by (male) revolutionary action—the classic heterosexual male gaze. Karen Cordero Reiman goes even further and suggests that the whole viewing experience of Chapingo follows the logic of penetration: "Podríamos decir que al traspasar las puertas de la capilla, al entrar en este recinto largo, oscuro y repleto de estímulos sensoriales, el espectador—implícitamente masculino—penetra en una vagina simbólica, uniendo su signo masculino (activo) con el signo feminino (pasivo)." [It could be said that on going through the doors of the chapel, on entering this long, dark space, full of sensorial stimuli, the spectator—implicitly masculine—penetrates into a symbolic vagina uniting his masculine sign (active) with the feminine sign (passive).][40]

Modotti's position as possible model for *Virgin Earth* is further complicated by the fact that she was also actively involved in the photographic dissemination of the murals. (One of her biographers, Margaret Hooks, even goes so far as to suggest that she made a photograph of her representation as Virgin Earth.) That is, Modotti participated in a project that subsumed her image into a dominant definition of femininity as space to be territorialized and dominated by the gaze. In other words, we get back to the classic feminist argument of woman as object of the gaze and not subject, which is figured by the canvas in the film-still and came under attack in Mulvey and Wollen's work on Modotti.

I do not wish, however, to dwell for too much longer on this argument. I want, rather, to use the impasse that it presents as a springboard in order to get to a zone that exists elsewhere to what Griselda Pollock terms the "negative aesthetics" of 1970s–1980s feminist visual theory. As I have suggested, in the light of developments in feminist theory, Mulvey and Wollen's work on Modotti is long overdue for critique. Questions of female marginality and the construction of the female body as essentially docile typify contestatory strategies that belong to an earlier phase in feminist theory. In their analysis, Mulvey and Wollen posit the possibility of a non-objectifying, "exemplary" female gaze. They state: "Tina Modotti, whose career had begun as a film-actress and a model, redirected the look which had focused on her outwards when she herself became a photographer. . . . Modotti's [art became] one of depiction of others—predominantly women, but seen with an eye quite different from the one that had looked at her."[41] I take issue with the notion of the "positive aesthetics" that is implicit in this statement. However, it is one thing to say that Modotti somehow made "good" images of women and that her gaze was on some level "exemplary." It is quite another to raise questions about the status of the female gaze and its relationship to the prevalent economy of vision. Or, to put it another way, is it really the case that we cannot say anything about the female gaze, that it is so imbricated in the prevalent visual economy that there is no getting beyond it?

I suggest that we cannot say anything about the female gaze and its contemplation of the body without first thinking about the relationship between bodies and space. In order to think this space-body relationship through, I look at one particular Modotti photograph that is all about space and more specifically the framing of space. Made in 1925 at the time when Modotti started to become engaged in the photographic representation and dissemination of the muralist project, the photograph is entitled *Open Doors*. I propose to bring *Open Doors* into dialogue with Rivera's murals especially, but not exclusively, those at Chapingo, in order to tease out some of the problems inherent in any discussion of the female gaze.

Space Body Frame

At first sight, a comparative reading of *Open Doors* and Rivera's murals might seem to confirm what we already suspect about the relationship between gender and space: Modotti's photograph represents interior, private, diminutive space, in short, the feminine domain; Rivera's murals represent exterior, public, monumental space, that is, the masculine domain. It is by now a commonplace of feminist theory to underscore the binaries that structure femininity, masculinity, and space. Indeed, Mulvey and Wollen pick up on this issue in the Whitechapel essay when they claim (somewhat problematically):

> The contrast between their work [Kahlo and Modotti's]—its smallness of scale, both in subject-matter and actual physical size—and the monumentalism of the muralists is immediately striking. Yet this "smallness" is deceptive. It springs in part from the traditional constraints of women's art, which the

Figure 2.
Tina Modotti, *Open Doors*, ca. 1925, platinum print,
9 1/2" × 5 3/8" J. Paul Getty Museum, Los Angeles, California.

Mexican revolution has done nothing to loosen. Yet within these constraints they were able to produce work quite as innovative and explosive in its implications as the mammoth productions of their confreres.[42]

However, beyond the particular configuration of space—interior/ exterior, private/public, masculine/feminine—that Modotti and Rivera articulate in their work, a tandem reading of their images raises questions more specifically about the framing of space and the body. This might seem a strange observation to make, given that Rivera's murals are literally full of bodies, whereas in Modotti's photograph, the body is most palpably registered in its absence. But this, precisely, is the point. In fact, what particularly interests me here is not so much the representation of the body in the images (although this factor does come into play) as the question of the viewer's body as it is engaged in the process of looking at these two different articulations of space.

By definition, the viewing of a mural is an intensely bodily experience. To take in a mural viewers have to circulate in the space around which it is painted, walk up and down stairs (in the case of the murals at the Palacio Nacional), step back in order to get an overview of a particular wall, step forward to inspect a detail. Viewing a mural can also involve momentary bodily discomfort. The murals at Chapingo, which span onto the ceiling, require viewers to crane their necks, thereby heightening the sense of viewing as an embodied experience. Furthermore, viewers are engaged with the fixed, stationary bodies of others as they are represented on the walls that are being surveyed. If there is one generalization we can make about Rivera's murals, most certainly in the early phase, it is that walls become saturated with bodies.[43]

Rivera's return to Mexico from Europe in 1921 at the behest of Vasconcelos marks a move away from European-inspired cubism back to figurative art that could articulate a vision of Mexico's historical and contemporary identity, which was to be found in the recently expanded definition of the body politic. The murals were ostensibly created for consumption by this newly defined body politic, which in turn, was to be actively created by the murals. The body, therefore, and its incorporation into national, monumental space, was the key issue at stake in the muralist project.

Radical in many ways—most notably in their celebration of the

indigenous and working-class subject—the murals nevertheless promoted a wholly conventional relationship between the viewing subject
and the viewed object, one that was predicated on the presence/
absence of the frame. The frame is a form of boundary, a cultural con-
vention that establishes the distinction between inside and outside,
image and world, self and other. Mural painting, on one level, trans-
gresses traditional notions of the frame insofar as the muralists aban-
doned the conventional frame by painting not on canvas, but on walls.
In fact, in a manifesto published in the newspaper *El Machete*, the
muralists articulated their objection to easel painting and its conventional use of the frame in class terms, rejecting it as elitist and limiting:
"we reject so-called salon painting and the ultra intellectual art of the

Figure 3.
Tina Modotti, Diego Rivera Mural: *In the Arsenal* (with Frida Kahlo
and Tina Modotti), from *Corrido de la Revolución*. Throckmorton Fine Art,
New York.

aristocracy and exalt the manifestation of monumental art because it is useful."[44] This did not mean, however, that muralism was to dispense with the notion of the frame altogether. While Rivera's murals certainly promoted a different kind of viewing experience, one that theoretically opened up art to the "masses," the densely "bodied" surfaces are offered for contemplation from within the ultimate in authoritative frames: the public buildings that are in turn framed within the space of the city. From within the safe form of the nation's official spaces, urban viewers were to peruse the largely rural Indian bodies in a visual experience whereby the embodied gaze conferred upon the viewers a combination of scopic and physical mastery.

Modotti's photograph *Open Doors*, like Rivera's murals, invites the viewer to engage with the image on a corporeal level. And, like the murals, this bodily engagement with the photograph is one that has the potential to undermine the authority of the frame and to challenge the conventional structure of the gaze. Two aspects of Modotti's photograph are especially striking in this context. First, *Open Doors* contains not a proliferation of bodies but a proliferation of frames: the invisible frame constituted by the four edges of the photograph; the first door frame that is surrounded by the wall frame, itself bisected by the picture rail; beyond the first door another space is framed; and beyond it another in the form of the second open door that gives out onto a space we cannot see; finally, the door panels are divided into smaller panels. Of these panels some are transparent (the upper six of the main door panel and those within the second space I outlined), and some are opaque (the panels on the first door). This play on transparency and opaqueness heightens a sense of framed spaces as containing and giving onto further framed spaces. Second, among this proliferation of frames, the space that is most visually significant insofar as it arouses the viewer's curiosity is precisely the space that cannot be seen: the lighter, "shinier" space beyond the second door that tantalizes the viewer with its inaccessibility. What exactly is there?

In a 1992 essay, "Pandora: Topographies of the Mask and Curiosity," Laura Mulvey outlines three themes underpinning the myth of Pandora and what she denominates as a feminist aesthetics of curiosity. The themes are "first, an active look, associated with the feminine; second, the drive of decipherment, directed towards riddles or enigmas; third, a topography of concealment and investigation, the space of secrets." This notion of a feminist aesthetics of curiosity seems immensely productive for an understanding of *Open Doors*, a photographic image that actively invites the viewer to explore, to investigate the secret space that exists beyond its frame. The pull of this space, the urge to investigate engages the viewer bodily with the image; it arouses a strong desire in the viewer to project herself into the second space from whence this other space might be glimpsed. I think of this space as the space of invitation to "the active look associated with the feminine." Within the frame of this image, this association between the feminine and the active look comes into sharper focus when we consider that Modotti's image is specifically a photographic image. Abigail Solomon-Godeau points out that in photographic images there is a "structural congruence of the point of view (the eye of the photographer, the eye of the camera, and the spectator's eye)." In other words, as viewers of this photographic image we are positioned and see what the woman photographer, Modotti, saw at the moment of making the image. It is her gaze that structures our gaze, awakening in us a desire to explore that other frozen space both within, and at the same time beyond, the image.[45]

This desire is, of course, ultimately thwarted. There simply is no gaining access to the off-frame space. This is, after all, just a photographic image. It is representation and not "reality." However, a combination of the proliferation of frames and a momentary detachment (can we call it out-of-body experience?) elicits a certain awareness in the viewer. And this awareness involves a more complex response to the body and its relationship to framed space. In other words, to look at the other "feminine" space that is hinted at in the photograph, a certain bodily maneuver is required. In order to enter the space of the image, the viewer must relinquish her position of visual mastery outside the frame, in a conceptual leap that problematizes the stability and fixity of the subject-object relationship. The significance of this problematization can be understood in the light of classic feminist theories of vision and psychoanalysis. If the body is the locus of the gaze, the gaze in turn is determined by psychic investments. Psychoanalysis has identified vision and the gaze as key issues in the structuring of sexual difference. Feminist theories of vision and psychoanalysis (notably the earlier work of Laura Mulvey) have revealed what is at stake in the organization of sexual difference around the binary of the male as locus of the active gaze and woman as erotic spectacle. Within this phallocentric visual economy—in which woman signifies lack, the fear of nothing to see—the visual field has conventionally been structured in such a way as to allay anxiety by affording the viewer scopic mastery over the scene. Modotti's photograph *Open Doors*, I suggest, potentially offers an altogether different kind of viewing experience, one in which the feminine gaze is associated with curiosity and therefore with agency. By "inviting the viewer in," Modotti's photograph brings about a momentary encounter with the self (back there) which, in turn, is recognized as other. In this temporary, yet strategic split second, the viewer's control over the visual field is radically called into question and revealed as terrifyingly, or invigoratingly, illusory.

Opening Doors

If, in the late 1990s, feminist cultural theory generally has moved into a more dynamic phase, in this chapter, my aim has been to think about ways in which it might be possible to push Modotti scholarship beyond the Mulvey moment of the 1980s in which it has become stuck. The Whitechapel exhibition and essay re-presented Modotti (and Kahlo) and provided a strategically useful framework within which to locate her photographs. My own work is very much indebted to Mulvey and Wollen's groundbreaking text. It is time, nevertheless, to clear some space in order to think beyond this moment in the 1980s. Clearing space, as Sue Best states, "means drawing upon the work of others. Although we cannot really claim to have 'cleared' a space, complete erasure does not take place; rather we write over that already written space, such that our writing remains legible, for a time at least before it is covered over. Through this process we remain defined, tied and indebted to that from which we differentiate ourselves."[46]

I draw frequently on Mulvey and Wollen's work in an attempt to negotiate a position from which to write on Modotti's photographs. Writing on, or reading, these photographs necessarily involves attending to questions of framing, the body, and space—elements that are present in the film-still of *The Tiger's Coat*. The irony implicit in that film-clip has fascinated me, has aroused my curiosity for some time. A footnote from an essay by Griselda Pollock, writing on Degas, has had a similar effect: "In a system which recruits the image of woman as a fixed object mastered by a masculine look, feminine desire will figure itself or find forms of representation as that which exceeds fixing, picturing, framing, containing, objectifying. Not because women are good and do not objectify, but because the social screens of representation negate feminine desire, deny it forms of representation. It is not to be represented by objects, but in relations."[47]

It is these relations that I attempt to articulate in my discussion of Modotti's photograph *Open Doors*. This discussion does not claim to offer a "solution" to the dynamic of the representation of either sexual or racial others. For to do so would imply that we indeed could glimpse that secret space off-frame. Instead, I attempt to develop further strategies for reading Modotti's photographs, strategies that might bring that secret space ever closer.

Commodity Feminism
and the Reading of *Roses*

At Auction

"Although a record price for a single photographic print at auction was reached at Christies on April 16 for Lissitzky's photomontage *Pelikan Tinte* ($120,000), . . . it was quickly topped at Sotheby's just 24 hours later by Modotti's *Roses, Mexico*, which went for $150,000. The second highest price realized was also at Sotheby's; $140,000 for Weston's *Palm Trunk, Cuernavaca* set a record for the artist."[1] It is ironic that at the very same sale at which Modotti's *Roses* fetched a (then) record sum for a photograph at auction, Weston's *Palm Trunk, Cuernavaca* should be outsold by Modotti's image. This fact does not tally with the positions Modotti and Weston occupy within the history of photography. In Ian Jeffrey's *Photography: A Concise History*, Weston is allotted three full pages, which offer biographical detail and a résumé of Weston's photographic aesthetic. Modotti is allotted five brief lines and is, significantly, defined first and foremost in her capacity as the "Italian companion of Edward Weston in Mexico in the twenties." Similarly, in Naomi Rosenblum's *World History of Photography*, Modotti is barely mentioned, while Weston receives an individual profile and is referred to frequently in the chapter entitled "Art, Photography, and Modernism, 1920–1945."[2]

The discrepancy between Modotti's virtual absence from the texts of photographic history and her contemporary status as a photographer who "outsells" Edward Weston underlines how the whole question of conferring value within the visual arts is a deeply ideological practice.[3] Until the recent critical reevaluation of Modotti, set in motion by the Whitechapel exhibition and essay, her work remained undervalued and on the margins of culture. In the wake of feminist excavation, a critical practice that purports to challenge the canon, Modotti's photographs start to accrue value from within the very system under attack. If feminist excavation is a question of plotting female signatures back onto the cultural map, then what I explore in this chapter is what happens to Modotti's signature in the wake of its "excavation" in the United States. Having established the Whitechapel essay's seminality within a British context, I now shift my focus to the United States, a location to which the exhibition later traveled.[4] Just under ten years after the Whitechapel exhibition, the signature "Modotti" inscribed on the surface of the photograph *Roses* sold for a record-breaking $165,000. This chapter explores why.

The constellation of factors that led to the elevated commodity value of the signatory of *Roses* include the literature and events preceding and surrounding the 1991 sale, which are linked to the cultural conditions underpinning the production of the photograph in the 1920s. I suggest that the female body has to be a crucial issue in our understanding of the sale of an image in which the female body is (apparently) not represented. My argument, in other words, is that in the 1990s Modotti's body was codified as specifically Mexican and Communist, where both categories connote radical chic. This process of codification was a crucial factor leading to the record-breaking sum fetched by *Roses*. Modotti's fetishized body now circulates as a commodity in a marketplace that ascribes value to images made by "exotic" women in "exotic" locations. This commodification of Modotti is a form of colonization that makes it difficult to plot either Modotti or Mexico onto the cultural map as anything other than paradigms of exotic otherness. Certain issues raised in the Whitechapel essay, such as the emphasis placed on the discourse of the body and on the Mexican context, have (albeit unintentionally) fueled Modotti's commodification. The whole process of the salability of the signature/body "Modotti" illustrates how feminism, despite its ongoing critique of the commodification of the female body, is itself subject to market forces. As Griselda Pollock points out, feminism is "something that can be packaged by publishers and curated by art historians and the museum."[5]

I offer a reading of *Roses* as a form of contestatory gesture to its own commodification. This reading will draw on Roland Barthes's ruminations on photography in *Camera Lucida*. According to Barthes, society seeks to shield itself from the full impact of what he terms the "intractable reality" (or the ontological link between the image and its referent) of photographic images. It does this by two means. First, photographs are tamed by being contained within the "safe" space of the art gallery, in a process whereby they are consecrated as art objects and thereby lose their specificity as photographic images. Second, Barthes argues that as the spaces in which we live become increasingly saturated with photographic images, these images become "banalized" and lose both their significance and specificity. This chapter focuses on the second means that society possesses to tame photographic images. In my reading I confront the notion of the "intractable reality" of *Roses* by attending to issues of framing and the photographic image. I contend that issues of taming are bound up with issues of framing, that is, with those processes whereby the image gets framed in a number of different and conflicting discursive contexts. These contexts have tended to diffuse the potency of Modotti's photograph, sapping it of its cultural meaning before it has ever had a chance to signify.

Commodifying the Mexican Body: The Signature Collection/Print

I return now to the moment in the 1950s when the anonymous donor deposited his brown paper parcel containing a number of Modotti prints into the custody of the Museum of Modern Art in New York. This moment in the trajectory of Modotti's prints raises key issues around visual representation, the signature, and the female body. The anecdote provided a striking opening image, the brown paper parcel suggesting, among other things, that Modotti comes to us prepackaged, insofar as the ample biographical material to have appeared recently means that one element of the "phenomenon" Modotti—her life—is well known. An emphasis on Modotti's biography has meant that nonbiographically oriented modes of reading her photographs have been foreclosed.

The brown paper package not only conjures up a notion of preknowledge but also lends itself to two additional and, to some degree, opposing interpretations. First, the notion of a bundle of photographic images concealed inside a plain wrapper conjures up images of pornographic material, that is, visual material deemed unsuitable for public consumption. If we take a conventional definition of pornography as graphically explicit material, usually depicting the human body, that is designed to provoke or arouse sexual stimulation, then it is helpful to take a peek at those images contained in the parcel. Sarah M. Lowe's catalog offers a representative selection of the images that were anonymously donated to the Museum of Modern Art and includes the following photographs: *Staircase* (ca. 1924–26); *View of Housetops* (n.d.); *Convent of Tepoztlán* (1924); *Exterior of Pulquería* (ca. 1926); *Nopal Cactus* (1925); *Calla Lily* (1924–26); *Baby Nursing* (ca. 1926–27); *An Aztec Mother* (ca. 1926–27); *Labour 1 or Hands Washing* (ca. 1927); *Fiesta in Juchitán, Oaxaca, Mexico* (1927–29); *Child in Sombrero* (ca. 1927); *Mella's Typewriter* (1928); *Tehuantepec Type* (1929).[6] The majority of the photographs depict inanimate objects, rather than human subjects. With one exception, the human subjects represented are fully clothed. That exception is *Baby Nursing*, where part of the mother's breast is visible. However, the function of the breast here is for sustenance, not titillation. Following a loose definition of pornography as graphically explicit material, usually depicting the human body, that is designed to provoke or arouse sexual stimulation, none of the images contained within the parcel should be considered pornographic.

Nor are they representative of any of what have been considered Modotti's more overtly political or sloganistic images. This brings me to the second layer of meaning suggested by the parcel.[7] With the possible exception of *Mella's Typewriter*, none of the images in the donated parcel are in any way overtly political. Or to be more precise, none of the images are explicitly and directly Communist. (See *Hammer and Sickle* [1927] for a clear example of a "Communist" photograph.) The donation was made in the 1950s during the anti-Communist purges of McCarthyism, hence, we must presume, the donor's desire to rid himself of potentially risky property. Yet the prints are not overtly "Communist," so their concealment has *nothing* to do with what they graphically represented as photographic images. Instead, what was at stake was something else inscribed upon their surface: the signature "Modotti." This signature leads back to the inscribing body that in the 1950s had been codified as a Communist body. The intersection of the body and Communism does come into focus in one particular photograph contained in the parcel: *Mella's Typewriter*. This image of the typewriter that belonged to the prominent and well-known political activist named in the title implicitly links Modotti to Communism through her body insofar as Julio Antonio Mella was one of Modotti's lovers. What I suggest here is that it was the Communist body, in its manifestation as signature, from which the donor was at pains to disassociate himself.

Two antithetical positions with regards to the donation of the photographs to the Museum of Modern Art emerge: first, the parcel image conjures up notions of the containment of pornographic material, which, nevertheless, was not the case; second, the images themselves were not representative of Modotti's overtly political images, and instead it was the signature on the prints, rather than the prints themselves, from which the donor wished to distance himself. In other words, this moment in the 1950s, with its emphasis on biography and the body, is symbolically representative of the continuing erasure of Modotti's photographs as visual objects in their own right. In what follows, I will pursue the ramifications of the latter position, that is to say, the prints were concealed because of their signatory, which in turn leads us back to the Communist body. But my aim in doing so is to work around to the second position, namely, the "unsuitability" of the prints for consumption. In this way, I hope to carry forward the process of uncovering the images and, most important, reading them.

In *Raiding the Icebox*, Peter Wollen comments on the purges that were taking place among North American political and artistic radicals in the 1950s, particularly in the movie industry, identifying those who were directly or indirectly attributable to McCarthyism and citing the names of radical artists fleeing to Europe as a result.[8] Given the historical circumstances of the 1950s, it stands to reason that, to be found in possession of a "Modotti," that is to say a photograph signed by a card-carrying Communist, at the height of McCarthyism in the United States posed a potential danger. The hypothesis that it was Modotti's signature and its Communist connections, rather than what the prints themselves depicted, that motivated the anonymous donor to make his gift, seems probable. The trace of the signature "Tina Modotti" on the surface of the prints ultimately leads back to the inscribing body. The containment of the Modotti prints within the parcel therefore represents a brief and significant moment of disembodiment. The prints and their signature become detached from the body that produced them in order to sever their link with another body, that of the donor.

Chapter Two

The anonymous donor of the Modotti prints to the Museum of Modern Art is unlikely to ever be identified. The identity of the current owner of *Roses*, however, is well and truly in the public domain. The image was purchased by the San Francisco–based entrepreneur Susie Tomkins, who "gained business fame as the spirit behind Esprit sportswear, but her claim to photographic glory was her . . . acquisition of Tina Modotti's blockbuster photo *Roses, Mexico*. Now Tomkins is combining her art with her commerce: She's reproducing the Modotti image (albeit sideways) on the handtags of her Susie Tomkins line of clothing."[9]

Tomkins's interest in *Roses* is based only indirectly on the photograph itself. She purchased the image, I suggest, because of the symbolic associations that the signature "Modotti" evokes. There are two factors worth underlining. First, Modotti was a woman photographer, and second, she was politically radical. Tomkins is not only a successful businesswoman but also considers herself something of an art connoisseur. These two activities are not unrelated. Tomkins was clearly looking to invest in a signature whose cultural capital would complement her own status as a woman entrepreneur. (She, like Modotti, is a woman who operates in a man's world.) That gender was on the agenda on 17 April 1991 is clear from Sotheby's postsale review:

> Although the market had calmed by the spring of 1991, the auction still provided some fireworks with the sale of Tina Modotti's *Roses, Mexico* and Edward Weston's *Palm Trunk, Cuernavaca* to clothing designer Susie Tomkins for $165,000 and $154,000. It was a fortunate coincidence that these images, both taken in Mexico while the two artists were lovers, came up for auction at the same moment. Each a stunning example of the photographer's work, the two images seemed to embody the very essence of female and male, yin and yang, exactly those forces which must have so powerfully drawn those forces together at that important period in their creative lives.[10]

Looking at the two images in question—Modotti's *Roses*, which is reminiscent of the kind of gyno-images produced by feminist artists in the 1970s, and Weston's undeniably phallic palm trunk—it is almost too tempting not to go along with the idea of the masculine and feminine principles in operation. However, what I want to underscore here is the fact that this review of the sale of the photographs in 1991 pushes a certain kind of understanding of gender to the forefront. Implicit in this understanding of gender is the perception that, in the 1990s, it was a category that sold images. It is ironic that gender, for so long an invisible, unmarked category within the realms of visual representation (both in terms of curatorial and critical practice) should play such a key role in the sale of Modotti and Weston's photographic images. In the light of feminist interventions into the history of art, it has become clear that issues of gender and visual representation are riven with conflict and tension, which become particularly acute when the image-maker in question is a woman. Images by women have traditionally not been endowed with either cultural or economic capital. But there can be no

Figure 4.
Tina Modotti, *Roses*, 1924, platinum print. 7 3/8" × 8 3/8"
Throckmorton Fine Art, New York.

doubt that the fact that Modotti was a woman photographer was an important feature for the purchaser of *Roses*.

Susie Tomkins is not only a female entrepreneur but also an entrepreneur with a difference. She is renowned for her middle-class, liberal credentials. The Esprit public relations blurb states that "Esprit has always been known as much more than just a fashion company. The company operates with a social conscience and has made a commitment to support causes and speak out on issues that are of global concern."[11] Tomkins has used Esprit advertising and marketing campaigns to raise public awareness about such issues as the environment and AIDS. The combination of associations implicit in Modotti's signature, connoting as it does a politically radical woman working in an underdeveloped country, matches Tomkins's style. Its associations with issues of gender and marginality suit Tomkins's sales agenda. The signature "Modotti" has come to represent the ultimate in radical chic—glamorous, gutsy, exotic, sexy, and with just a hint of danger. Tomkins and her publicity team could not have harnessed a more desirable string of adjectives to the name Esprit. However, these attributes have little to do with any photograph that Modotti might have made. Instead, these attributes are predicated on Modotti's status as an iconic body.

It seems likely that Tomkins would have been aware of Modotti's role as the model and muse of Edward Weston. It is, after all, in Weston's images that Modotti's body assumes its iconic status. His series of images *Tina on the Azotea* precedes any photograph that Modotti herself made. And Weston's photograph is responsible for another factor that contributes to the elevated commodity value of *Roses*. That factor is evoked in the title of Modotti's image in the Sotheby's catalog, where it gains the appendage "Mexico."[12] Despite the fact that Modotti was Italian American, a great deal of emphasis has been placed on the Mexican context in which she lived and worked. Although this context was the one in which Modotti produced the bulk of her photographs, the location of her body as a Mexican object in Weston's *Azotea* series was probably also a contributing factor in her "Mexicanization." This objectification functions on two levels. First, Weston's image functions as a transparent representation of Modotti's body, which is located within a specifically Mexican context, as the Spanish word *azotea* (or rooftop) in the English title indicates. This conjunction of image and text powerfully contributes to the objectification of Modotti's Mexican body. Consider José Vasconcelos's reaction to Weston's photograph and its model: "The photographer [Weston] brought with him a beauty of Italian origin, sculptural and depraved who was the axis of the group [of bohemian artists] and held them united by a common desire; divided by bitter rivalry. La Perlotti, let us call her thus, practiced the profession of vampire. . . . She was seeking, perhaps notoriety, but not money. *We all knew her body* because she served as a gratuitous model for the photographer and her bewitching nudes were fought over. Her legend was a dark one" (my italics).[13] Bertram D. Wolfe, who quotes Vasconcelos's description of Modotti at length, suggests that this section of the memoirs tells us more about Vasconcelos's "erotic mysticism" than it does about Modotti. Nevertheless, Vasconcelos's sense that "we all knew her body" is significant here, for it highlights the force of transparency with which photographic representation has traditionally been invested.

Second, Weston's photograph of Modotti-as-Mexican-body exists alongside a series of other images of Mexican objects, such as the *pulquerías* and toys that so fascinated Weston during his fabled stay in Mexico. Modotti's Mexican status therefore has nothing to do with any sense of a "real" national identity; it is predicated on having been photographed as a Mexican object. Furthermore, her objectification as Mexican is ultimately based upon a question of bodily identity.

That Tomkins's investment in the signature "Modotti" hinges on its bodily and Mexican connotations is confirmed by the events surrounding the sale of *Roses*. On the successful purchase of *Roses*, Tomkins's "photographic consultant" Merrily Page issued a press release in which she revealed the identity of the other bidders for the image. These included the pop icon Madonna. Page exultantly declared that she understood that Madonna was bidding for the image because she "had an intense interest in feisty women."[14] Madonna's drive to possess *Roses* is revealing on a number of counts and underscores the way in which the codified body figures at the center of a complex promotional web. As a popular artist working within the global public arena, Madonna herself "has come to represent the perfect post-modern body in both theoretical and popular discourse."[15] Both women then, signify the body in what is effectively a two-way interchange. Modotti's signature is replete with cultural capital for Madonna, a well-known collector of images by radical women artists.

She already owns a number of paintings by Frida Kahlo, and at the time of the sale of *Roses* she was interested in completing her collection with a Modotti. Despite the fact that Madonna was outbid by Tomkins, she later went on to confirm her interest in the photographer. The 1995 Philadelphia show of Modotti's photographs was funded by Madonna, who auctioned off her 1969 Mercedes convertible, donating $56,350 to the exhibition. Coinciding with the opening of the Modotti exhibition in Philadelphia, an article entitled "Lucky Star" in the magazine *Philadelphia*, draws an explicit parallel between Modotti and Madonna:

> In her 45 years, photographer Tina Modotti lived many lives. She was an artist, a globe-trotting activist, an intellectual, a humanitarian, an olive-complected beauty with a healthy appetite for men. Everywhere she went, controversy and romance were sure to follow. And everybody had an opinion on her politics, her work, her promiscuity. Sound like someone we know? Someone whose name has been linked to everyone from Warren Beatty to Dennis Rodman? Whose art involves simulated masturbation and tasseled pasties? It should come as no surprise that Madonna has taken a keen interest in the life and art of Tina Modotti.[16]

This parallel is confirmed by Madonna herself, who suggests that her interest in Modotti should be self-evident. "Tina Modotti was an actress, an artist, a muse and a freedom fighter, unbelievably talented and completely misunderstood. Need I say more?"[17]

Writing about Madonna's interest in Frida Kahlo, Janis Bergman-Carton calls the kind of cultural interchange between Madonna and Kahlo "an old and reliable advertising device, the artist-celebrity validation code. By this measure, Kahlo is considered a better artist (investment) because she is collected by Madonna, and Madonna is considered a more serious and respected celebrity (investment) because she collects Kahlo."[18] This notion of cultural investments and exchanges is equally applicable to the events surrounding the Philadelphia exhibition and to the sale of *Roses* in 1991. However, in the sale of *Roses*, the artist-celebrity validation code becomes a three-way process once Susie Tomkins enters the game. Madonna, I should point out, is believed to have an interest *not* in the *images* made by "feisty" women but in the feisty women themselves, where "feisty" connotes a particular kind of sexual/sexy female body. Her interest in feisty women is underlined in her comments in *Philadelphia* magazine, where Modotti's status as actress, artist, muse, and freedom fighter precede any mention of Modotti's photography, which is after all the ostensible subject of the exhibition and indeed, the article.

Modotti, like Madonna, was Italian American. Yet this link is nowhere evident. Madonna's interest in feisty Mexican women, however, is well-documented. She owns a number of paintings by Frida Kahlo and is said to have purchased the rights to the artist's life story.[19] Madonna, then, has an intense interest not only in feisty women but also in feisty women working within a specifically Mexican context, where feisty-ness would even seem to be derived on some level from the Mexican setting.[20] This context becomes overdetermined at the time of the sale of *Roses*. Besides the addition of the word "Mexico" to the photograph's title, the Mexican context becomes a key selling point in a number of ways. This fact is borne out in the short fragment of text that appears below the reproduction of *Roses* in the Sotheby's catalog: "In 1926 Diego Rivera captured the essence of Modotti's work in the following words: 'Tina Modotti has done marvels in sensibility on a plane, perhaps more abstract, more aerial, even more intellectual, as is natural for an Italian temperament. Her work flowers perfectly in Mexico and harmonizes with our passion.'"[21]

The Rivera quotation comes from an article on the photographs of both Modotti *and* Weston that originally appeared in *Mexican Folkways*.[22] The fragment selected for the catalog entry omits any mention of Weston, nor does it mention Modotti's North American connections, either in the form of Modotti's 1913 immigration to California or in the form of the influence of Edward Weston. On one level, the exclusion of Weston might appear liberating. His presence problematizes any critical approach to Modotti's photographs informed by an interest in issues of gender. However, the argument that Weston's exclusion from the catalog takes place in the name of some sort of feminist strategy is difficult to sustain. Feminism, in the guise of radical chic, does have something to do with the sale price, in that Tomkins was almost certainly interested in Modotti as a specifically woman photographer. This, after all, is the world of dealers and speculation. There is more at stake in the exclusion. On the one hand, the Rivera quotation *does* acknowledge Modotti's Italian roots. On the other, the catalog entry prioritizes her location within a specifically Mexican cultural context both in terms of its content and in terms of what Rivera himself represents. Rivera's voice functions as another signifier in the chain of celebrity endorsements surrounding the image and its sale. For the kind of consumer who would frequent Sotheby's sales, Rivera would be an established name, with specific connotations of Mexicanness. In turn, Mexicanness would be imbued with a particular set of cultural and historical associations for this consumer.

Peter Wollen states that "the Mexican Renaissance is the one recent Third World art movement that has had a significant impact on the metropolis."[23] This impact was felt particularly in the United States. All three of the major proponents of muralism, Rivera, Orozco, and Siqueiros, traveled north to paint in the United States, where California represented a specific of point of entry. Wollen further notes that the traffic between California and Mexico has been particularly intense, providing a gateway to Mexico for, among others, Weston, Jackson Pollock, and Philip Gusto, and from Mexico, for the "rey gordo" of Mexican art, Diego Rivera.[24] Furthermore, it is important to recall that California, until relatively recently, *was* Mexico.[25] California is also home base to Esprit, Susie Tomkins's international company.

Rivera's name and its reifying invocation of Mexicanness is underlined by the muralist's words, which feed into the worst kind of stereotypes of Mexican exoticism: "Modotti's work flowers perfectly . . . and harmonizes with our passion." And conveniently, there above the quotation, the photograph seems literally to illustrate this flowering passion. The catalog entry therefore promotes the notion of Mexico as a mythical and exotic space. It omits to mention Modotti's significant collaboration with Edward Weston. It seems likely that the catalog aligns her instead with the Mexican Rivera because, in an economy of desire, his "otherness" as opposed to Weston's "self" is simply more valuable. Ironically, today California is also home to a sizable Mexican American community and Mexicanness is loaded with negative connotations. However, Rivera belongs comfortably to a distant past. According to Helen Delpar, "during these years American intellectuals, journalists and artists, most of them of a leftist persuasion, were drawn to Mexico because of their interest in the Revolution's impact on society and the arts and their desire to defend Mexico from attack in the United States."[26] Their number included Ella and Bertram Wolfe (the latter went on to write a biography of Rivera), the painter and critic Carlton Beals, Anita Brenner (author of *Idols behind Altars*), and Frances Toor (editor of *Mexican Folkways*).

Just as the Mexican context inhabited by Modotti and Rivera exists at a safe enough distance in the past to be glamorous, so too does another factor they have in common, which would be tacitly understood by Sotheby's clientele. Both were committed Communists and, in the post–Cold War era, the threat of Communism would simply not represent the same kind of menace it had during McCarthyism in the 1950s. But there is a fundamental difference in how the political activity of both is interpreted. Whereas Rivera is constructed as an artist whose radical ideals are manifest in the murals he painted across Mexico and the United States, Modotti's status as a Communist is set out in terms of the sexual relationships she had with prominent Communist men, among them, it was rumored, Diego Rivera. The Mexican poet and Nobel Prize winner Octavio Paz makes this case emphatically in an article on Modotti and Frida Kahlo: "A riesgo de desilusionar a alguna feminista, agrego que en algo se parecen Frida y Tina: ninguna de las dos tuvo pensamiento político propio. Al seguir una causa, siguieron a sus maridos y amantes. Nos interesan no como militantes sino como personas complejas y pasionales. Sus figuras pertenecen más a la historia de las pasiones que a la de las ideologías. [At the risk of disillusioning the feminists, I will add that Frida and Tina are alike in something: neither of the two had their own political belief. By following a cause, they followed their husbands and lovers. They are not interesting as militants, but instead as complex and passionate people. As figures, they belong more to the history of passion than to the history of ideology.][27]

Although I would most certainly not endorse Paz's viewpoint, he is not entirely wrong. Despite Modotti's overtly "political" or "slogan" images (for example, *Hammer and Sickle*), despite her involvement in organizations such as International Red Aid, Modotti *does* belong more to the history of "passion." But this is because critics like Paz choose to consign her to that place, conflating the ideological with the bodily, thereby denying Modotti any political agency whatsoever. As if to prove Paz's point, an anonymous piece that follows Paz's text, both literally and thematically, cites the testimony of one

Jean Rivaud Valdés, a combatant in the Spanish Civil War. Although Rivaud Valdés's testimony does not dismiss Modotti's political activity out of hand, he nevertheless seeks to implicate her in the crimes of Vitorrio Vidali, another of Modotti's Communist lovers, and thereby discredit her: "Nuestro corresponsal se escandaliza del silencio de estos intelectuales [Elena Poniatowska y Rascón] sobre los aspectos sombríos y bien conocidos de la vida de Vitorrio Vidali. . . . Agrega que es imposible que Tina Modotti no conociese las actividades de Vidali, acusado de haber sido el exterminador de la izquierda española." [Our correspondent is scandalized by the silence of these intellectuals (Elena Poniatowska and Rascón) over the dark and well-known aspects of Vitorrio Vidali's life. . . . He adds that it is impossible that Tina Modotti did not know about Vidali's activities, accused of having been the exterminator of the Spanish left.][28]

Given that for these critics, Modotti's politics ran no deeper than her current lover (and they did all tend to be Communists), it is ironic to discover that Modotti discusses Rivera's political activity at some length in a letter to Weston dated 17 September 1929. She elaborates on Rivera's expulsion from the Communist party, revealing her strongly held political principles:

Reasons: That his many jobs he has lately accepted from the government—decorating the Nat. Palace, Head of Fine Arts, decorating the new Health Department are incompatible with a militant member of the p[arty]. Still the p[arty] did not ask him to leave his posts, all they asked him was to make a public statement declaring that the holding of these jobs did not prevent him from fighting the present reactionary government. His whole attitude lately has been a very passive one in regard to the p[arty] and he would not sign the statement, so out he went. . . . He will be considered, and he is, as traitor. I need not add that I shall look upon him as one too, and from now on all my contact with him will be limited to our photographic transactions.[29]

What is more, Modotti's own attitude to the Party could never be described as a passive one. At a crucial moment in her career in Mexico, Modotti's photography came into conflict with politics when she was offered the post of official photographer of the Museo Nacional in Mexico City. She turned the offer down because she felt she could not accept an official post from a government that had done nothing to bring to justice Julio Antonio Mella's murderers.

Whatever the truth about Modotti's political activity (and owing to the dearth of material written by her, it is unlikely we will ever know the extent of her involvement in Vidali's affairs), in 1991, at the time of the Sotheby's sale, positioned within the safe space of a bygone age, Modotti's Communist body circulated in the post–Cold War era as a commodity in a market in which it signified the ultimate in radical chic. Sotheby's photography expert, Beth Gates-Warren, issued a statement to the magazine *American Photo* that concerned the political dimension of the sale of *Roses* and its latter-day location on Tomkins's handtags. Seemingly without a trace of irony, she declared: "Tina Modotti, who was a communist, would probably have loved it—everyone will have access to the image now."[30]

She could not have been further from the truth. The sale of *Roses* represents a moment at which the signature "Modotti" becomes excessively overdetermined with bodily connotations in a process whereby Modotti's image itself becomes occluded. By investing in Modotti's signature, Tomkins was investing in an iconic body to promote herself and thereby to enhance the salability of her products. These products, we should not forget, clothe the female body. Modotti's body becomes a site at which a number of key signatures converge: Modotti's, Madonna's, and Rivera's. These signatures in turn become appended to Tomkins's own signature. This is graphically illustrated by the handtag on which the image is reproduced. *Roses* occupies the top quarter of the handtag on which it appears sideways. Below the image there is a brief section of typewritten text by Tomkins herself stating, "I don't buy a lot of things for myself. But when I do it's something I'd want to have for a long time. That's the premise of this collection. It feels like it's been around forever, but you still want to keep wearing it over and over again." Below the text the bottom quarter of the handtag is occupied by the flamboyant signature "Susie Tomkins." In other words, on the handtag, Tomkins's signature is as visually important as *Roses*. Tomkins's marketing device implicitly draws a parallel between herself, the fashion artist and author-designer of a "signature collection," and the photographic artist, Modotti, author of what has become her signature work, *Roses*. In the light of Tomkins's assertions about the durability of her collection, it is ironic that once the body/signature had served its purpose she simply discarded it. Tomkins is quoted in *Vogue*,

"Actually, we don't credit the picture [on the handtag], which we're using as icon material. Though we use big blow-ups of it in the shops, we're not celebrating Tina Modotti. We're just celebrating a beautiful image, linking it with a line of clothes (and it's been very successful)."[31]

The erasure of the signature at this point in the 1990s represents a second moment of disembodiment that mirrors that other moment back in the 1950s when the anonymous donor concealed the signature in the paper parcel in order to avoid its association with himself. If the signature represents the trace of the signing body, at these two moments in the 1950s and the 1990s, this body/signature is simply voided. The body/signature, and the very real danger that it represented in the 1950s, first passed into the care of the museum and was then co-opted by the fashion industry; its charge of danger has, effectively, been defused. The commodification of *Roses* represents an act of appropriation that has foreclosed the possibility of reading *Roses* as an image in its own right made by a specifically female subject. The Third/First World dynamic of this act of voiding is elaborated by Celeste Olalquiaga, who states: "In the First World . . . the cultural production of Third World countries is integrated into mainstream culture as a marker of difference and exoticism. Here, what is appropriated loses its original meaning, whatever that may have been. It is pre-emptively voided of any signification that could prove destabilizing to the receiving culture."[32]

The ultimate paradox, considering the role that the complex cultural framing played in the commodification of Modotti's *Roses*, is that once commodified and in the marketplace, *Roses* loses its significance as a cultural statement. What is perhaps even more alarming is that at certain points in the events surrounding the sale of *Roses*, one cannot help but remark on the overlap between issues raised in the Whitechapel catalog and the selling points of Modotti's image. The Whitechapel essay, working from within debates around feminist aesthetics, focuses on the female body in a bid to deal with the implications that this body has for an understanding of Modotti's position as a photographer. It also positions Modotti firmly and unproblematically within a specifically Mexican context. It is the particular connotations of the Communist body and its specifically Mexican context that drew Susie Tomkins to Modotti's signature. That Modotti had been appropriated by an explicitly feminist project of excavation, and that her name was linked with Kahlo's, could only have added to the allure for Tomkins. Gender and marginality, words that did not exist in the vocabulary of the auction room before the sale at Sotheby's, all of a sudden signify chic. And chic in turn means money. Tomkins therefore invested money in Modotti's signature, which became briefly appended to Tomkins's own signature in an outburst of publicity surrounding the sale (involving Madonna, fortunately enough for Tomkins). And then the signature was simply voided, effectively having served its purpose. After the sale had taken place, the image, minus its original signature, appeared for an indeterminate period with its context suppressed, on the handtags of a line of women's clothing. The handtag itself, it is worth noting, is an item that is discarded once the purchase of the goods has been made.

The sale of *Roses* graphically illustrates the precarious boundaries that separate the marketplace, the art world, and the academy. The academy here includes what might be termed its more radical elements, in this case feminist scholarship and theory. Abigail Solomon-Godeau succinctly sums up the way in which the three institutional practices overlap:

> The discipline of art history and its newest offshoot, the history of photography, differs from all other self-contained histories of cultural production (e.g., musicology, architectural history, literary studies etc.) in that the object of study exists also as a commodity within a market system. Thus the enterprise of scholarship—no matter how disinterested—is inevitably linked to a parallel world of dealers and collectors, investment and speculation. When, for example, art historians "rediscover" the neglected glories of American luminist painting . . . a certain train of events is set off.[33]

However, the question remains, beyond recapitulating and thereby to some degree exposing the imbrication of the marketplace, the art world, and the academy, what more can we (in this case I, located within the academy) do to reappropriate Modotti's photographs and to reinfuse them with cultural meaning?[34]

In what follows I elaborate on a reading of *Roses*, with the aim of answering the question as to how we might both reappropriate Modotti's photographs and reinfuse them with cultural meaning.

Chapter Two

A Rose is a Rose

Victor Burgin points out that had Roland Barthes never written specifically on photography, his work on other forms of textual production would nonetheless be central to its study. According to Burgin, Barthes's pioneering work on semiology enables us to understand the way in which visual images are structured through and by language. As it was, Barthes did write specifically on photographic representation at a number of points in his career. *Mythologies*, which originally appeared in French in 1957, includes two sections with an overt interest in photography: "Photography and Electoral Appeal" and "The Great Family of Man."[35] In neither of these essays does Barthes venture "inside" any individual photographic image to offer an analysis. He chooses instead to decode the ideological subtexts of a particular genre of photography, in the case of the first section, and the resonances of a photographic exhibition, in the second. However, at a later point in his work, he does take the important step of "entering" the photographic image, to offer a formula for decoding it. Barthes published two influential essays on photographic meaning, "The Photographic Message" (1961) and "The Rhetoric of the Image" (1964).[36] In these essays Barthes elaborates a system of meaning in photographic images that hinges on the key concepts of connotation and denotation. Denotation is concerned with information and with what I describe (borrowing the terminology of Abigail Solomon-Godeau) as the photograph's "purchase on the real." It is what one sees when one looks at a photograph, the basic information that the image renders:

> In front of a photograph, the feeling of "denotation," or, if one prefers, of analogical plenitude, is so great that the description of a photograph is literally impossible; to describe consists precisely in joining to the denoted message a relay or second-order message derived from a code which is that of language and constituting a relation to the photographic analogue, however much care one takes to be exact, a connotation: to describe is thus not simply to be imprecise or incomplete, it is to change structures, to signify something different to what is shown.[37]

Connotation, therefore, which functions on a symbolic level, is concerned with the cultural codes that are activated when the viewer looks at a photograph. Both levels of meaning are triggered when one looks at a photograph. So, for example, to turn to *Roses*, the image denotes roses, a kind of flower, but on a connotational level roses have a whole range of meanings, contingent on the viewer's formation within a specific cultural context, that might include the rose as a symbol of love, time, beauty, and so on.

In *Camera Lucida*, an intensely personal meditation on photography, Barthes introduces two new key concepts into the vocabulary of photography theory: *studium* and *punctum*. Their significance lies in the emphasis they place on the active role of the viewer in the production of photographic meaning. In many ways this position is not so far removed from other of Barthes's theories of textuality, most famously of course his proclamation of the death of the author. And on a superficial level the terms appear to correspond with the notions of denotation and connotation. Organized around a binary principle, *studium* and *punctum* represent two elements in the apprehension of a photographic image. As he attempts to elucidate how photographs affect him, Barthes makes a distinction between photographs that contain only *studium* and those that have the additional element of *punctum*:

> What I feel about these photographs derives from an average affect, almost from a certain training. I did not know a French word which might account for this kind of human interest, but I believe this word exists in Latin: it is *studium*, which doesn't mean, at least not immediately, "study," but application to a thing, taste for someone, a kind of general, enthusiastic commitment, of course but without special acuity. . . . The second element will break (or punctuate) the *studium*. This time it is not I who seek it out (as I invest the field of the *studium* with my sovereign consciousness), it is this element which rises from the scene, shoots out of it like an arrow, and pierces me. . . . This second element which will disturb the *studium* I shall therefore call *punctum*; for *punctum* is also: sting, speck, cut, little hole— and also a cast of the dice. A photograph's punctum is that accident which pricks me (but also bruises me, is poignant to me).[38]

The first element, the *studium* roughly corresponds to a notion of intentionality—the photographer's aims in making the image; the second, the *punctum*, is a detail in the image that strikes out beyond the

Chapter Two

photographic frame and is what, therefore, for Barthes makes the photograph special or poignant.

In the closing pages of *Camera Lucida* Barthes states:

> Society is concerned to tame the Photograph, to temper the madness which keeps threatening to explode in the face of whoever looks at it. To do this, it possesses two means. The first consists of making Photography into an art, for no art is mad. Whence the photographer's insistence on his rivalry with the artist, on subjecting himself to the rhetoric of painting and its sublimated mode of exhibition. . . . The other means of taming the Photograph is to generalize, to gregarize, banalize it until it is no longer confronted by any image in relation to which it can mark itself, assert its special character, its scandal, it madness.[39]

A number of points interest me about this notion of the way in which photographs get tamed. First and most important, taming is subtended by issues of framing. Barthes describes the way in which photographs tend to be contained within framing discourses, the art gallery or the market, and these framing discourses circumvent or check elements present in the image. So in the first example that Barthes cites, the museum or art gallery functions as a form of framing device that draws the photograph within its boundaries and determines the response that the photographic image will elicit. This response is predicated on the photograph's conferred status as an aesthetic object for contemplation. I suggest that the treatment of Modotti's photograph *Roses* at the hands of the institutions of the art world and the marketplace is symbolic of the way in which her photographic output has been "tamed." Moreover, the anonymous donor is involved in one stage of this process of "taming" the photograph when he deposits his gift into the safekeeping of the Museum of Modern Art. In the donor's case, the stakes are personal: he does not wish to have his name associated with the signatory of the prints, "Modotti." The act of donation defuses the perceived danger of the photographs and their maker in the face of a McCarthyist society that would perceive the images as Communist and therefore "mad."[40] The donor sets in motion a chain of events resulting in the eventual purchase of *Roses* by Susie Tomkins.

In the second mode of taming the photographic image posited by Barthes, a photograph is "generalized," "gregarized," and "banalized" "until it is no longer confronted by any image in relation to which it can mark itself."[41] Barthes's second notion of taming the photograph applies appositely to Modotti's photographs and more especially to *Roses*, once they enter the marketplace. "Banalize" is the operative word here. After all, *Roses*, located on the handtags of Esprit products, becomes an empty, meaningless image, totally divorced from any form of "original" context.

Barthes goes on to conclude that, in a culture saturated by images, photography can be either "mad" or "tame." Which one of these two binaries photography represents is ultimately up to the spectator who can "subject [the photograph's] spectacle to the civilized code of perfect illusions, or to confront in it the wakening of intractable reality."[42] In a move toward reinfusing *Roses* with cultural meaning, we need to reappropriate and reread *Roses* against the grain of the process of banalization to which it has been subjected by the twin institutions of the art gallery and the marketplace. First, we need to realign it with "images in relation to which it can mark itself"; second, we need to read it. In this way, the "scandal" of the photograph can be brought back into focus.

The paradoxes underpinning the sale of Modotti's *Roses* have tended to proscribe readings of the image. This proscription is subtended by debates around the status of photography in modern society. Therefore, I want to work through Barthes's notion of framing/taming by bringing into play an additional consideration. I contend that we need to understand the notion of taming in conjunction with an awareness of the issues of framing and sexual difference that inform the production and consumption of visual images. I take my cue again from Griselda Pollock, who states: "Within a visual system which recruits the image of woman as a fixed object . . . feminine desire will figure itself or find forms of representation as that which exceeds fixing, picturing, framing, containing, objectifying."[43] What especially interests me about Pollock's formulation is this notion of exceeding the frame, because *Roses* is a photographic image that is all about framing and excess. Questions of framing and excess also underpin Barthes's notions of the *studium* and the *punctum*.

Roses exists first within an iconographic frame that, in turn, corresponds to a specific historical period in the history of painting. It

Chapter Two

meshes within a tradition of flower painting that has historically been associated with women artists. In *Old Mistresses*, Parker and Pollock trace the history of flower painting, which they argue became a prominent branch of still-life painting that was widespread in Europe in the sixteenth and early seventeenth centuries.[44] Although early practitioners were, on the whole, men, by the late eighteenth century flower painting had become a genre largely associated with women. This period saw a shift in the institutional basis of art practice. Art education became increasingly professionalized and now took place within the newly formed academies.[45] Although women were admitted into the new academies (albeit in small numbers), they were not permitted to participate in the life class, which was of prime importance for the most elevated genre of painting of the period, history painting. Thus women artists were often limited to painting subjects that were considered more "suitable" for their sex, for example, flowers. As the genre of flower painting became increasingly associated with women, so too did its standing and status within the hierarchy of the fine arts diminish.

By the twentieth century, flower painting had become debased and discredited. Parker and Pollock illustrate this point by citing one commentator who wrote, "flower painting demands no genius of a mental or spiritual kind, but only the genius of taking pains and supreme craftsmanship." The association of the genre with women practitioners was not simply a one-way process whereby the genre became linked with women. Parker and Pollock note that with the increasing feminization of the genre came the tendency to conflate the women artists who practiced it with their subject matter: "Paintings of flowers and the women who painted them became mere reflections of each other. Fused into the prevailing notion of femininity, the painting becomes solely an extension of womanliness and the artist becomes a woman only fulfilling her nature."[46]

Where does this historical/iconographic frame take us with respect to Modotti's *photograph* of roses? By making the image, was she just doing what women "do best," depicting flowers, to which as a woman she would have a "natural" (read "cultural") affinity? On one level *Roses* is certainly imbued with such connotations. Nevertheless, on another level, as a photograph, that is to say as an object produced mechanically, *Roses* would not require the "pains and supreme craftsmanship" necessary to capture the neat and intricate detail associated with flower painting. Not only could this photograph not be considered "high" art, in that images of flowers have traditionally been associated with women and are therefore second-rate *avant la lettre*, it could not even be considered crafted because it was produced by a machine. So what is the relation between *Roses* and the historical frame of flower painting? My reading of the photograph posits that although by definition the image invokes the historical frame of flower painting, it also exists beyond that frame. Furthermore, I suggest there *is* a correlation between women and roses. However, this correlation runs contrary to the reductive conflation of woman-with-rose-with-femininity that Parker and Pollock expose in their text as a masculinist myth.

If the painstaking manual effort required to produce a flower painting is not an issue in a photograph, the labor required to produce the intricacy of detail can nevertheless be recast in terms of the complex formal composition of *Roses*. Modotti's image displays meticulous attention to detail in the way it renders the irregular curved shapes of the arrangement of the rose petals that saturate the frame. What at first sight seems to be an image about irregularity is in fact organized around strictly geometrical principles. The right-hand corner is occupied by the largest, most open rose, thereby creating an off-center center. This central rose is framed above and to the left by three smaller and less open roses. The bottom right-hand corner forms a square that is encased neatly by the inverted L-shape, composed of the three surrounding roses. The image therefore is full of frames within frames, which divide the picture plane along its vertical and horizontal axes. However, if a frame is that which separates inside from outside, then this image is also full of transgressed frames: the irregular, round shapes of the petals overspill the straight horizontal and vertical lines within the main frame that in turn is transgressed. The petals overspill the edges of the photographic frame. What are we to make of these transgressed frames within frames?

Just how significant the "discourse of the frame" is becomes apparent when we consider it first in terms of the spectator and second in terms of subject matter. In an article on feminism and photography theory, Lindsay Smith describes the way in which geometral perspective "assumes an established linear relationship between a vantage-point (the eye of the subject looking) and the vanishing-point (the culmination of the look upon an object) according to the eventual convergence of lines of geometral projection." The linear relationship between viewer and image is established partly by perspective and partly by the frame. The frame instructs the viewer how to position herself in relationship to the image. This schema translates itself into what Victor Burgin calls the "cone-of-vision" metaphor, which predominated in theories of representation during the 1970s and 1980s. This has been an especially useful model for feminist theory, as it allows for an account of the spectator's psychic investment in the visual image. However, critics, among them Burgin (and indeed Mulvey herself), have expended a considerable amount of energy in critiquing the cone-of-vision metaphor. This critique of previous theoretical models is based on the grounds that they are "responsible for a reductive and simplistic equation of looking with objectification" where objectification is by definition "bad."[47] The cone-of-vision metaphor therefore lends itself to a form of analysis that leads us down a blind alley from which we can only articulate a critique based on the condemnation of objectification. Such a position does not allow us to offer an account of female agency. I therefore propose that *Roses* is an image that calls into question this "simple equation of looking with objectification." *Roses* is an image that lacks clear instructions as to the viewer's positionality. Instead it provides the perceptive viewer with a number of frames alongside which she can line up. None of these in turn are clearly delineated. There is always spillage, which is both internal and external. In this way the image at once plays to and thereby acknowledges a straightforward notion of the subject-object relationship of the cone-of-vision metaphor. At the same time, it problematizes this relationship, which is one constantly being undermined by the transgression of frames.

Nevertheless, it is perfectly legitimate to ask what is so destabilizing for the viewer about an image of roses, that is to say a bunch of innocuous flowers, that does not clearly demarcate its frame? This leads us to question the cultural resonance, or connotations, of the rose. In an article entitled "The Immutable Still Lifes of Tina Modotti," Sarah M. Lowe suggests that *Roses* can be read in formalist terms. But it can also be read in terms of the cultural significance of the rose as subject matter:

Its rich content has both an intellectual and popular appeal. On the one hand, it falls into art historical discourse as a *memento mori*, for these roses, not upright in a vase but heaped together, appear to have outlived their usefulness as things of living beauty and their differing degrees of deterioration signal human mortality. On the other hand, even an unschooled interpreter would instantly understand the rose as a time-honored symbol of love, from its Roman association with Venus to its role in contemporary Mexican courtship.[48]

Undoubtedly, as Lowe indicates, the rose is resonant of love and death. However, what Lowe does in her reading of *Roses* is to draw the image into the safe and conventional domain of art-historical discourse with her emphasis on the roses as *memento mori*. I am not suggesting here that we simply eschew the art-historical framework within which the photograph exists. To do so would be to underestimate the inextricable relationship between painting and photography. Instead, it is necessary to find another angle from which to approach the question of framing/framework. To do this we need to align *Roses* with another image. This image is *Temptation* (1920) by Modotti's first husband, Roubaix de l'Abrie Richey, for which Modotti modeled and in which the rose figures as a familiar trope representing the pubis. This alignment of images means the relationship between the play on framing in *Roses* and the subject matter becomes especially complex and we can start to discern something of the "scandal" of Modotti's image.

Lynda Nead explores this notion of scandal in her study of the female nude. She describes the crucial role the frame plays in constructing an "acceptable," nonscandalous image of the female body within a visual economy grounded in the psychic need to project a flawless image of "woman." Nead describes the sets of values that subtend the categories of art and obscenity within this economy: "Art is . . . defined in terms of the containing of form within limits; obscenity on the other hand, is defined in terms of excess, as form beyond limit, beyond the frame and representation."[49] Nead here is referring specifically to the female nude. By obscenity we are to understand those images of the female body that exist beyond the realm sanctioned as acceptable within the prevalent visual economy. Within the parameters of Nead's argument, *Roses is* obscene.

The bodily connotations surrounding Modotti's signature became overdetermined during the sale of *Roses*, despite the apparent absence of the represented body in the photograph. But the body, or at least a part of it, *is* represented in the image. This bodily part comes into focus if we read *Roses* in conjunction with *Temptation*. The rose in

Chapter Two

Figure 5.
Roubaix de l'Abrie Richey, *Temptation*, 1920.

Roubaix de l'Abrie's sketch stands in for what is located below it, the pubis. In other words, the rose represents the female genitalia metaphorically and metonymically. This metonymic displacement takes place because visual culture does not sanction the depiction of the female genitalia. As Ludmilla Jordanova argues, "women's bodies and, by extension, female attributes, cannot be treated as fully public, something dangerous might happen, secrets be let out, if they were open to view."[50] If they were open to view, they would unleash a whole series of psychic anxieties concerned with lack and castration. These anxieties must be contained by careful attention to framing, which serves the dual purpose of distancing viewers from the object and providing clear instructions as to their positionality. Therefore, in Roubaix de l'Abrie's sketch the rose functions as an opaque screen concealing what lies below it; this, in turn, is framed by the outline of the female body. Furthermore, the female body in this image has been encased by a hand-drawn frame. De l'Abrie's is an "acceptable" image of the female body, in that although simply a sketch, its representation of the naked female body draws the body into the safe iconographic domain of the nude. The iconographic and literal framing of the body allows the viewer critical distance from which to contemplate the image. This distance reinforces the viewer's objective mastery of the female form.

In Modotti's image the viewer is not afforded the same critical distance in relation to the roses as in *Temptation*. The body that frames the pubis is not represented. Conventionally, this body-frame (absent in *Roses*) would also be framed by the image's physical frame, offering the viewer a kind of double security insofar as the instructions as to the viewer's positionality are clear. The stabilizing presence of the clear body/conventional frame in *Temptation* is replaced in *Roses* by a proliferation of frames contained within the image. What is at stake here becomes evident if we look closely at *Temptation*, for we discover that the psychic anxiety that the loss of this distance would imply is symbolically figured. In the bottom right-hand corner of de l'Abrie's image is a skull. The skull, with its distinctive hairstyle, visually echoes the head of the female form representing the figure of *Temptation*. This female skull is shown, significantly, devouring a snake. The Freudian connotations of the snake hardly need spelling out. In *Temptation* a metonymical displacement takes place, from the castrating skull/mouth to the rose/genitalia. We can theorize this displacement in de

Chapter Two

l'Abrie's image and the implications for a reading of Modotti's photograph by returning to Barthes's notions of the *studium* and the *punctum* and more specifically to Jane Gallop's fascinating interpretation of these terms in *Thinking Through the Body*.

In "The Prick of the Object" Gallop reformulates Barthes's notions of *studium* and *punctum* in terms of their relationship to issues of framing and to the positionality of the viewer. What particularly interests me about Gallop's reading of Barthes's text is the link she makes between the *studium* and the frame, and the way in which this relationship makes possible an encounter with alterity. She suggests "if you think of the *studium* as a kind of enclosure, breaking it up [*punctum*] suggests breaking something open, allowing seepage." Recognizing seepage is another way of approaching the relationship between the viewer and the object. In the traditional cone-of-vision metaphor, the image is conceived as an inert and bounded entity that receives the aggressive look of the gaze, whereby the gaze has conventionally been associated with the masculine, predatory viewing position. However, the recognition of another element in the photograph, the *punctum*, is to imagine another kind of relationship between the viewer and the image, which hinges on the contrast between "the photograph where everything is contained within the frame and the photograph where things continue to happen outside the frame."[51] Gallop elaborates on her understanding of the relationship between the viewer and photograph, destabilizing any simplistic equation between the passive/female and aggressive/male viewers and objects:

> A picture that is all *studium* is just a passive object: inert, immobile, lying there. But when there is that second element, the element that breaks up the *studium*, something happens which is quite the opposite of the relationship which occasions complaints about the male gaze and the female object of the gaze. Something happens: the second element goes off from the scene like an arrow and comes and pierces the viewer. There is a reversal: something in the photograph is aggressive and penetrates the viewer.[52]

The presence of the *punctum* in a particular photographic image disrupts the stability of the boundaries framing the relationship between the viewer and object, which now becomes based on an interchange, what Gallop describes as a "gesture toward some sort of contact with alterity."[53] That is to say, a photograph with a *punctum* stops being an inert, bounded object and starts to offer the possibility of a fluid interchange between the viewer and the image.

Now it could be argued that there is a problem when we apply Barthes's notion of the *punctum* to Modotti's *Roses*, in that the *punctum* has decidedly phallic connotations: "it is this element which rises from the scene, shoots out of it like an arrow, and pierces me." Reminiscent of a certain style of 1970s gyno-images, *Roses* is therefore decidedly unphallic. However, the *punctum* is "also: sting, speck, cut, little hole."[54] By bringing *Roses* alongside *Temptation*, the photograph is confronted by an image "in relation to which it can mark itself, assert its special character, its scandal, its madness."[55] *Roses* then becomes pure *punctum*, in that it is an image all about seepage and, in this sense, is a "photograph where things continue to happen outside the frame." *Roses* can be inserted into a whole range of discursive frames. Each discursive frame, likewise, produces a different viewing position. Certain discursive situations (the marketplace) rob the photograph of its cultural resonances. Others (art-historical discourses) draw the image into the safe space of the art gallery. In both instances, the viewer is accorded the stable position of objective mastery over the inert image. However, when we line *Roses* up alongside *Temptation*, an altogether different dynamic starts to inflect the viewer's relationship with the photograph.

Sarah M. Lowe was right about the rose symbolizing death. It does. But I suggest that the rose here is not an abstract image about the mortality of human beings in any "real" sense. Instead, it is an image shot through with psychic implications insofar as, viewed in tandem with *Temptation*, *Roses* forces the viewer to confront a potent symbol of lack. This reading of *Roses* as lack functions on two levels. First, the roses, as the subject matter of the photograph, represent the female genitalia and thereby represent a metonymic symbol of lack. Second, the proliferation of frames within frames in the photograph invokes lack in that the photographic frame, insofar as it is present, is formed by the layers of rose petals. Here it is possible to trace a link between the frame and lack. John Tagg, in his discussion of framing and discourse, articulates just such a relationship between the frame and lack: "The frame is all show and yet it escapes visibility, like the labia which, to the infibulating eye Freud gives the little boy, already present the desolate spectacle of 'nothing' to be seen, enframing the sight of pure difference."[56] Modotti's photograph, on both a thematic and compositional level, stages an encounter with alterity, with the "sight of pure difference." This encounter takes place in a space in which the viewer is not only denied the security of the frame, but this frame itself comes to figure lack, the sight of nothing (and everything) to see. *Roses*, through its total lack of boundaries and borders, is a truly scandalous photograph. But what ultimately makes *Roses* utterly scandalous, beyond its lack of boundaries and borders, is the fact that this is a photographic image. That is to say, photography's "intractable reality"—its purchase on the real—inevitably points toward a direct reference between the signifier and the signified, the rose/genitalia.

Concluding Remarks

In this chapter I have been concerned to show first how a number of seemingly discrete discursive spaces in fact overlap in significant ways. The academy (including its radical elements such as feminism), the art world, and the marketplace exist in a tightly knit web. Tracing the trajectory of one particular Modotti print through this web shows how, in the aftermath of the "feminist excavation" of the signature "Tina Modotti," the urgent political issues subtending the excavation have been appropriated by the marketplace and repackaged. For a short time the signature "Modotti" circulated as a consumer product imbued with connotations of radical chic. As a consequence of the repackaging of *Roses* by the entrepreneur Susie Tomkins, the image has lost its cultural significance. The photograph has been "tamed" to the point of banality. This is nothing new. As David Tetzlaff states, "the fashion industry has long expropriated images of the exotic other in order to extract value from their affective charge of mystery and danger."[57] To which I would add, in the process the fashion industry also defuses that charge of danger.

If we are ever to get beyond either biography, or approaches to the photographs that rely too heavily on issues of gender and marginality, then contestatory readings are a matter of political urgency. My aim in this chapter, therefore, has been twofold. First, to explore and thereby to unpack the commodification of Modotti, and second, to move beyond the impasse represented by issues in the development of feminist theories of visual representation. These were, namely, the conflation of issues of gender with debates around marginality; and the question of the cone-of-vision metaphor as a useful tool for analysis of visual images. These theoretical positions tend to smooth over the complexities embodied in Modotti's photographs and the discursive frames in which they exist. As such, readings of the photographs that focus wholly on these theoretical positions compromise the potential to offer readings of Modotti's images that enable us to offer an account of her agency as a woman photographer. At the outset of this chapter I argue that the anonymous donor of the Modotti prints to the Museum of Modern Art was concerned more to conceal the signature on the prints than the prints themselves. I now revise this argument. In a move to reinfuse Modotti's photographic prints with cultural meaning, we need to realign the images with others, against which we can discern the real scandal of these photographs. In this way it becomes possible to argue that the images themselves contained within the brown paper parcel donated to the Museum of Modern Art, and not just the signature on their surface, were indeed potentially dangerous and scandalous images. Their scandal and danger emanate from a space unbounded by the frame. Or at least from a space in which the authority of preexisting frames is called into question. Only by attending to issues of framing can we unwrap the brown paper parcel in which Modotti's photographs have been contained, in order to produce readings of her photographs that restore to them their sense of scandal.

3
Photography and
the Politics of Signature

Snapshot

I begin this chapter with a snapshot and a quotation. The snapshot (1924) is by Edward Weston and depicts, from left to right, Federico Marín, Jean Charlot, and Tina Modotti. The quotation is from the feminist art historian Griselda Pollock: "It is normal to see paintings of women's bodies as the territories across which men artists claim their modernity and compete for leadership of the avant-garde."[1] Although the quotation refers specifically to painting, it opens up questions around notions of signature and originality that are equally pertinent to photographic representation.

If the avant-garde is a site of struggle where male artists vie for authority, then some form of classificatory system must be in place. Such a system has been theorized by Rosalind Krauss in *The Originality of the Avant-garde and Other Modernist Myths*. Krauss asserts that "one thing only seems to hold fairly constant in vanguardist discourse and that is the theme of originality." She puts forward the view that the whole notion of originality is predicated on that which it is not: namely repetition or the copy. The categories of the original and copy are "bound together in a kind of aesthetic economy, interdependent and mutually sustaining, although one (originality) is the valorized term and the other (repetition or copy or reduplication) is discredited."[2] In the realms of artistic practice and art history the mark that distinguishes the original from the copy is the signature. If, as Pollock claims, the female body represents the territory where male artists jostle to occupy the valorized term of the original/copy binary, the female

59

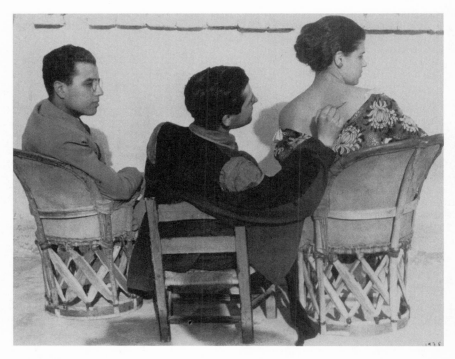

Figure 6.
Edward Weston, *Federico Marín, Jean Charlot, and Tina Modotti,*
ca. 1924–26. Throckmorton Fine Art, New York.

body is therefore the site of the signature. Signature is also a key issue
in Weston's snapshot. It depicts a male artist, Jean Charlot, inscribing
(his name?) on the body of a woman, Tina Modotti. This act of
inscription is viewed by the bespectacled gaze of Federico Marín. We
see here, then, that configuration of inscription, gaze, and body that
lies at the heart of Pollock's formulation. This configuration cannot
help but raise important questions as to the status and significance of
the signature in the images of Tina Modotti, whose body both represents the site of signature and inscribes its own signature. In this chapter, I read Modotti's photograph *Hands Resting on Tool* (1926) in the
light of a notion of the avant-garde as a site of (male) struggle for originality.[3] In a visual culture that pivots on the dual axis of the origi-
nal/copy opposition, Modotti's signature had, until recent feminist
excavations that have been the subject of the preceding chapters, been

erased from the history of photography. There will be a number of interconnected strands to my argument. The first is concerned with the status and significance of signature within recent critical work on Modotti that, derived from art historical models more commonly associated with painting, revolve around the issue of signatural style. Drawing on crucial distinctions between painting and photography, I suggest that Modotti's photograph *Hands Resting on Tool* problematizes the very notion of the signature.

Second, through a close examination of *Mella's Typewriter* I will propose that this photograph, which is also concerned with questions of signature, at the same time points toward a particular kind of photographic reading, based on context and on a notion of signature as a highly complex issue. The shift in focus in this chapter is, in a nutshell, predicated on a move toward dealing with the specificity of photography, with its "intractable reality" and recontextualizing Modotti's photographs.

Counter Signatures

The question of Modotti's signature as a contested site for feminism has gained particular significance since the Whitechapel exhibition. This renewed interest, however, should not eclipse the fact that the question of signature is no new phenomenon to enter either discussions of the photographs of Tina Modotti or more general debates surrounding photographic representation. This concern with signature is characteristic of approaches to photography that have become increasingly influenced by a certain type of art-historical discourse.

At a striking moment in 1924, Edward Weston exclaimed: "I have been doing the best work of my life. . . . Tina has one picture I wish I could sign with my name—that does not happen often in my life!" This throwaway comment reveals that for Weston the signature appropriates the stamp of artistic merit. The signature for Weston was a key factor that confirmed the photograph's status as art object. Weston, in fact, was a photographer who devoted considerable time and effort to photography's elevation to the status of art. Weston's comment, with its emphasis on the signature, is also symptomatic of subsequent critical speculation about the attribution of photographs by Modotti and Weston. A degree of confusion, which has bothered some critics, surrounds the signature on a number of individual photographs and collaborative projects in which the two photographers were involved. A 1929 edition of the magazine *Creative Art*, for example, reproduces "'Colonial Mexican Christ-Head,' attributed to a certain Robert [*sic*] Weston." Typographical errors aside, subsequent sources attribute the image in question not to Weston but to Modotti. In fact, the Christ-Head image belongs to the disputed series of photographs that Modotti and Weston made for Anita Brenner's book *Idols behind Altars*. Depending on the political agenda of the critic in question, this series is alternately attributed wholly to Weston and his son Brett or is viewed as a collaborative project carried out by Weston and Modotti. Weston himself fuels the debate in his *Daybooks* where he suggests that Modotti's role was that of assistant to himself and Brett, saying that "if a woman had not been in our party, especially Tina, with her tact and sympathy for the Indians, a woman which made the group seem less aggressive, Brett and I would never have finished the work."[4]

I do not wish to intervene in this particular debate, as it is a speculative and ultimately futile activity. Instead, using it as my focus, I examine the implications of the practice of attribution by focusing on the work of the North American art historian Amy Conger. Conger is one of a number of critics who have endeavored to "set the record straight" on the question of attribution surrounding this particular series of photographs, which has troubled conventional critics of art and photography. Conger prefaces "Tina Modotti and Edward Weston: A Re-evaluation of their Photography" with comments made by critics concerning questions of attribution and the two photographers. These include: "Weston, at least, felt that some of Tina's photographs were indistinguishable from his," and "it would be impossible to say whose photographs are which." Conger launches her essay by categorically denying the plausibility of these comments, arguing that "neither facts nor careful visual studies of their prints, however, offer evidence to support these claims."[5] Conger's essay is concerned with mapping out the individual style of each photographer by adhering to strictly art-historical principles. These principles focus on dating, attribution, and stylistic analysis of the image. Conger alights, therefore, on examples where Weston and Modotti photographed the same or similar objects, in order to show how the photographs produced by each diverge. So, for example, she looks at the photographs that both Modotti and Weston made of Mexican popular art. Conger's text has a particular art-historical flavor:

Chapter Three

Modotti's *Painted papier-mâché Toys* is undated, but it had to have been made before November 1926, since it was included in a large assignment completed then. She placed the dolls on a white marble table top and in front of a clean white wall so they would stand out clearly. Most of the toys, the *juguetes*, cast delicate shadows against the wall that do not distract from the overall high key of the picture.

Weston, on the other hand, in his *Petate Soldiers* chose to photograph in a very strong natural light so that the shadows from the toys became an important part of the composition, in effect repeating the horizontal line on the back wall.[6]

Note the insistence here on dating and on the presence and intervention of each "artist" in the images produced. Reading Conger's text, we get a sense of the activity that took place before the shutter was pressed. This emphasis on activity serves to play down the role of the camera as a mechanical form of reproduction that has the potential to call into question the photographs' status as art objects. This maneuver allows Conger to distinguish critical differences between the two compositions, differences that reside in the mood that each conveys: "This, of course, reflects the attitudes of the photographers towards their work and towards the toys at that moment."[7]

As a critic, at no point does Conger seek to value the work of either Modotti or Weston above the other's, to say that she is "better" than he is or vice versa. She is merely interested in showing how the signature of each is testimony to the unique styles of Modotti and Weston. Conger's approach is typical of much critical work carried out on Modotti's photographs that is inflected by the issues and concerns of a traditional form of art history. Abigail Solomon-Godeau has traced the way in which a particular form of art-historical methodology has tended to inflect the newly formed discipline of photography history and criticism. She describes how at a crucial moment in the sixties, the study of art history experienced a dramatic change: "Infusions of modernist critical theory, the influx of émigré art historians from Eastern and Western Europe, the new importance of social history and iconographic analysis—all these combined to shift art history away from a dominant emphasis on attribution, dating and stylistic analysis. While these would remain staples of thesis mill grist, a new generation . . . approached the history of art in a way that stressed the cultural and religious meanings . . . that made the work of art a site of signification." The discipline of photography history has, on the whole, remained immune to the changes that have taken place within art-historical scholarship, and as Solomon-Godeau suggests, "a closer scrutiny of current approaches to the history of photography suggests that the particular kind of art-historical model most widely employed is, even within art history, fast becoming either discredited or simply obsolete."[8]

Amy Conger is not the only critic to latch onto this discredited art-historical model. Another critic whose comments display all the trappings of it wrote a short article for the Mexican magazine *Vuelta* in 1983. The article was written in response to the Whitechapel exhibition "Frida Kahlo and Tina Modotti," which ended its run in the Museo de Arte Moderno in Mexico City. Unlike Conger, however, this critic was unable to refrain from value judgments: "Para Tina la fotografía fue un incidente, ligado a sus amores con su maestro y amante, el fotógrafo Edward Weston. . . . La *obra* fotográfica de Tina es más bien escasa y ostenta la *huella* de la personalidad de Weston. Es una obra derivada." ["For Tina, photography was just an incident, linked to her affair with her teacher and lover the photographer, Edward Weston. . . . Tina's photographic oeuvre is at best scarce and reveals the *imprint* of Weston's personality. It is a derivative oeuvre."][9]

The critic in question, identified by his initials O. P. alone, was none other than Octavio Paz. Effectively, for Paz, the issue is not that Modotti and Weston's photographs are indistinguishable from each other nor that they are unreadable. The issue is that Modotti's are not *worth* reading. Paz's comment was made in response to an overtly feminist exhibition that focused strategically on issues of gender and marginality. Such issues may have constituted an attractive proposition for Susie Tomkins some years later when she purchased *Roses*. However, they were clearly not to the liking of Paz, who categorically rejected their validity as modes of analysis, in a reassertion of traditional art-historical values. If, as Krauss argues, the "first constant in vanguardist discourse is the theme of originality," Paz's condemnation of Modotti evokes the second and third constants, namely, the exclusion of women in the role of cultural producers and their prominence as cultural products. As Bridget Elliot and Jo-Ann Wallace have noted, the theme of originality depends on the existence of its opposite, the derivative or repetitive. Moreover, they

Chapter Three

point out the conspicuous lack of women writers and artists classified as avant-garde. Making connections between these two constants of vanguardist discourse, Elliot and Wallace describe the way in which the work of women writers is constantly condemned as "derivative, deviant, old-fashioned and second rate."[10]

In a cultural sphere where the notion of originality depends on the devalorization of its other, the copy, Paz does not hesitate to cast Weston as the original talent, Modotti as his derivative, whose primary function is linked to her body as Weston's lover. As editor of Mexico's most influential cultural magazine, *Vuelta*, as a poet and essayist, *and* as a future Nobel Prize winner, "Octavio Paz" the signature carries clout. Indeed, the signature is so laden with cultural capital that Paz only needed to use his initials at the end of his comments in *Vuelta*. The signature that these initials represent belongs to one who is arguably the father of Mexican culture and letters. Paz speaks, therefore, as someone who occupies the "right" side of the original/copy opposition. He obliterates Modotti's potential signature, and thus potential to signify, with the crushing force of his own. As an authority, he proffers his final word on the trivial matter of Modotti's photographs. His statement offers a straightforward account of the way in which the work of a male photographer, Weston, is valorized over that of a female photographer, Modotti. As such it is unremarkable.

However, I suggest that the deceptive banality of Paz's comment, its unremarkability, masks an altogether more interesting and complex issue, which turns on the words *obra* [oeuvre] and *huella* [imprint]. The Spanish word *huella* is particularly significant in the development of my argument, which revolves around a tension between photographic prints and signatures. The connotations of the word *huella* in this context are threefold. On the one hand, the word conjures up an image of the fingerprint (*la huella digital*) as a marker of the individual's unique identity. On the other, within the specific historical context of prerevolutionary Mexico, the link between the fingerprint and the signature becomes quite literal, insofar as the illiterate peons working on the haciendas would *pintar su huella* in the *tienda de raya* where the *huella* would stand in for the signature.[11] Finally, the word *huella* also conveys a sense of physical inscription, of marking or scoring of a surface. By using the word *huella*, Paz is claiming that it is possible to trace the influence/inscription of Weston's personality/signature on Modotti's photographic oeuvre. Weston's unique personality, his signature, for Paz is somehow etched onto the surface of Modotti's photographs. The words *huella* and *obra* are laden with cultural values and assumptions that require careful examination. They belong to the sphere of art history where the concepts *oeuvre* and *influence* hold currency. As such, their significance lies in the way in which they construct Edward Weston as the author/originator, as someone whose unique presence is somehow recognizable in the photographic images of Modotti. In using them, Paz joins the vast enterprise dedicated to the legitimization of a particular area of photographic practice: the "art" photograph. And the main thrust of this enterprise has been to "reinvest this most ubiquitous of image-making systems with the attributes of individuality, rarity and aura."[12]

In his assessment of Modotti's photographs, Octavio Paz is missing a key point with respect to photographic representation, a point that is set out by Walter Benjamin in "The Work of Art in the Age of Mechanical Reproduction." Although Benjamin's famous proclamation—"that which withers in the age of mechanical reproduction is the aura of a work of art"—is almost too well-known to need repetition, I invoke it here because of its relevance to questions of signature. For Benjamin, the aura of the work of art was predicated on the presence of the original, which in turn was authenticated by the signature. In the wake of mechanical reproduction, the notion of authenticity, of the viability of the original and therefore the status of the signature was radically undermined. The invention of the camera meant not only that the original could be reproduced infinitely but also that the act of reproduction could "put the copy of the original into situations which would be out of reach for the original itself."[13]

However, Benjamin's account did not take into consideration the arriviste mentality that has plagued photography since its inception in 1839. For Benjamin, the age of mechanical reproduction was truly revolutionary, "the total function of art [was] reversed."[14] Photography, in other words, had the potential to overturn the authority of the signature. Others, including practitioners of photography, were less sanguine about its status and function in the face of its established rival in the realm of visual representation, namely, painting. Indeed, the history of photography has been the history of a series of crises of legitimation that stem from a troubled relationship with painting. At its inception, many commentators believed that the birth of photography meant the traditional graphic artist would be upstaged by a mechanical counterpart in the form of the photographer with his camera.[15] However, these initial reactions were soon supplanted by an altogether different relationship between the two forms of representation, one in which photography would come to occupy the role of the "poor relation."

In the early days of photographic practice, photography enjoyed a fairly equal relationship with painting, in that technology dictated that photography was still very much an artesanal practice and practitioners were consequently considered artists. The crises of legitimation that characterize the history of photography were precipitated principally by three factors concerned with technological changes. First, the negative-positive process was gradually perfected in the mid-nineteenth century. Multiple copies could be made from a single negative, robbing the photographic image of its status as a unique object. Second, in 1888 George Eastman marketed the handheld camera. This brought photography within the reach of the masses, potentially robbing the photographer of his status as a producer of art objects. Third, since its inception, photography has been associated with the "real," with the social. It belongs to a tradition of reportage. It records people, places, and events. It furnishes evidence. These factors conspire to challenge photography's smooth and easy acceptance as art object. In other words, the accessibility and the sheer diversity of photographic practice, from the family snapshot to the police mug shot, from pornography to advertising, constantly threaten to invade and undermine the practice known as art photography. If photography has had any currency as an art form, it is because this status has had to be negotiated discursively and institutionally in order to be established.

Hands and the Connoisseur

In his *Vuelta* article Paz is essentially involved in the negotiation of Weston's status as an art photographer. In the process of negotiation, two discredited terms, two "copies" must be suppressed. First, Modotti, the apprentice who is only able to produce poor copies of her original master, is condemned as second-rate. Second, Paz elides the specificity of the medium of representation with which he is dealing. That is to say, by using the language of art history, Paz willfully overlooks the fact that he is dealing with photography. Instead, he claims that the authority of his eye is able to trace the presence of another author, Weston, in the images of his pupil, Modotti. In so doing he adopts the time-honored role of the most "retrograde" of art historians: the connoisseur.

Connoisseurship is concerned with the identification of authorship in the work of art through an examination of its style. It is about how to distinguish copies from originals, about how to fix signatures and how signatures fix value. Central to the theory of connoisseurship is a fundamental belief in origins and originals, in the singularity of the individual as the signatory of a unique work of art. What is often left unsaid is that the practice of connoisseurship is driven not by some detached, disinterested "aesthetic" ideal but by market forces. It makes a difference that an image is attributed to Weston and not Modotti in so far as its commodity value alters according to its perceived signatory.[16]

The practice of connoisseurship dates back to antiquity and continues to pervade the discourses of art history to this day, as the remarks of Octavio Paz clearly illustrate. However, I take as my paradigm of connoisseurship a practice that has come to be known as the "Morelli method," based on the theories of the nineteenth-century Italian Giovanni Morelli.[17] Morelli developed a theory of attribution whereby the connoisseur focused on the minor details of the painting, for example, on the ears or, more important for the purpose of this discussion, the hands. In Morelli's view, "these marginal details were revealing . . . because in them the artist's subordination to cultural traditions gave way to a purely individual streak."[18] Morelli designed and implemented his method of attribution in order to call into question the authorship of a number of works of art. In so doing, he was involved in a process that had ramifications beyond the frame of the individual image. Morelli was effectively challenging the very authority of the institution involved in the fixing of signature, the art gallery. Ironically, for one in the business of disputing signatures, when Morelli first published his theory of attribution between 1874 and 1876, he did not use his real name, which he only revealed some years later. Instead he adopted a pseudonym, Ivan Lermolieff.[19]

Morelli was concerned specifically with the attribution of paintings. Indeed he developed a quasi-scientific scheme based on the hands of the Italian "great masters." Morelli illustrated the method in his 1892 book *Italian Painters*, in which he reproduced tables that brought together the isolated details, extracted from the paintings of the great masters. In his tables, the name of the author of each is printed below each hand. Thus the art historian could use the table as a guide to making the correct attribution to the image in question. I relate the "Morelli method" of attribution here not to painting but to Modotti's photographs of hands in order to problematize the whole-sale importation of art-historical discourse to photographic representation. Far from being susceptible to the practice of print connoisseurship, Modotti's photographs of hands call into question its practice and its relevance to photographic representation. And in so doing, these photographs undermine the very "foundation stones on which the integrity, value and supposed autonomy of the work of art rest," namely, the signature and originality.[20]

Figure 7.
Typical hands, from Giovanni Morelli, *Italian Painters: Critical Studies of Their Work* (London: John Murray, 1892).

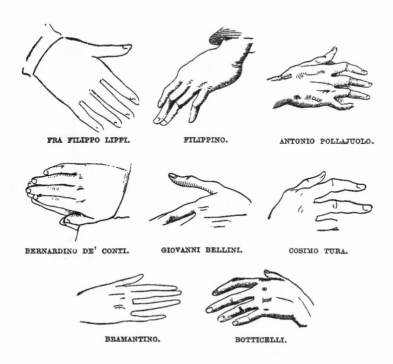

FRA FILIPPO LIPPI.   FILIPPINO.   ANTONIO POLLAJUOLO.

BERNARDINO DE' CONTI.   GIOVANNI BELLINI.   COSIMO TURA.

BRAMANTINO.   BOTTICELLI.

If the minor details, the hands, reveal the artist's "purely individual streak" in the painterly tradition, then what do they reveal in the photographic tradition? Following Morelli, within the painterly tradition, the hands represent an adjunct to the signature, a mark of authenticity. In order to implement his method of attribution, Morelli abstracted the minor details, that is, the hands, from their visual context in the painted canvas in order to scrutinize them for the idiosyncrasy of the individual artist's brush stroke. By contrast, in Modotti's photograph, *Hands Resting on Tool*, the hands appear in close-up and occupy the center of the frame. That which for Morelli constituted the minor detail is the major detail in Modotti's photograph.

Hands provide a clue to the identity of the author because the canvas is a textured surface and the "idiosyncrasy" of the unique individual's brush stroke, his signature, is traceable on the surface of the image. A noticeable characteristic of Modotti's photograph is the grainy effect that appears to rest on the surface of her image. In *Hands Resting on Tool* attention is focused on the indentations on the skin surface of the hands, the furrows and skin tone at the knuckles, the roughness of the hands, which are clearly depicted as working hands, the dried-on earth at the base of the fingernails. The significance of texture is underlined by a play on depth in the image. Depth is created by the direct, frontal camera angle, by the shadow that is cast behind the hands onto the worker's clothing, and by the contrast between the softer (un)focus of the worker's clothing, which is contrasted with the sharp central focus of the hands. The hands are given further prominence by the way in which the arms and the body recede toward the left and the right of the image, creating a sense of roundness. The highly textured hands seem literally to sit on, or indeed, to protrude beyond the surface of the print.

This play on texture appeals to the haptic gaze. According to Claude Gandelman, the haptic gaze "penetrates in depth, finding its pleasure in texture and grain."[21] The haptic gaze exists both in opposition to and in conjunction with the optical gaze, which "corresponds to a certain way of looking . . . based on the scanning of objects according to their outlines." The haptic gaze conjures up a notion of the possibility of "touching with the eye." In Modotti's *Hands Resting on Tool* this possibility is underlined by the subject matter itself: the hand. Surely hands embody the very notion of tactility. The interplay of surface texture and the hand as motif creates the illusion that if the

Chapter Three

Figure 8.
Tina Modotti, *Hands Resting on Tool*, n.d., gelatin-silver print, 7 1/2" × 8 1/2"
The Museum of Modern Art, New York. Anonymous gift. Copy print
© 1995 The Museum of Modern Art, New York.

print were touched with the hand, it would reveal a textured surface. And if the surface were textured, following the Morelli method, this texture would offer the possibility of attribution.

The practice of attribution and the sense of tactility are connected in an important way. Attribution is intricately concerned with questions of economic value. The commodity value of an image accrues when that image is perceived as desirable and therefore purchasable. This matrix of economics and desire is played out in *Hands Resting on Tool* in the conjunction of tactility and attribution. The sense of tactility conveyed in the image, both on a compositional and thematic level, "enhances the viewer's feeling that they can almost touch what is in the image, reminding them that they might, in fact, possess it."[22]

Yet on closer inspection this appearance of tactility is, of course, found to be illusory on two counts. First, the haptic element is only one element of the spectator's gaze. The photographic image is an apparently transparent rendition of a three-dimensional object into two dimensions. The transparency of the medium is of crucial significance insofar as the realism of the photograph at once underscores the potential of "touching with the eye," while at the same time negating it. The haptic gaze, and its fixation on depth, is always circumvented by the optical gaze of the camera. Second, texture gives way to the inevitable smoothness of the photographic print. The surface is coated with a layer of emulsion and the image, which came about as a result of a chemical reaction, lies quite literally below the surface. The texture that would yield the "purely individual streak," the signature in the painted image, is patently absent in its photographic counterpart.

The absent signature is further underlined by the fact that *Hands Resting on Tool* does not exist in isolation in Modotti's oeuvre. It is part of a series of images of hands produced over a number of years. This series includes *Assunta Modotti's Hands* (ca. 1926); *Labour 1 or Hands Washing* (ca. 1927); *Hands of the Puppeteer* (1929). All these photographs feature hands as their central theme.[23] What is more, the insistence on the hand as a motif is not limited to the representation of its human form. The photograph *Flor de manita* (1925) draws a visual analogy between the human hand and its plant "incarnation," thereby adding greater emphasis to the hand as motif. The seriality of these photographs of hands is significant. It reminds us of the fact that an infinite number of images can be reproduced from a single negative. Photography's basic reproducibility illustrates Benjamin's notion that "to ask for [an] 'authentic' print makes no sense."[24] To ask for the "authentic" print, the one that bears the signature, makes no sense because the photographic print is the product of a negative. And the existence of the negative ultimately subverts the circumscription by signature of the "authentic" print. This idea lies at the heart of Rosalind Krauss's notion that "photography's technical existence as multiple thus joins the theoretical possibility that all images taken of the same object could end up being the same image and thus partake of sheer repetition. Together these forms of multiplicity cut deeply against the notion of originality as an aesthetic condition available to photographic practice."[25]

Of course, in Modotti's series of photographic images the hands in question are different in each image, and each print is reproduced from a discrete negative. However, the hand series disavows the singularity of each individual image, for seriality serves as a reminder that each print exists in relation to the others, and each to a negative. As such, *Hands Resting on Tool*, and its status as one in a series of photographic prints, invokes the impossibility of containing photographic images within the auteurist boundaries of the signature. Indeed, at a significant moment in her essay "On Photography" ["Sobre la fotografía"], Modotti herself states:

Siempre que se emplean las palabras "arte" o "artístico" en relación a mi trabajo fotográfico, recibo una impresión desagradable, debida seguramente al mal uso y abuso que se hace de ellas.

Me considero una fotógrafa y nada más, y si mis fotografías se diferencian de lo generalmente producido en este campo, es que yo precisamente trato de producir no arte, sino fotografías honradas, sin trucos ni manipulaciones, mientras la mayoría de los fotógrafos aún buscan los "efectos artísticos" o la imitación de otros medios de expresión gráfica, de lo cual resulta un producto híbrido y que no logra impartir a la obra que producen el rasgo más valioso que debería tener: LA CALIDAD FOTOGRAFICA.

[Always, when the words "art" and "artistic" are applied to my photographic work, I am disagreeably affected. This is due, surely, to the bad use and abuse made of these terms.

I consider myself a photographer, nothing more. If my photographs differ from that which is usually done in this field, it is precisely because I try to produce not art but honorable photographs, without distortions or manipulations. The majority of photographers seek "artistic" effects, imitating other mediums of graphic expression. The result is a hybrid product that does not succeed in giving their work the most valuable characteristic it should have: PHOTOGRAPHIC QUALITY.][26]

If, as my reading of *Hands Resting on Tool* indicates, Modotti's photograph posits a challenge to critical practices that would contain photographic images within the auteurist boundaries of the signature, then urgent questions regarding this form of critical activity are inevitably raised. What is at stake when critics, even those with conflicting views, from Amy Conger to Octavio Paz, attempt to perform the impossible, namely to circumscribe photographic practice by the signature and thereby designate it as art? Is it possible, or indeed desirable, to discard the signature? Is it possible when reading photographic images to escape art-historical models altogether?

Photography and Cultural Legitimacy

The work of Pierre Bourdieu on the sociology of culture, and more specifically on the sociology of photography, provides a key to understanding why critics like Octavio Paz and Amy Conger insist on privileging the photographic signature. In "The Social Definition of Photography," Bourdieu plots photography as a cultural activity into what he calls "the hierarchy of legitimacy." He delineates three spheres of cultural legitimacy within this hierarchy, indicating the particular kinds of cultural activities that fall within each category. These categories are the Sphere of Legitimacy, the Sphere of the Legitimizable, and the Sphere of the Arbitrary. The first sphere, with claims to universal value, includes such activities as music, painting, and literature. These practices, which are designated as "highbrow," are culturally perceived as fixed and therefore representative of "eternal" values. These activities also have strong associations with the signature and originality. The second sphere, which is constantly in the process of claiming legitimacy and authority, includes "middlebrow" activities such as cinema, photography, and jazz. The cultural value of these activities is not fixed and any activity may move "up" to the Sphere of Legitimacy, or highbrow activity. Conversely, these activities might move "down" a category, to the Sphere of the Arbitrary. This third category comprises "lowbrow" activities such as fashion, decoration, and cookery. There is a certain degree of overlap between the three spheres as they compete for cultural consecration and legitimacy. Thus photography, which exists in the Sphere of the Legitimizable, can equally exist within either of the other two spheres located "above" or "below" it. That is to say, when photography is critically consecrated as an art practice, it can cross over into the sphere of legitimacy and become a cultural product, with claims to universal highbrow value.[27]

How has Modotti's oeuvre been appropriated as art/commodity? Photography represents a liminal cultural activity, insofar as it teeters constantly on the border between the Spheres of Legitimacy and the Arbitrary. Turning first to the question of Modotti's construction as artist, we find her photographs, together with a number of Weston's, reproduced in Mildred Constantine's reissued biography of Modotti. Constantine states in her preface that her aim is to "introduce to the public the work of this gifted artist and shed light on her courageous life."[28] Constantine's large-format, luxuriously illustrated book contains not only reproductions of "art" photographs by the two photographers but also a number of snapshots. The two kinds of photographic images appear in significantly different formats. The status of those images designated as snapshots and their simultaneous location alongside, and segregation from, other images by Weston and Modotti that are clearly denominated as "art" photographs is of critical significance. The snapshot by Weston with which I opened this chapter is among those in the book. This is not an image across which Weston "claim[ed] his modernity and compete[d] for leadership of the avant-garde." It is, nevertheless, emblematic of Weston's right to the status of original signer; a status that critics like Octavio Paz deny to Modotti. That Weston's image is a snapshot and that it is important to display it as such is abundantly clear. The snap is framed by white borders; two other images, with more claim to the status of snap (one commemorates a family meal; the other, an outing) are "casually" arranged upon it. Lest there should remain any doubt as to the image's status, the curled edges of these mere "album" snaps cast shadows across the white page.

These images must be revealed as mere snaps in order to distinguish them from "art" photographs made by Modotti and Weston. These art photographs, by contrast, appear flatly framed only by the whiteness of the page. Thus within this particular context, the border between the Sphere of the Legitimate (the art photograph) and the Sphere of the Arbitrary (the snapshot) is graphically figured by the way in which each kind of photograph is perceived to lie on the page. At the other extreme, as someone engaged in the world of fashion, Susie Tomkins's enterprise is located within the Sphere of the Arbitrary, her activity is almost irremediably lowbrow. She seeks to legitimize her activity as a fashion entrepreneur by buying into a more legitimate cultural sphere: art photography. The status of the photograph at any given moment, it should be clear from these examples, is determined by the mediation of the institutions of cultural criticism: the editor, the curator, the auctioneer, and so on.[29]

However, despite the most strenuous efforts of those involved in the consecration of photography as belonging to the Sphere of Cultural Legitimacy, for Bourdieu, photography is always destined to occupy an ambiguous position within the hierarchy of legitimacy that he sets up: "half-way between 'vulgar' practices . . . and noble cultural practices." Thus, even when photography is considered highbrow, it is also, given the diversity of photographic practice, always simultaneously lowbrow. And photography, "unlike a legitimate practice, [is] a practice in the process of legitimation [and] poses and imposes to those involved in it, the question of its own legitimacy." At the heart of the struggles for legitimation that take place within the cultural arena lies a factor of singular importance: class. This factor is figured in Bourdieu's use of terminology (i.e., highbrow versus lowbrow). In other words, what one says about photography is more an indicator of class status than anything intrinsic to photography as a cultural practice. Therefore, so-called objective norms of aesthetic taste for Bourdieu "are organized according to a type of systematic arrangement which has nothing more to do with individual psychology than that which structures the preferences and knowledge of 'cultivated' people, but which, without attaining systematic explanation, tend to organize the 'conduct of life' of a social class."[30]

The "value" of Bourdieu's insights lies precisely in the fact that they reveal the "universal" and supposedly "impartial" value judgments of critics like Conger and Paz for what they really are: class-bound and partial. To position Modotti either as an art photographer and therefore signatory of the print, as Amy Conger does, or as a bad art photographer whose prints bear the signature of another, as Octavio Paz does, amounts to the same thing. This position can be challenged on two interrelated fronts. First, it can be unmasked as a legitimizing device employed in the name of the maintenance of a class-bound, hierarchical system. Second, as my reading of Modotti's image *Hands Resting on Tool* reveals, this position can be challenged from within the very frame of photographic representation itself. This particular photograph with its play on tactility and texture resists the

Chapter Three

rigid categorization of photographic prints as art photographs. The existence of this photograph within Modotti's work and an understanding of the discursive frameworks that surround that work, point toward the possibility of constructing a critical practice that instead of being based on the ritualization of the photographic image, begins to be based on another practice: politics. Or more precisely, the politics of context.

Mella's Typewriter and the Politics of (Il)Legibility

My analysis of Modotti's image *Hands Resting on Tool* poses a challenge to the whole notion of photographic signature. Read in conjunction with Bourdieu's notion of photography's status as a decidedly middle-brow practice, with its implications for the status of criticism and critics, it raises a troubling question. Namely, does this mean we can say nothing meaningful about photography? Clearly, it is possible to articulate some form of critique of the photographic image under certain conditions. Critique becomes possible once we are able to jettison the kind of value judgments based on a form of art-historical analysis that fails to take into account the specificity of photographic representation. However, this does not entail discarding the apparatus of art-historical discourse wholesale. It is necessary to read the visual language of photographic images not for "who said what" (connoisseurship) but for "how what is said." In this way we are able to move toward readings of the photographs themselves.

Mella's Typewriter, a 1929 photograph, provides further insight into the question of the photographic signature that I plan to introduce to my analysis of Modotti's photographs. This shift in focus marks a break with the kinds of readings in which I have been engaged as critic up until now; readings that, I now suggest, have tended to transform Modotti's photographs into theoretical battlegrounds. While the readings that I have offered in this study constitute an attempt to take an important step—that of venturing inside the photographic frame, providing a combination of formal analysis with theoretical and cultural contextualization—they are not without their pitfalls. That is to say, my readings have shown a marked tendency to turn Modotti's photographs into sites of contestation that tease out theoretical points concerned with issues of commodification, signature, and framing. Although as readings they represent a form of corrective to the lack of close critical analysis that typifies much work on

Modotti's photographs (and indeed on photography in general), they require a more detailed understanding of the historical and cultural conditions under which Modotti's photographs were produced. However, just as it is important not to jettison art-historical discourse altogether, I am not proposing the banishment of the insights of theoretical discourse. I now move toward a form of photographic reading that takes place within a nuanced understanding of the cultural and political context in which Modotti's photographs were produced. In a gesture that dramatizes this movement, I read *Mella's Typewriter* as theory in order to posit that the photograph itself demands a contextual reading.

Modotti made a number of photographs of and about her partner the Cuban political activist Julio Antonio Mella (1904–29). These ranged from conventional bust portraits to the nude photographs that were to cause so much trouble after Mella's death, to a death portrait published in *El Machete* alongside the news of Mella's assassination.[31] Unlike these photographs, which belong in varying degrees to conventional modes of photographic portraiture, *Mella's Typewriter* invokes its subject, Mella, only indirectly, through the conjunction of title and image. In the absence of his bodily representation, Mella is figured through the tool of his trade, the typewriter. Margaret Hooks claims that *Mella's Typewriter* is Modotti's "truest portrait of Mella" and that Mella himself "believed this photograph of his typewriter to be a synthesis of Tina's photography and politics." She cites a letter from Mella to Modotti in which he refers to the "keyboard which you [Modotti] have socialized with your art."[32] I am equally convinced that this photograph offers a synthesis of photography and politics, but not for the same reasons as Hooks. Hooks construes politics in a straightforward manner, in this case, as Communist politics. The photograph therefore conveys for Hooks a sense of politics by dint of its subject matter. The whole notion of the politics of the photograph becomes more complex, however, if we reformulate the image as one whose subject is the politics of photography. The politics of this photograph issues from a synthesis of its formal composition, which articulates a certain relationship between what is represented, that is to say, the typewriter, and the process by which the subject comes to be represented, namely, photography. The relationship between subject and process in Modotti's photograph, in turn, stages an encounter that is inscribed within and beyond the photographic frame and that is

Figure 9.
Tina Modotti, *Mella's Typewriter*, 1928, gelatin-silver print, 9 3/8" × 7 1/2"
The Museum of Modern Art, New York. Anonymous gift. Copy print
© 2000 The Museum of Modern Art, New York.

between questions of photographic textuality and signature. I privilege an examination of the formal composition of the photograph in order to pursue a reading that focuses on the encounter between photographic textuality and the signature.

The overwhelming visual impact that *Mella's Typewriter* creates is one of clarity and sharpness, coupled with a meticulous attention to balance. The sense of sharpness is enhanced by the way in which the metallic sections of the typewriter form regular points of brightness, as the light is reflected and bounced off these silver-toned metallic surfaces. The brightness of these silver surfaces is intensified by contrast with the darker tone of the rest of the typewriter that encases them. However, although encased, the sharpness and clarity of these sections heighten their angularity and make them seem to jut out of the surface of the photograph. The picture plane itself is divided diagonally into three discrete areas. The bottom left-hand corner is occupied by the round keys of the typewriter, where the bold gray tone of the letters, set against the whiteness of the keys, makes them clearly legible. This left-hand corner cuts a neat triangle that is echoed in the upper right-hand corner of the image, in which we see the edge of the paper imprinted with a number of words in Spanish. Among these words, those that are complete and therefore legible are "inspiración," "artística," "en una síntesis," and "existe entre la." We can also make out the ends of two words "ción" and "ón," which might be supposed to be abstract nouns. The middle band of the image is occupied by the hammers of the typewriter and the ribbon spool. The hammers fan out in a regular, regimental semicircle. Once again, the inverse letters engraved on the end of the keys are clearly visible and become darker as they converge with the left edge of the photographic frame. Like *Hands Resting on Tool*, *Mella's Typewriter* plays on a sense of tactility and texture. The letters on the hammers are figured in sharp relief and were we to run our finger over the photographic surface, we would almost feel able to trace the letters below, like a kind of Braille. The regular roughness of the letters is set off against the smoothness of the paper above and the shiny, cold smoothness of the keys below. The sense of the smoothness of the keys is enhanced by the warmer, woven texture of the fabric below them.

The tripartite composition of the image and its play on tactility and texture serve to highlight the fact that the typewriter is a piece of mechanical equipment. The photograph invites the viewer to press the keys with the finger/eye. The photograph makes its appeal to the haptic gaze, which would "penetrate the image in depth, finding its pleasure in texture and grain."[33] Although it is not shown in action and only a portion of the typewriter is visible, the image nevertheless provides the viewer with plenty of detailed graphic information. The photograph therefore mobilizes cultural information in the viewer, to whom it is clear how the typewriter produces text: the writer presses a key, a hammer embossed with an inverse letter strikes the page through the inked ribbon, and the letter is inscribed on the white page. Additionally, this photographic representation of Mella's typewriter draws a visual parallel between the process by which the typewriter inscribes text on the page and way in which the camera produces an image on photographic paper. That is to say, it reminds us that when the photographer presses a button, a negative copy is made (echoed in the inverse letters) and then the negative becomes a positive image in the process of development. The relationship between the two representational media—the act of writing "mechanically" and the photographic act—is also underlined by the fact that both are essentially mechanical. Two further tropes of reciprocity are articulated in the image. Namely, the writer and photographer are aligned, insofar as they both operate a piece of mechanical apparatus, so too, therefore, are the photograph and the written text. Consequently, it is no exaggeration that the photograph figures itself in a gesture of self-referentiality, in the written text in the top right-hand corner. In *Mella's Typewriter* the text and the words written upon it symbolize the photograph and the image imprinted upon its surface, by virtue of a complex play on the visual and the textual whereby the visual becomes textual and the textual becomes visual.

If the written text in *Mella's Typewriter* represents not only Mella by metonymy but also the photographic image, what does this tell us about photography and the photographer? First, *Mella's Typewriter* is a photographic image that comments on the legibility of the photographic image. Katherine Adler and Marcia Pointon describe the text of photography as "super-legible." Their point is that the ontological link between the photographic image and what it represents promotes a certain kind of relationship between viewer and image. This relationship has been dissected by Rosalind Krauss in her account of the most common form of photographic judgment as one "that reads things generically; that figures reality in terms of what sort of thing *x* or *y* is." This kind of photographic judgment leads to a reductive approach to the image. For example, the photograph under scrutiny here would be read in terms of its subject matter, that is, a typewriter. However, by figuring itself in the form of the written text, Modotti's photograph is telling us something about the textual nature of the photographic image, something about its status as an object to be read.[34]

Mella's Typewriter, and its configuration of the photograph-within-in-photograph, effectively plays on and simultaneously undermines that ostensibly transparent relationship between the photograph and reality that has for so long determined what can be said about the photographic image. In order to see how it does so, we need to remind ourselves of how, basically, the photographic image is usually read. Commentary on photographic images has tended to polarize around two positions. The first position is that occupied by professional critics (Amy Conger, Octavio Paz et al.), who seek to consecrate photography as an art and therefore recruit the terminology of art history to legitimize their position. These professionals strenuously avoid engaging with the "intractable reality" of the photographic image. The second position is that adopted by the amateurs who are unable to see beyond the "intractable reality" to any further considerations. Modotti's image plays on these two positions. On the one hand, it confirms, in terms of both its formal composition and subject matter, the notion of the transparency or legibility of photographic representation. The sharpness of focus and high definition of the image and its almost fetishistic insistence on the perfect circularity and linearity of form produces a photograph that is absolutely legible. The section of *Mella's Typewriter* that most forcefully confirms the legibility of the image is significantly that upper right-hand section, which is almost perfectly readable. This section of the image is also that which represents the photograph-within-the-photograph. And yet, it is in this section that the sense of legibility created by the formal composition of the image breaks down in a number of important and interrelated ways.

The text itself, which is represented in the photograph, is only readable up to a certain point. The text that appears as a result of the action of typing is bisected by the upper photographic frame. The text does not appear in full, comprehensible sentences. Instead, we are left with disjointed words. These words themselves are abstract rather than concrete nouns and adjectives: "inspiración," "artística," "síntesis." If there is a commonplace in the language of theoretical discourse, then it is to do with the inevitable gap between language and reality, between words and the world. In this photograph the abstract nouns that are represented and that are, by definition, one step further removed from that notional reality serve to draw attention to that gap. Last but not least, the text ends on a conjunction: "entre la." What is more, it ends on a conjunction that precisely figures the space or gap between terms, in that "entre" serves to link two elements in a clause. The text is, therefore, patently unfinished. It does not tell us the complete story. Therefore, all those formal, compositional factors in the photograph that conspire to create an illusion of legibility are undermined by the written text itself, which is on one level illegible. It deals in abstractions that in turn are abstracted from the context of the sentence of which they form a part.

This notion of abstraction operates on another level that serves to reinforce the relationship between the abstract written text and the photographic text. That is to say, the photograph itself is an abstraction insofar as the particular camera angle selected means that we do not see the whole typewriter, only a part of it. This part is abstracted from the whole and thereby denies us the possibility of seeing the whole. This denial acts as a reminder that photography is essentially about abstracting visual information from its context by imposing a frame upon the external world. By definition, photographs never offer the complete picture they purport to present. Instead, as *Mella's Typewriter* demonstrates, photographs exist within the structure of language. They are culturally encoded products that deal in signs and symbols that the viewer must decode in order to imbue the image with meaning. As Victor Burgin contends: "The intelligibility of the photograph is no simple thing; photographs are *texts* inscribed in terms of what we may call 'photographic discourse,' but this discourse like any other, engages discourse beyond itself; the 'photographic text,' like any other, is the site of a complex 'intertextuality,' an overlapping series of previous texts 'taken for granted' at a particular cultural and historical conjuncture."[35]

Mella's Typewriter is not only an image in which the viewer is made aware of the textuality of the photographic image but also an image that issues a proscription regarding the act of photographic reading that, in turn, leads to a prescription. This prescription concerns the practice of reading photographs. This particular practice is anticipated in Burgin's formulation of the photographic text as "the site of a complex 'intertextuality,' an overlapping series of previous texts 'taken for granted' at a particular cultural and historical conjuncture." The prescription, I suggest, is concerned with sketching out new strategies for reading, which become possible when the viewer refuses to take the (inter)textuality of the photographic image at face value.

As in the image *Hands Resting on Tool*, the proscription is concerned with questions of signature and authorship. Having established that both typewriter and camera permit mechanical forms of reproduction, I now undo this established commonality and underline one fundamental difference between the two pieces of equipment, or more precisely between those subjects involved in their operation, the writer and the photographer. Despite the fact that the writer might have recourse to a mechanical mode of production in the form of a typewriter (or today, a word processor), the fact that a mechanical object is employed to produce text does not detract from the writer's claim to the status of author. Within the parameters of Western culture, which privileges the signature as the mark of the individual, as the originating source of her own discourse, the typewriter as mechanical means of production is a laborsaving device. The writer could equally well produce her text manually. The fact that a text has been produced mechanically does not alter in any way the authority of the signatory as its unique author. By contrast, the camera is both the mode of production and the means of production. The question of what can be represented by the photographer, and how, is determined as much by technology as by the photographer. Solomon-Godeau underlines this point when she asserts that "the photographer's aspirations to formal invention, individual expression, and signatural style are perpetually circumscribed by industrial decisions. Indeed, the very size and shape of the photographic image are the result of such decisions; the requirements of artists were only taken into account in camera design for a brief historical moment well before the industrialization of photography."[36]

Mella's Typewriter calls into question the dubious status of the photographic signature by placing special visual emphasis on the typewriter as a mechanical object. Our gaze focuses on the functional parts of the typewriter. We are encouraged to view the written text as a product that came about as a result of what is essentially a three-stage, mechanical/chemical process that is highlighted by the tripartite structure of the photograph.

The dubious status of the photographic signature is further reinforced in a play on authorship that takes place both within and beyond the frame, whereby the photograph becomes a site of struggle for authorship. The struggle for authorship, which is played out in and around the image, comes into focus when we consider that the photograph offers up not one but three potential authors for a single image. First and most straightforwardly, there is Modotti the author and signatory of the portrait-photograph *Mella's Typewriter*. The second author present in the image is Julio Antonio Mella, the owner of the typewriter and, we might presume, the author of the text issuing from the typewriter. However, Mella is *not*, a number of sources claim, the author of the text. Both Pino Cacucci and Elena Poniatowska concur that the text represented in the photograph is a fragment authored by Leon Trotsky. Poniatowska reproduces the fragment in full in *Tinísima*: "La técnica se convertirá en una inspiración mucho más poderosa de la produccción artística; más tarde encontrará su solución en una síntesis más elevada, el contraste que existe entre la técnica y la naturaleza." ["Technique will be converted into a much more powerful inspiration of artistic production; later it will find its solution in a higher synthesis, the contrast that exists between technique and nature."][37] The play on questions of signature engendered by the presence of three authors within a single photograph raises questions about the photographic signature. It also touches on issues of gender and authorship, insofar as the image, produced by a woman photographer, is traversed by the signatures of two male authors. Indeed, in many ways this photograph seems ironically to prefigure Octavio Paz's erasure of Modotti's signature in his *Vuelta* article, insofar as it is a site of struggle for signature.

What especially interests me about this conflictive encounter between the textuality of the photograph versus its challenge to the notion of photographic signature is that it is not an encounter that ends in a stalemate. The photograph, on the one hand, proscribes a certain form of reading. This form of reading, which only has dubious claim to the status of "reading," is again one based on traditional print connoisseurship, where the author is the ultimate arbiter of value and meaning. It is one that is defined by the fact that the critic, looking for the signature as the trace of the single author, will instead find an image traversed by three competing signatures. On this level, the image therefore ultimately confounds the connoisseur and his reading.

However, these signatures, while confounding the connoisseur, also hold the key to the prescription that I suggest exists in the photograph. To arrive at a reading of the photograph as one traversed by three signatures, the viewer requires a certain amount of contextual knowledge in order, first, and most obviously, to identify and comprehend the significance of the typewriter's owner, and second, and more cryptically, to trace the author of the written text. The photograph *Mella's Typewriter* is an image that, on the one hand, urges the viewer to confront the textuality of photographic representation and, on the other, offers a suggestion as to *how* to confront this textuality. This suggestion is based on contextual information, on a nuanced understanding of elements that exist both within and beyond the frame of the photograph. The need to move beyond the frame is signaled from within it, insofar as the words of the text/photograph, like the flower petals in *Roses*, spill over the edge of the photographic frame. Whereas the critic following the kind of agenda set by the art-historical model looks exclusively *within* the frame in the search for the photographic signature, *Mella's Typewriter* is a photograph that encourages the viewer to look both within and beyond that frame.[38] It is an image that, on a compositional level, poses questions concerning the status and function of the photographic image, leaving them, however, unanswered. It is up to the viewer to deal with these questions by paying careful attention to both text and context.

4

Aesthetics and the Body Politic
Building Contexts

Mexican Hats

This chapter is all about hats. Not just any old hats, but Mexican hats, or sombreros. More specifically, the sombrero in a 1926 photograph entitled *Workers Parade*. By focusing on a single image, which I insert into a number of different contextual situations, I produce increasingly refined readings of the photograph. As in the reading of *Roses* in chapter 2, the contextualizing process essentially involves a juxtaposition of *Workers Parade* with other images against which it can be seen to signify. This and the following chapter shift the focus of critical work that has appeared to date (including my own) on Modotti and her photographic output.

To date, critical work on Modotti has, broadly speaking, proceeded on three fronts. First, her photographs have been discussed in the Whitechapel essay within a feminist framework in terms of their status as the product of a marginalized cultural producer. Second, they have been discussed in terms of their signature style by critics such as Amy Conger and Octavio Paz, who work from within a traditional, art-historical context. Third, within the parameters of my own argument, individual images (*Open Doors, Roses, Hands Resting on Tool*, and *Mella's Typewriter*) have been read in the light of theories of photography in response to Modotti's appropriation by feminist discourse, her commodification within the global marketplace, and efforts to contain the photographs within the auteurist boundary of the signature. Running parallel to these efforts to evaluate the photographs have been the fleet of biographies on Modotti. The major focus of the biographies has obviously been the photographer's life, which is plotted into a cultural and historical context. But whereas Modotti's life has been contextualized within a specific historical moment, analysis of her photographs has tended to remain in a state of historical disjuncture.[1] As a corrective to this disjuncture, I produce a close analytical reading of *Workers Parade*, which draws together critical analysis of the photograph itself with a historically and iconographically grounded account of the context within which the photograph was produced.

There are a number of pressing reasons why such a shift in focus is necessary: the urgent need to restore a sense of Modotti's agency as a woman producing photographic images within a specific historical and cultural context and the need to contest the exoticizing appropriation of the Mexican context in which Modotti produced her images. By establishing iconographic, historical material and theoretical contexts within which to read, I build up layers of nuance around the photograph. These layers of nuance are designed to avoid the kinds of pitfalls that I have outlined in approaches thus far to Modotti's photographs.

The word *nuance*, the organizing principle of this chapter, is a particularly appropriate and productive term to use when discussing visual representation, and especially when looking at black-and-white photographs. By definition, black-and-white photographic images require the viewer to focus on variations in tonality. Nuance and the perception of nuance are predicated on the apposition of more than one shade or tone. In this chapter, nuance therefore represents a conceptual metaphor and structuring device, whereby each layer of context formed around *Workers Parade* is to be understood in the light of the other layers. The chapter is punctuated at various points by readings of the photograph within these layered contexts. The aim, with each successive contextualizing step, is to bring into relief sharper, more complex readings of the photograph in question. This complexity, I contend, revolves around an understanding of the relationship between the aesthetic dimension of the image and what is represented. The aesthetic dimension of the image is also bound up with questions of framing and photography.

In the first section, I plot *Workers Parade* into a broadly construed notion of the cultural and political renaissance emerging in Mexico in the 1920s. I explore the way in which Mulvey and Wollen's analysis of

Workers Parade tends to focus on a number of key issues that they treat separately: on the one hand, the marginal status of Modotti as a woman photographer working within the context of postrevolutionary Mexico; on the other, the irreconcilable tension between the aesthetic and political dimension of the image. There is a marked tendency in their analysis to approach what are effectively three categories—gender, politics, and aesthetics—as mutually exclusive entities. Moreover, while all three categories are bound together in a kind of critical economy, aesthetics occupies the devalorized position. I call into question this devalorization and toward the end of this first section of the chapter, I will undertake my first reading which reveals the boundaries between these three categories to be permeated, and contends that the aesthetic occupies a central but charged and ambivalent position.

In the second section, I explore the charged and ambivalent role of aesthetics in our understanding of the photograph by plotting *Workers Parade* into a specifically Mexican photographic tradition. I read Modotti's image in tandem with a photographic image from the Casasola archive of the Mexican Revolution. I also consider how Modotti's photograph, and the way in which it aestheticizes its subject matter, raises problematic issues that point to the photographic gaze as predatory and appropriatory. In other words, bearing in mind a reformulated notion of the status of the aesthetic dimension of the image, I offer an experimental reading of *Workers Parade* as bespeaking Modotti's status as a cultural tourist in Mexico.[2]

As I said, this chapter is all about hats. But the issues the hats raise come into sharper focus and converge at a site/sight that is nowhere clearly depicted in *Workers Parade* itself: namely the body.

The Absent Body

In a letter dated 9 March 1930, written from the U.S. Immigration Station, New Orleans, after her deportation from Mexico, Modotti jokes to Edward Weston:

> I hope, Edward that you enjoyed a good laugh when you heard I was accused of participating in the attempt to shoot [President Pascual] Ortiz Rubio—"who would have thought it eh? Such a gentle looking girl and who made such nice photographs of flowers and babies—." I can just imagine comments of this

order being made by readers of Mexico's yellow press on reading all the sensational "informations" headed by huge titles on
the front pages, calling me "la inquieta agitadora comunista" "la
célebre fotógrafa y comunista" and so forth.[3]

Modotti's ironic tone and her bitter amusement about the perceived
discrepancy between the subject matter of her photographs and her
political activities could not be clearer. "Nice" pictures of flowers and
babies are by definition *not* political and as such are construed by the
"yellow press" as entering into conflict with Modotti's political activities. Underpinning Modotti's almost flippant observation is a basic
assumption: to all intents and purposes, the political dimension of a
photograph is predicated on its subject matter, where certain kinds of
subjects are considered more "political" than others. Indeed, the division between the political and the aesthetic dimensions of Modotti's
photographs is not one made by the press alone. This division also
represents a recurrent and enduring motif in critical approaches to
Modotti's photographs. Of the more "serious" commentators on
Modotti's photographic output, the Mexican photographer Manuel
Alvarez Bravo lends weight to this division. In an interview with
Raquel Tibol, Alvarez Bravo states that Modotti's oeuvre can be neatly divided into two separate strands that correspond with the phases
in her political activity:

> Tina tuvo dos períodos: el romántico y el revolucionario. En
> el primero, con gran influencia de Weston, fotografiaba flores,
> objetos delicados, superponía negativos para conseguir efectos
> más sensibles del cristal. En contacto con el medio revolu-
> cionario mexicano se desarrolla su segunda etapa. En el perí-
> odo de transición produjo algunas obras que van a pasar a la
> historia, como las de las manos del campesino agarrando la
> pala, o las manos de la lavandera. Para mí ese momento es el
> más alto en la fotografía de Tina, las prefiero a las que
> vinieron después como las fotografías de los estribadores, la
> hoz y el martillo, las cananas, la mazorca.
>
> [Tina had two periods: the romantic and the revolution-
> ary. In the first, under the great influence of Weston, she pho-
> tographed flowers, delicate objects; she superimposed
> negatives to obtain more sensitive effects on the glass plate.

Chapter Four

Her second phase developed in contact with the Mexican revolutionary scene. In her transitional period, she produced some of the images that are going to pass into history, like the hands of the peasant holding a spade or the hands of the washer woman. For me this moment was the high point of Tina's photography, I prefer these photographs to those that came later like the photographs of the estribadores, the hammer and sickle, the bandoleers, the corn cob.][4]

Speaking as an authority on Mexican photography, Alvarez Bravo has influenced subsequent critical approaches to a surprising degree. And yet, as demonstrated by my reading of *Roses*, pictures of flowers, for example, can be, indeed are, political. It is all a matter of the context in which we elect to read photographs, not to mention the inflection we give the word *politics*. The antinomy between Modotti's photographs and her political activity is echoed in a further opposition that has been established by critics influenced by Alvarez Bravo's notion of Modotti's two periods. This opposition turns on a perceived conflict between the visual language of an image, its semiotic productivity, and its subject matter. Following the conventional logic that governs the form/content binary, the latter is the factor that determines whether an image is political and the aesthetic dimension is set up as potentially antithetical to the political dimension. In other words, the aesthetic is seen to exist in some kind of apolitical zone. This tendency to set up an opposition between the political (content) and an apolitical aesthetic (form) and its implications for a reading of the photographs can be seen in the Whitechapel essay.

Mulvey and Wollen effectively set up two notions of the political in their essay. First, they insert the work of Modotti and Kahlo into a feminist political framework. This feminist framework is political on a number of levels. Within the wider framework of the art establishment, the exhibition and accompanying essay posed a challenge to the exclusions of the art world by drawing attention to those subjects that had remained on its margins: women cultural producers working within a Mexican context. The essay itself further seeks to politicize Modotti and Kahlo by reworking their significance through the critical focus of feminist aesthetics. In other words, the essay imposes a discursive frame around Modotti and Kahlo by politicizing them through a notion of feminist aesthetics. This discursive frame was in turn inserted into the wider context of the art establishment as a form of political challenge to its tradition of exclusions and elisions.

Mulvey and Wollen's argument sets up an opposition between two notions of context and subsequently two formulations of the political. If feminism is the first formulation of the political within the essay, it also maps out another sphere that might be described as politics with a capital P. Discussing Modotti's photographic trajectory, Mulvey and Wollen comment: "[Modotti's] photography was initially dominated by [the] aestheticism [of her teacher, the North American photographer Edward Weston]. Gradually her work shows her searching for her own direction, and gaining confidence as her political commitment changed her way of looking at the world. Her photographs do not lose their sense of form; but her priorities change."[5]

As Modotti becomes more actively engaged in postrevolutionary Mexican politics, the subject matter of her photographs changes. In crude terms, she starts off making ("nice") photographs of flowers and ends up making photographs of, for example, workers. What emerges in Mulvey and Wollen's account is a second notion of the political predicated on subject matter.[6] Now, there is a basic assumption concerning aesthetics underpinning their argument that needs teasing out. *Despite* Modotti's aestheticizing approach to her subject matter, the photographs are political per se, by virtue of their political subject matter. In other words, Mulvey and Wollen imply that an emphasis on the aesthetic, formal quality of an image has the potential to diminish its political punch.

With oblique reference to *Workers Parade* Mulvey and Wollen state that "in her photographs of Mexican political life [Modotti's] . . . use of formal patterns gives a sense of detachment from the people photographed and a commitment to the political ideas expressed. She must very often have been the only woman present at the meetings she photographed." "Political life" as represented in this photograph was in the process of being reformed by the defining event in modern Mexican history: the revolution. The photograph coincides with a period of cultural renaissance that occurred in the aftermath of the 1910–20 armed struggle. The revolution had been a popular uprising, toppling the twenty-seven-year dictatorship of Porfirio Díaz, replacing it with a new, modernizing notion of the state. The new state actively set out to define and promote a specifically Mexican identity, one in which the fragments that constituted Mexico before the revolution would cohere. But while the revolution sparked off intense debates about what it meant to be Mexican, Mulvey and Wollen note that it did nothing to loosen "the traditional constraints of women's art."[7] And politics, they add, remained "primarily the sphere of men." This wider notion of the "political" stands in contradistinction to "politics" in the form of feminist aesthetics. Modotti fits conveniently into the context of feminist aesthetics that Mulvey and Wollen construct. However, when it comes to the construction of a more generalized notion of context, in the form of the main political and cultural activities taking place in Mexico in the 1920s, Modotti's participation within these events becomes engulfed. This, in turn, has led to her erasure from texts of cultural and visual history in Mexico. And once again we lose sight of a notion of Modotti's agency.

As I suggested earlier, a failure to read was one of the shortcomings of the catalog essay. Following Mulvey and Wollen's analysis, *Workers Parade* is about issues of marginality. However, by reading this image in terms of marginality, I hope to pick up on, and at the same time move beyond, the argument set out in my earlier chapter, with reference to this particular photograph. That is to say, if in chapter 1 I argued that the conflation of debates around gender and marginality ultimately produces a form of circular and, therefore politically untenable analysis, I now wish to demonstrate this point with my reading of *Workers Parade*. A return to what has been set up as an "original" frame (namely the analysis of Mulvey and Wollen) within my project is an essential and strategic step if we are to break with the circularity of the debates subtending questions of gender and marginality. For this return to origin makes it possible to start to deal with the contradictions and complexities of this image.

Without doubt, the single element that transfixes the viewer's gaze in *Workers Parade* is the sombrero. Within the context of 1920s Mexican cultural politics, the sombrero was heavily invested with revolutionary connotations. Indeed, the sombrero achieved iconic status during the armed struggle when unprecedented mass mobilization was photographically documented and widely disseminated in the form of images from the Casasola archive.[8] In Modotti's image, the sombrero figures as a symbol of the continuing surge of popular power as the revolution entered its institutional phase. As viewers, we are immediately drawn to the sombreros: to their circular shape with their indented peaks, to the way in which the light bounces off them, producing points of focus set against the grainier, textured bodies below. As the sombreros flow up the image, they are converted into a form of visual rhythm. Whereas, as a general rule, hats tend to sit on the head, in this photograph the head is occluded, and the sombreros seem to rest directly on the bodies. This occlusion of the head and the visual privileging of sombrero over body means that the body becomes an adjunct to the sombrero. By extension, the surge of sombreros that traverse the image come to function as a metaphor for the body politic.

Such a formulation of the body politic is not a new concept. Elizabeth Grosz traces the history of what she calls the parallelism, or isomorphism, between the body and the state. She argues that one way of understanding the relationship between the body and the state is as follows:

> The two are understood as analogues, congruent counterparts, in which the features, organization, and characteristics of one are reflected in the other. This notion of the parallelism between the body and social order (usually identified with the state) finds its clearest formulations in the seventeenth century, when liberal political philosophers justified their various allegiances (the divine right of kings, for Hobbes; parliamentary representation, for Locke; direct representation, for Rousseau, etc.) through the metaphor of the body politic. The state parallels the body; artifice mirrors nature.[9]

However, Grosz then goes on to identify a problem in such a formulation specifically for feminist analysis: "If there is a morphological correspondence or parallelism between the artificial commonwealth (the 'Leviathan') and the human body in this pervasive metaphor of the body politic, the body is rarely attributed a sex. If one presses this metaphor just a little, we must ask: if the state or the structure of the polis/city mirrors the body, what takes on the metaphoric function of the genitals in the body politic? What kind of genitals are they? In other words does the body politic have a sex?"[10] In Modotti's photograph we can see that the sombrero here is not only a readily legible political symbol but also a trope in which questions of sexual difference are present, even in the absence of a clearly depicted body. As a culturally specific marker of gender identity, this kind of sombrero is

Figure 10.

Tina Modotti, *Workers Parade*, 1926, gelatin-silver print, 8 3/8" × 7 3/8"
The Museum of Modern Art, New York. Anonymous gift. Copy print
© The Museum of Modern Art, New York.

overridingly codified as masculine. Thus I suggest that three meanings
are telescoped into one within the photographic frame: sombrero =
body politic = masculine. Or to put it another way, in this photograph,
the body politic does have a sex and it is overwhelmingly male.

However, the workers' bodies are not the only bodies palpably present in this peculiar state of presence/absence. So too is Modotti's body, which although visually absent from the photographic frame, is inevitably present as the site of representation. The photograph can be seen to chart two spaces: a "political" space occupied by the workers and "another" space occupied by the photographer's female body. Modotti's body is thus doubly absent from an image in which the political is codified as specifically masculine.

This reading goes some of the way toward breaking down the division between gender and revolutionary politics that Mulvey and Wollen set up in the Whitechapel essay. In its attention to the constant slippage between sombreros and bodies, the reading draws together questions of gender and a notion of the wider political sphere. In addition, through its insistence on attention to aesthetic detail, the aesthetic is restored to an integral and central position. In other words, if *Workers Parade* can be read as a political image (both in terms of gender *and* revolutionary politics) it is *because* of its formal, aesthetic concerns and not *despite* them. In this way, the aesthetic is drawn out of the apolitical zone to which it has been relegated and instead becomes a crucial factor in the dynamic of the photograph.

The Aesthetics of Violence: The Violence of Aesthetics

Having established the aesthetic as a central category for an analysis of *Workers Parade*, I move to a more complex understanding of the slippage between the sombrero and the body. So far I have fixed upon the body within the photographic frame as representative of a notion of a specifically masculine body politic, which exists in opposition to Modotti's female body, a body that is located beyond the frame. The inscription of gender on the body in this reading of *Workers Parade* is governed by a binary dynamic based upon notions of empowerment and disempowerment. In brief, the photograph describes the aspiration to power represented by a body politic codified as specifically masculine, which stands in opposition to the photographer who, as a woman, cannot form part of this body politic but instead must look on as an observer. This analysis is the logical conclusion to a reading that focuses on questions of gender and marginality. But there is something that still bothers me about the troubling convergence of sombrero, body, and aesthetics. The bothersome aspect of the image comes into focus if we return to Mulvey and Wollen, who draw a parallel between *Workers Parade* and another of Modotti's photographs, this time, of wine glasses. They suggest that "the hats of the peasants on a demonstration echo the same circular forms as the glasses on a table."[11] In drawing this parallel, in effect Mulvey and Wollen ensure that the subject matter of *Workers Parade*—the workers' bodies and hats—once again becomes subsumed into the visual language of the image, where that language has already been posited as apolitical. Mulvey and Wollen ignore the fact that *Workers Parade* does not depict glasses. It depicts hats. These hats can only be understood in relationship to the bodies below them. Both bodies and hats are charged with cultural values.

Just as the sombrero codifies the body below it as specifically male, it also inscribes that body with racial difference insofar as it invokes the stereotype of what James D. West calls the "native male subject [who] is similarly represented as a depersonalized cipher, a masked or faceless character hidden under a sombrero."[12] When making a reading of any of Modotti's photographs, it is perhaps too easy to become carried away by questions of gender and marginality and to ignore the fact that while in Mexico, Modotti became integrated into the cultural elite of the period. And this cultural elite was largely middle-class and white/mestizo. Furthermore, Modotti, of course, was one of many foreigners involved with this cultural elite. She was *not* Mexican. To focus too overtly on questions of gender and marginality is therefore flawed on two counts. Not only does such a narrow reading constitute a circular argument that basically serves to reinforce the status of marginality: Modotti was marginalized, therefore *Workers Parade* bespeaks that marginalization. By relying too heavily on a totalizing concept of the body—one that can only understand the body in terms of sexual difference—such a reading also runs the risk of erasing a number of politically fraught dimensions of the photograph.

When Elizabeth Grosz asks "does the body politic have a sex?" she does so in order to interrogate what she terms the "implicitly phallocentric codifying of the body politic, which, while claiming it models itself on the human body, uses the male to represent the human."[13] Her question, therefore, is motivated by a drive to reveal the universalist use of what is effectively a gender-specific term. In my application of Grosz's theorization of the body politic to *Workers Parade*, I use the notion of the body politic in an account that stresses Modotti's marginal status as a woman photographer working within the broadly defined context of postrevolutionary Mexico. However, in the light of J. D. West's observation about the cultural resonance of the sombrero as a marker of racial difference, and bearing in mind Modotti's status as a foreign photographer working within Mexico, Grosz's question requires modification. It is necessary to ask not only if the body politic has a sex but also can we offer a reading of the sombrero that is historically grounded, and how can we account for an inscription of race onto that historically grounded body? My analysis of the photograph forecloses both these considerations. That is to say, the privileging of issues of gender and marginality to the exclusion of other notions of difference and specificity leads, invariably, to the erasure of complexity.

Complexity in Modotti's image lies in the unavoidable aesthetic response that the photograph elicits in its conversion of sombrero into visual rhythm. If, in the first instance, the viewer's gaze is drawn to the rhythmic flow of the sombreros, it soon alights on the blurred bodies below. The inscription of racial difference onto the blurred body and its configuration as stereotype point up and problematize the tendency to read the image as visual rhythm, raising a pressing issue: what is going on in a photograph that casts a stereotype as aesthetic spectacle?

To approach these issues, I establish further contexts within which to locate and read *Workers Parade*. The construction of the more generally defined context, in the form of the political and cultural events of 1920s Mexico, on the one hand, allows us to account for questions of gender and the body politic but, on the other, forecloses an understanding of the photograph in terms of questions of racial difference and historical specificity. The remainder of this section is devoted to the establishment of a photographic context that, in turn, leads to my second reading of *Workers Parade*. This section posits the Casasola photographic archive of the Mexican revolution as an important iconographic intertext to Modotti's photograph; traces the inscription of race onto the sombrero within the Casasola archive; takes a brief detour, in order to discuss the etymological roots of the word *aesthetics*; and provides a comparative reading of *Workers Parade* and *Calle de Plateros* from the Casasola archive.

In 1912 Agustín Víctor Casasola founded the Agencia de Información Gráfica. The agency collected photographs made by a range of photographers, representing all phases of the revolution in Mexico, to sell to the foreign and national press in order to compete with the foreign photojournalists who were arriving in Mexico to cover the historical events taking place. Once the violent phase of the civil war was over and the events photographed became less instantly newsworthy, images from the agency were used to produce a visual history of the events that were shaping the radical changes in Mexican society. The culmination of this project was the publication, in 1960, of the *Historia gráfica de la revolución mexicana* under the editorial control of Agustín Víctor's son, Gustavo Casasola. The ten-volume *Historia gráfica* charts the revolution from the dictatorship of Porfirio Díaz through the first years of the presidency of Luis Echeverría.[14] The images from the archive are firmly located within a tradition of documentary photography, which is founded on the belief in photography's power of objective transcription. Flora Lara Klahr suggests that despite the fact that the Casasola family was convinced of photography's role as a tool that bore faithful witness to the events that it recorded, nevertheless, "por más que se declararan [los Casasola] 'ajenos a todo partidarismo' su trabajo editorial tuvo, desde las primeras publicaciones, el propósito de orientar políticamente las convicciones de los lectores." ["However much they (the Casasolas) declared themselves "distanced from any form of partiality," their editorial work, from the first publications, aimed to shape politically the convictions of their readers."][15] Photographs from the archive not only shaped political convictions but also influenced the formation of the nation's visual iconography. In these photographs the sombrero becomes specifically associated with racial difference.

Within the context of Mexico and of Latin America as a whole, the sombrero is an icon with a number of resonances. The sombrero, for a start, has come synecdochically to represent the whole of Latin America both on the continent and beyond. This is evident in the cartoon "High Sierra," which appears in John J. Johnson's *Latin America in Caricature*. The cartoon is clearly a commentary on the iniquity of class and race relations in the hemisphere. Johnson notes that a number of factors guided the cartoonist's choice of object: "In this cartoon the artist chose a most effective means of transmitting to the public a greatly oversimplified version of the social issue in Latin America. Throughout this century the sombrero has been the one unmistakable, all-purpose cartoonists' symbol for the area. Several considerations contributed to giving the sombrero that status. It has been and remains a readily recognizable item of apparel in Mexico, the area best known to the average United States citizen."[16]

In *The Jaguar Smile*, Salman Rushdie notes how in Nicaragua the sombrero becomes associated with Sandino, where "it was Sandino's hat, and not his face, that had become the most potent icon in Nicaragua. . . . Infinity and eruptions: the illegitimate body from Niquinohomo was now a cluster of metaphors. Or, to put it another way: Sandino had become his hat."[17] The symbolic resonance of the sombrero on the American continent is, undoubtedly, wider-ranging than these two examples. However, to return to Mexico, how did the sombrero become associated with race within a specifically Mexican tradition of photographic reportage?

Figure 11.
Bill Mauldin, "High Sierra," 1963. Reprinted with special permission from the *Chicago Sun-Times*, Inc., © 2000.

As the revolution progressed, the sombrero became a defining mark for the different factions engaged in battle. One particular style of sombrero, the large *charro* sombrero, became the personal trademark of Emiliano Zapata. Through its association with Zapata the sombrero came to take on its significance as a marker of racial difference. Zapata has become an instantly recognizable symbol of the revolution precisely because of his sartorial style and especially his *charro* sombrero: "La indumentaria del General Zapata en el vestir, hasta su muerte, fue de charro: pantalón ajustado de casimir negro con botonadura de plata, sombrero charro, . . . espuelas de las llamadas amozoqueñas y pistola al cinto." [Until the day he died, General Zapata dressed in "charro" clothing: tight, black cashmere trousers with silver buttons, a "charro" hat, . . . so-called amozoqueño spurs and a pistol on his belt.][18] By extension, Zapata's followers—who were on the whole, but not exclusively, indigenous peasants—also came to be identified by their sombreros, which although less elaborate than Zapata's, shared its basic shape and size.

I am not suggesting that, come the revolution, the population suddenly donned a new style of hat and took to the streets and countryside, where they were then photographed. But during the dislocation of the violent phase of the revolution, the streets and countryside were filled with crowds of people sporting hats, and they were captured by the lenses of the multiple photographers covering the conflict. In turn, these hats acquired new meanings and came to signify the different factions involved in the struggle. In the aftermath of the revolution, one particular style of hat—the *charro*-style sombrero associated with Zapata and his followers—predominates in the visual vocabulary of the nation. Furthermore, through its association with Zapatismo, this specific style of hat has implicit racial connotations. As the historian Alan Knight observes: "Zapatismo, it is important to note, was linked to the 'Indian' cause first by outraged planters, who similarly shrilled the dangers of caste war, and later by indigenista reformers like [Manuel] Gamio (and even Vasconcelos), who chose to see Zapatismo, in retrospect, as the awakening of the Indian people of Morelos."[19]

Race is a formidably complex concept within the context of Mexican cultural politics. Attempts to fix or establish racial categories (for whatever purpose) are ultimately inflected by sociopolitical factors, and "it bears repeating that these slices [of the population] are socially, not racially, determined; even in respect to inherited somatic features 'Indian' and 'Mestizo' people may be indistinguishable, individually or collectively."[20] Also, it is essential to underscore the fact that the revolution was *not* fought in the name of race. But in the aftermath of the armed conflict, race became a key and controversial issue as the state attempted to forge a new notion of *mexicanidad*.[21] In so doing, the state projected its concern with race back onto the revolution, in a maneuver whereby the revolution was constructed as a site of retrospective racial conflict.

The impact that the photographs from the Casasola archive have made on the interpretation and definition of the Mexican Revolution cannot be overstated. Many of the images have achieved iconic status. It is rare to read a historical account of the revolution without encountering one of these photographic images. The Mexican cultural critic Carlos Monsiváis points out that in the aftermath of the armed struggle images from the collection came to signify the revolution for those who had not experienced it directly: "Al publicarse la *Historia de la Revolución mexicana*, una generación que ya no vivió la experiencia armada inicia un asombro que se repitirá y elegirá, con sospechosa monotonía, unas cuantas fotos para extraer de ellas ejemplos, moralejas, lecciones históricas, autocomplacencia estatal, estímulos de pequeña burguesía ilustrada o radical. Usted ya los conoce: unos zapatistas con expresión indescifrable desayunan en el palacio porfirista de Sanborns." ["On the publication of the *Historia de la Revolución mexicana*, a generation that had not lived through the armed experience initiates an astonishment that will repeat and choose, with suspicious monotony, a handful of photographs in order to extract from them examples, morals, historical lessons, state complacency, stimuli for the educated or radical bourgeoisie. You know them well: some Zapatistas with an indecipherable look on their faces breakfast in the Porfirian palace, Sanborns."][22]

Monsiváis further notes that during the early phases of the revolution, the violence depicted in these photographic images had the power to incite fear and to repel. However, with repeated exposure the photographs lost their power to shock and, like the ideals of the revolution itself, underwent a process of institutionalization: "Repetidas, comentadas (casi podría decirse 'impresas en el inconsciente colectivo'), las fotos seleccionadas muestran que el centro del interés no es el examen de la violencia popular sino la *estetización* mitológica del proceso revolucionario." ["Repeated, commented upon (it could almost be said, "engraved in the collective unconscious") the selected photographs demonstrate that the center of interest is not the examination of the popular violence, but the mythological *aestheticization* of the revolutionary process."] Monsiváis's comments articulate what has by now become a commonplace of writing on photography. That is, with the proliferation of images of violence, the potential impact of witnessing that violence in what is effectively a realistic medium diminishes. As Susan Sontag states: "To suffer is one thing; another thing is living with the photographed images of suffering, which does not necessarily strengthen conscience and the ability to be compassionate. It can also corrupt them. Once one has seen such images, one has started down the road of seeing more. Images transfix. Images *anesthetize*. An event known through photographs certainly becomes more real than it would have if one had never seen the photographs. . . . But after repeated exposure to images it also becomes less real."[23]

At this point, I take a brief etymological detour to discuss the words *estetización* [aestheticization] and *anesthetize*. *Aesthetics* derives from the Greek *aisthesis*, pertaining to the domain of human perception and sensation. Terry Eagleton points out that "aesthetics is born as a discourse of the body." Before it becomes associated with art in the eighteenth century, aesthetics charts "territory [that] is nothing less than the whole of our sensate life together—the business of affections and aversions, of how the world strikes the body on its sensory surfaces, of that which takes root in the gaze and the guts and all that arises from our most banal, biological insertion into the world."[24] *Anaisthesis*, its opposite, pertains to the absence of bodily sensation. These terms represent a productive antinomy that can help us understand Modotti's photograph by turning the formulation of violence and aesthetics around. Instead of the aesthetics of violence—the way in which violence becomes pure aesthetic spectacle and, in turn, the viewer is anesthetized or desensitized— I consider the violence of aesthetics by reading *Workers Parade* alongside a photograph from the Casasola archive, *La calle de Plateros*.

La calle de Plateros is a photographic precursor to the revolutionary images in which the sombrero gained its iconic status. It foreshadows the photographs where the sombrero comes to represent the unruly, revolutionary body politic engaged in violent struggle. And it is particularly (but not exclusively) in the photographs portraying Zapata and his followers that the sombrero comes into sharpest relief as an instantly recognizable symbol of the conflict and more especially the agrarian, peasant faction of the revolution, which in the process, becomes a marker of racial difference. *Calle de Plateros*, however, is a useful comparative image. Reading the two photographs in tandem, the viewer is inevitably struck by two interrelated formal concerns that both photographs display. Namely, both photographs are taken from the same vertiginous camera angle, and as a result, both share a formal interest in the shape of the hats of the crowds that visually eclipse the bodies below them. But here the similarities end. The Casasola photograph exists within a very specific context, which is revealed both within the photographic frame itself and beyond it, in the title. The title informs the viewer where the photograph was taken, when, and why. That is to say, it tells us that the photograph was taken to commemorate the "fiestas patrias," or independence celebrations, in Mexico City, in Calle de Plateros on 16 September 1910.

Within the photographic frame itself the crowds of hats are sandwiched between the two rows of buildings that occupy the upper third of the image, tapering off into the white space of the vanishing point, punctuated by what seem to be decorations. The buildings are bedecked with Mexican flags in celebration of Independence Day. At the center of the crowd of hats stands a figure clothed in military uniform, who, if not the immediate focal point of the photograph, becomes so once the eye alights upon him. This photograph, then, is brimming with visual and textual information that allows the viewer to insert it into a specific historical context. Taken on the eve of the revolution, this photograph marks the one hundredth anniversary of the declaration of Mexican independence from Spain. "In September 1910," write historians Meyer and Sherman, "Mexico appeared to many to be enjoying her finest hour. But with social reform still alien to the Porfirian mentality, the peace would soon prove to be fragile and the showy facade would collapse with it."[25]

In contrast to the historically grounded, "documentary" photographs taken before and during the revolution, Modotti's photograph, taken in the aftermath of the revolution's violent phase, works as a series of abstractions. The workers of the title are abstracted from their physical environment. The only suggestion of context is the ground across which they parade and what we assume is a streetcar line, in the top right-hand corner of the image. The workers themselves are abstracted from the crowd as the sombreros spill over and are bisected by the framing edges of the image. Finally, the workers

Figure 12.

*La calle de Plateros antes de iniciarse el desfile militar durante las fiestas patrias,
México City*, 16 September 1910. Fototeca de la INAH, Pachuco, Hidalgo,
Mexico.

are even abstracted from their bodies and instead are represented
metonymically by their sombreros. Whereas *Calle de Plateros* is replete
with visual and textual information, *Workers Parade* pares this information down to the minimum.

This series of abstractions is achieved by the framing of the photograph, whereby the sombreros are cast in a visual language of pure
form. Indeed, the key to understanding this image lies in the vertiginous camera angle. On the one hand, this camera angle, which clearly
signals that Modotti was positioned up above the crowd, stages
Modotti's distance as a woman from the body politic below her, which
is encoded as specifically male. But equally, the camera angle of *Workers
Parade* is emblematic of Modotti's position of power as she imposes
the frame of photographic representation. By imposing a frame on the

subjects below her, she fixes meaning. In the final analysis, framing always represents a gesture of authority, of power. And to overlook Modotti's power as the subject who imposes the frame, the subject who decides what goes into that frame and how, is to overlook an important facet of this photograph.

However, what is crucially important to understand is how Modotti's photograph frames the sombreros/bodies. When the two photographs are brought together, the full force of the sombrero's potential status as a stereotype becomes evident. To return to Monsiváis and Sontag, their observations are based on a notion of the way in which the representation of violence becomes pure aesthetic spectacle. According to this formulation, the viewer becomes desensitized, or anesthetized. By contrast, the violence of Modotti's image does not reside in the representation of a violent subject. What is violent in Modotti's image is its aesthetic representation of its subject as stereotype. By subsuming a stereotype—the sombrero and, by extension, the body that exists below it—into the visual language of pure form, aesthetics functions against its etymology, as anesthesia. Or to put it another way, aesthetics might numb us to the full impact of the image as stereotype. It is impossible to separate the aesthetic dimension from the content of the image. Once again, if aesthetics works against its etymology as anesthesia in the rendering of sombrero into stereotype in *Workers Parade*, then the implicit violence in this visual gesture is ultimately political.

The aestheticization of the sombrero as stereotype, therefore, raises a series of questions. Is Modotti's image simply a cultural stereotype taken through the lens of the camera of a cultural tourist? Or to put the question into another context, bearing in mind that Modotti was a nationalized North American citizen, what makes *Workers Parade* different from, for example, the cartoon "High Sierra"? Although Modotti's photograph predates the cartoon by some forty years, the juxtaposition of the two images raises some interesting questions. Given that Modotti herself was a foreigner in Mexico, does her "Mexican" photograph buy into the range of stereotypes associated with Mexico and Mexicans? What, if anything, distinguishes Modotti's representation of the sombrero from the moustaches, the serapes, the cacti that have come to stand in for Mexico in the North American and European (and Mexican) popular imagination?[26]

It would be almost too easy to read *Workers Parade* in terms of the sombrero's status as a stereotype and thereby dismiss the image as "morally" reprehensible and therefore unworthy of further discussion. In many ways, such a dismissal has much in common with the early feminist condemnation of the objectification of the female body, what Griselda Pollock has termed the "negative aesthetics" of earlier feminist visual theory.[27] Just as questions of sexual difference require a more complex approach, so too do issues of racial difference. Indeed, in an essay that directly addresses the stereotype, Homi K. Bhabha suggests that

> the point of intervention should shift from the ready recognition of images as positive or negative, to an understanding of the process of subjectification made possible (and plausible) through stereotypical discourse. To judge the stereotyped image on the basis of a prior political normativity is to dismiss it, not to displace it, which is only possible by engaging with its effectivity; with the repertoire of positions of power and resistance, domination and dependence that constructs colonial identification subject (both colonizer and colonized).[28]

Bhabha's formulation argues not for a dismissal of the stereotype but for an engagement with its effectivity. Within my discussion of *Workers Parade*, I suggest that such an engagement will require a more complex approach to the photograph itself and to its context. In order to engage more fully with the effectivity of this particular stereotype, we need to think again about the aesthetic dimension of Modotti's photograph and its particular status as a photographic image that depicts a stereotype because the notion of the sombrero as stereotype is bound up with the aesthetic dimension of the image. To denounce the image as a stereotype would be reductive and simplistic. It would amount to a failure to engage fully either with the stereotype in its own right or with the aesthetic language in which the stereotype is cast. In order to attend to these issues, we need to construct a further layer of context in which to locate *Workers Parade* and its representation of the sombrero/body. In the next chapter, I focus once again on the conjunction of body and sombrero in *Workers Parade*. But I offer a more nuanced reading of the photograph in the form of its publication in the journal *Mexican Folkways*. And I bring into play another body, a body that has constantly haunted the edges of this study—namely, the female body.

5

Beside the Abject Body

Toward Context

In a letter written shortly before her deportation from Mexico in 1930, Modotti comments that in her photographic work she has been at pains to avoid what she perceives as the usual visual clichés associated with Mexico and Mexicanness: "I feel that if I leave the country, I almost owe it to the country to show, not so much what I have done here, but especially what can be done, without recurring to colonial churches and charros and chinas poblanas, and the similar trash most fotographers [sic] have indulged in."[1] Given that, on some level, the photograph *Workers Parade* plays on the idea of the sombrero as stereotype, how are we to understand the image in the light of Modotti's comments? If, as Homi Bhabha argues, the displacement of a stereotype is only possible by "engaging with its effectivity," then it is productive to return *Workers Parade* to one of its original material contexts, namely the cultural magazine *Mexican Folkways*. In this way, it is possible to explore how Modotti's photograph articulates meaning at a specific historical and cultural moment in the development of Mexican identity politics.

Workers Parade is not the only photograph that Modotti published in *Mexican Folkways*. Some forty-five of her photographs appeared in this source, including two of her famous images of mothers and children, *An Aztec Mother* and *An Aztec Baby* (ca. 1926–27).[2] A return to material context will also involve a return to ideas and issues explored in earlier chapters. I first return to a reading of *Workers Parade* as body politic in order to shift the analysis of this particular image toward an understanding of the way in which, in the light of Julia Kristeva's notion of abjection, the photograph can be seen to dramatize the abject body. I then return to the female body. In chapter 1 I suggested that we cannot simply claim that as a woman photographer, Modotti looked on her female subjects with an "exemplary," non-objectifying gaze, but that instead we should attend to questions of framing, space, and the gaze. Here in my final chapter, then, framing my reading of the female body within the dual contexts of *Mexican Folkways* and Bracha Ettinger Lichtenberg's discussion of the possibility of the matrixial, I place another kind of reading of the female body on the critical agenda alongside (but *not* superimposed upon, and therefore occluding) those that already exist.

My intention in returning to context is not to reproduce a sense of what Mieke Bal calls "totally successful communication" between photographer and viewer, "wherein the message arrives unharmed at its destination and is decoded according to the intention of the sender. The receiver is totally passive, a container rather than a subject, and the sender is omnipotent. We all know, of course, that reality is not so idyllic, and that messages hardly ever arrive complete and undamaged. . . . Yet most art history and much of literary interpretation still aims at 'restoring' this ideal communication by retrieving the original intention and context."[3] I am keen, rather, to examine the wealth of interpretative constellations that open up once we re-view these photographs in their material context, which turns on issues of Mexican cultural identity, photographic representation, and sexual difference.

Indigenismo

In the aftermath of the revolution in Mexico, the need to articulate a coherent narrative of national identity became a key issue that cut across political and cultural practices. After a period of instability and disruption in the form of the armed phase of the revolution, which led to a period of continued conflict and change in the 1920s, the Mexican state urgently needed to renegotiate and modernize national identity. The revolution did not usher in a socialist state but instead "a new type of state . . . nurturing an indigenous capitalism."[4] In other words, the role of capitalism as a driving force behind the modernizing thrust of the nation should not be underestimated. It is particularly relevant to bear in mind this notion of "indigenous capitalism" when approaching the cultural activity of the period. One of the hurdles with which the state was confronted in its endeavor to "gel" and thereby modernize the nation was the sheer diversity of racial identities that coexisted within the national boundaries. Race, therefore, became a key and contentious issue within the emergent debates around national identity in the 1920s, manifesting itself in the discourse of *indigenismo*. In its quest for national definition, the state attempted to offset multiplicity and diversity against a notion of singularity and coherence, using *indigenismo* as a unifying tool.

In his invaluable and complex essay "Racism, Revolution, and *Indigenismo*," Alan Knight brings to light a fundamental paradox about postrevolutionary *indigenismo*. The paradox turns on the fact that while *indigenismo* emerged from the revolution as a crucial and nation-defining cultural concept, the revolution itself was not fought in the name of race. Instead, the conflict was couched in terms of class. "The Revolution that began in 1910 could be fought and was fought on the basis of considerable Indian participation . . . but in the absence of any self-consciously Indian project." Therefore, despite its name, *indigenismo* constituted an elite discourse in Mexico as the nation-state struggled to consolidate and legitimate its identity. Knight highlights the fact that the discourse of *indigenismo* is as old as post-Columbian Mexico itself. Europe invented the Indian "and this generic concept remained part of Spanish rather than Indian usage. It defined those who were not Spanish or *mestizo* and it lumped together a wide range of Indian groups, languages, and communities." In the 1920s it became necessary to overcome these time-honored binaries. According to Knight, at this point the state's aim was to create a sense of national identity in which "the old Indian/European thesis/antithesis [would give] rise to a higher synthesis, the *mestizo*, who was neither Indian nor European, but quintessentially Mexican." In other words, *mestizaje* is a singular term that is wholly predicated on multiplicity. And, again, despite the implications of its name, as a discourse *indigenismo* was not really about reinstating Indian culture. As David Brading argues: "The ultimate and paradoxical aim of official *indigenismo* in Mexico was thus to liberate the country from the deadweight of its native past or, to put the case more clearly, finally to destroy the native culture that had emerged during the colonial period. *Indigenismo* was therefore a means to an end. That end was cultural *mestizaje*."[5]

As the state strove to reinvent the nation, it looked to that dimension of its *mestizo* self that had previously remained in a state of cultural dereliction: the Indian. In the process of nation formation, the figure of the Indian—both rhetorical and real—came to play a new role. According to Francisco Reyes Palma: "De ahí provino la exaltación mítica de la imagen del indio como fuente de originalidad creadora y sustento de lo nacional. Encubierto en ese razonamiento se inició un proceso de colonización interna que buscaba incorporar al indio al idioma y a los patrones culturales del denominador, a la vez que se le expropriaba su particular herencia de raíz prehispánica." ["This is where the mythical exaltation of the image of the Indian as a source of creative originality and basis of national identity came from. Concealed behind this reasoning, a process of internal colonization was initiated that sought to incorporate the Indian into the Spanish language and hegemonic cultural paradigm, at the same time expropriating the Indian's particular legacy of pre-Hispanic roots."][6]

The terms "internal colonization" and "expropriation" are particularly useful for an understanding of the link between *Mexican Folkways*, official *indigenista* discourses, and the ultimate goal of cultural *mestizaje*.

Mexican Folkways

If, as Knight, Brading, and Reyes Palma concur, *indigenismo* represents a move to offset a singular *mestizo* identity against the potentially destabilizing multiple identities that the nation embraced, then social engineering had to take place on two fronts. First, the Indian communities that existed on the cultural, political, and social margins needed to be "educated" into the ways of the modern nation. Second, the elite sector of society had to learn to revalue its Indian heritage. Devoted to the description of "Indian folk practice," the magazine *Mexican Folkways* was designed to fulfill this educational function. On its title page, *Mexican Folkways* announces itself as a "Revista bimestral en inglés y español, dedicada a usos y costumbres mexicanas" ["bimonthly magazine in English and Spanish devoted to Mexican ways and customs"]. The magazine's bilingual status was due to its founder and editor, the North American writer and folklorist Frances Toor (1890–1956). Toor, who had studied anthropology at the University of California, traveled to Mexico after graduation and founded *Mexican Folkways* in 1925. The project ran to eight volumes, each comprising five issues, and eventually folded in 1933. Each issue consisted of a range of articles, either on a variety of topics or on a single theme, such as a 1927 edition dedicated to Mexican folk song. The table of contents of a random issue of *Folkways* gives a sense of its scope.[7] In the August–September 1927 issue we find a variety of articles and illustrations, including the words and music to the corrido "El 30–30" (accompanied by an untitled Modotti photograph of cartridge belt, scythe, and corn); an anthropological article by Carlos Basauri entitled "Creencias y Prácticas de los Tarahumaras" ["Beliefs and Practices of the Tarahumara,"]; an archaeological essay "Notas sobre las ruinas de Tizatlán, Tlaxcala" ["Notes on the Ruins at Tizatlán, Tlaxcala"] by Alfonso Caso; and a recipe for *mole de guajolote.*

Among the contributors to the magazine were some of the most prominent politicians and policy makers in Mexico in the 1920s. Indeed, the *Diccionario Porrúa de historia, biografía y geografía de México* singles out the following contributors to *Mexican Folkways* for special mention: Carlos Basauri, Alfonso Caso, Manuel Gamio, J. M. Puig Casauranc, and Moisés Sáenz. It is also noted that the magazine "contiene un inapreciable acervo documental enriquecido con la colaboración de los especialistas más conotados; asimismo ilustraron sus páginas Diego Rivera, José Clemente Orozco y David Alfaro Siqueiros, no sólo en lo gráfico sino también con pluma" ["contains an invaluable documentary archive enriched by the collaboration of the most distinguished specialists; Diego Rivera, José Clemente Orozco, and David Alfaro Siqueiros contributed to it both graphically and by pen"].

Considering the wealth of material that appeared in the magazine and the cultural and political prominence of many of the contributors to these eight volumes of *Mexican Folkways*, it has received surprisingly scant critical attention. One of the few critics to have recognized the importance of *Mexican Folkways* is the art historian Barbara Braun. She picks up on the magazine's relationship to state policy, highlighting the contributions made to the magazine by the intellectuals-politicians Manuel Gamio and Alfonso Caso.[8] Braun suggests that *Folkways* "helped [to] popularize these intellectuals' attitudes during the 1920s by celebrating indigenous forms and promoting a revival of popular arts as a means of fostering a new national unity." Both men made important contributions to cultural policy in the 1920s and both were passionate *indigenistas*. Moreover, in 1916 Gamio had published the book *Forjando patria*, in which he set forth his views on the future of national culture, enjoining "his countrymen to regard previously despised artifacts aesthetically, saturate themselves in aboriginal history, myths, cosmogony, and philosophy, and *use visual culture as a means of unifying the national consciousness*" (my italics).[9] Given the content and cultural politics of *Mexican Folkways*, it is not surprising that the magazine found official support from Gamio and Caso.

In a brief history of the trajectory of *Mexican Folkways*, Frances Toor acknowledges the support the magazine received from the Mexican state.[10] She explains how, during the early stages, she funded the project herself before securing funds from Manuel Gamio, then subsecretary for education, who offered her one hundred pesos a month and also contributed an article to the first edition. In fact, the Secretariat for Education was to have a noteworthy input into the magazine throughout its publication span. The magazine received the support of subsecretaries J. M. Puig Casauranc and Moisés Sáenz during their terms in office. Both men offered financial assistance and contributed articles. The magazine was also subsidized by a North American benefactor Mrs. Leonard Elmhirst, which attests to its appeal to a North American readership. Indeed, Toor confirms that it was enjoyed by North American and Mexican readers alike, and in its first year of publication, "small and humble though it was, *Folkways* was establishing itself in Mexico and abroad. It was on the subscription lists of the best libraries in the United States, and it was esteemed by those of the young Mexican writers who were not at all interested in the Indian." The magazine not only met with the approval of these "young Mexican writers" but also received praise from no less a figure than President Plutarco Elías Calles, who in a letter personally addressed to Toor, stated "*Mexican Folkways*, in addition to being very original, is making known to our people and to foreigners the real spirit of our aboriginal races and the expressive feeling of our people in general, rich in beautiful traditions."[11]

Toor makes explicit the link between her magazine and the events that were taking place on a political level in Mexico during the early years of its publication. Locating the impulse for change in Mexico within the revolution, she examines the way in which the magazine reflects the new revolutionary government's interest in "the Indian," a figure who had previously been neglected by the state. She notes that although the more tangible aims of the revolution, such as economic reform and land distribution, were slow in coming, one of the major achievements was the recognition of "the Indian":

> Everyone knows by this time that the Mexican Revolution of 1910 has brought about a social change—dozens of books and articles have been written about it. The change got underway with the first of the Revolutionary-Reconstruction Governments, beginning with the incumbency of General Alvaro Obregón in 1920, and has continued down to the present time.
>
> The change thus far consists chiefly in attitude. By this I mean that the Revolution has not yet made good in an economic sense all its promises to the people. It has been perhaps unnecessarily slow in its reconstruction work, and the Indian is still poor and illiterate. But at least he has been recognized as a human being. The new governing classes have discovered the value of the Indian just as the Industrial Revolution has discovered the value of the man on the street. They have realized that if Mexico is to progress, the masses of Indians, forming two-thirds of the population, must be taken into account.[12]

Toor's text is revealing on a number of counts. First, her status as an apologist for the slowness of governmental reform is abundantly evident.[13] Second, Toor's sense that the Indian can now be recognized as a "human being" underlines the profound lack of status of the Indian communities of the period. Third, the comparison between revolutionary change in Mexico and the Industrial Revolution is especially poignant, for it indicates that value here means more precisely use-value of "the Indian." In other words, in Toor's editorial we can see the convergence of cultural and economic factors, insofar as her words reveal the need to incorporate the Indian into the modernizing space of the nation for a specific purpose. The disparate Indian communities had to be drawn out of the "past" and into the capitalist present, in a process that involved the commodification of the Indian body to fulfill the demands of labor. Toor's choice of the term the "governing classes" here is also striking, underlining Braun's notion that the perceived backwardness and poverty of large sectors of *mestizo* and indigenous Mexico had to be corrected by the "reeducation of *elite* sectors of Mexican society about Indian traditions." In fact, the elitist, colonizing aspect of *Mexican Folkways* is embodied in its very title. That is, although the plural "folkways" would seem to suggest a recognition and perhaps even celebration of diversity, that diversity is effectively made singular and contained by the qualifier "folk." Or as Susan Ritchie states in an article titled "Ventriloquist Folklore": "Local diversity has always existed and is always present; yet the dynamic of representation is, in its very inclusiveness, always the same. Representation gathers people together in order to formulate them as a People subject to the inscription of a particular master narrative: usually that of the democratic nation-state."[14]

The dynamic of representation and the intervention of the state in that dynamic is made absolutely explicit in the first issue of *Mexican Folkways*, in which an article appears by Manuel Gamio, tellingly titled "The Utilitarian Aspect of Folklore." In his article, Gamio establishes the study of folklore as a subject that merits governmental attention: "The study of folklore is interesting not only for the specialist and the cultured man in general, but even for the statesman, who may deduce from it proper conclusions which will finally serve for the elaboration of rules of government." In his article, Gamio divides Mexican society into two sectors: an elite, educated minority and an uneducated, backward mass. He thereby establishes a wholly conventional self-other binary relationship, where readers of *Mexican Folkways* clearly belong to the former category. "It is obvious, then, that there is a lack of understanding and a conflict between the social Mexican majority and the minority incorporated into modern civilization, whose conception of the social phenomena is generally naturally based on information of a scientific character, which they derive from schools, books, etc., etc."[15] According to Gamio, if Mexican society was to progress in economic terms, that is, if the productivity of those who lived beyond the bounds of modern, "civilized" society was to be tapped, then something had to be done about the "uneducated mass":

> As it would be impossible to make that Indian-mestizo majority abandon their folkloric ideas all at once in order to incorporate itself with the minority of advanced civilization, it is indispensable to analyze and to know their diverse and peculiar modes of thinking, in order to formulate later educational means that may make progress easy for the gradual forming

of the Indian mentality until it is molded into the ways of modern thought. This of course, does not mean that we shall attempt to strip the Indian of his typical characteristics for we are enemies of standardization, above all with respect to that which refers to artistic expression. It is inevitable, nevertheless, to be modern and standardized from many points of view, in order to change from a stage of darkness, organic misery, and general malaise to one of satisfactory knowledge and of intellectual and material well-being.[16]

Gamio's article, especially this passage, underlines the paternalism that subtended the Mexican state's attitude to its indigenous subjects. Faced with a heterogeneous mass, the state needed to homogenize this mass in order to incorporate it into the body politic. Given the sheer diversity of the myriad Indian groups and groupings within the nation-space, it could never realistically hope to standardize them. It could, however, minimize the threat of diversity by containing the other through the discourse of *indigenismo*, a discourse that would essentially render that other knowable. It is the pursuit of this particular kind of knowledge that, for Gamio, makes *Mexican Folkways* an especially valuable publication.

Within the Western tradition, knowledge and objective mastery have always been closely associated with vision and visuality. To see is to know. To know is to be powerful. Or as James C. Faris puts it, "Since Plato's allegory of the cave, wisdom has been accepted in the West in illusions of and allusions to vision—knowing is insight, seeing is believing, light is privileged over heat, and rationalist epistemology rides heavily on ocular metaphor: the mind's eye." What is striking about Mexican *indigenismo* is that, following the exhortations of Gamio in *Forjando patria* and the impetus provided by José Vasconcelos as the first postrevolutionary secretary of education, it translates itself in specifically visual terms; artists rather than writers emerged as the intellectual vanguard in the 1920s. As Alan Knight notes, "the most celebrated representatives of this new official philosophy were, of course, the revolutionary muralists, [most prominent among them Diego Rivera] who provided pictorial affirmation of Indian valor, nobility, suffering, and achievement."[17]

As the muralists devoted their time to re-imaging national history on a grand scale across the public spaces of the nation, in keeping with the visual privilege of *indigenismo*, *Mexican Folkways* participated in this project on a smaller scale. Graphic artists, including Rivera and Modotti, figure prominently among the editorial committee.[18] Furthermore, considering that *Folkways* appeared at a time when illustrated print culture was in its infancy, its pages are replete with graphic material, from pre-Hispanic-style drawings to details of murals to anthropological photographs of Indian subjects. Toor states proudly that as official support grew for her magazine, she was able to increase the number of pages and the quantity and quality of its illustrations. Moreover, she adds that Mexicans of all classes have a special affinity to visual culture: "The Indians have conserved this plastic heritage in the construction of Christian temples, the finest on the American continent. And the middle and upper classes, although their tastes have been warped by the former tendency to imitate everything European, also have plastic ability and a love of decoration. Art, good or bad, is almost essential to the existence of Mexicans."[19] As a measure of the importance of the visual aspect of the magazine, the first art editor, Jean Charlot, was replaced within a year by Diego Rivera, whose name has become synonymous with visual representation in Mexico.

In the process of consolidating national identity, in terms of both the macro level of the state and the micro contribution of *Mexican Folkways*, the "Indian" effectively becomes a national spectacle in a visualizing gesture that reveals a drive to know, define, and control. And as the cultural historian Serge Gruzinski argues, such a gesture belongs to a long tradition in Mexico where visual representation is intricately bound up with issues of race. Just as *indigenismo* did not represent a new discourse when it emerged in the 1920s, the privileged status of the visual within the formation of Mexican cultural identity was not a phenomenon that arose in the early twentieth century. As Gruzinski states in the introduction to his book on the visual image in Mexican colonial society, significantly entitled *La guerra de las imágenes*: "La imagen ejerció, en el siglo XVI, un papel notable en el descubrimiento, la conquista y la colonización del Nuevo Mundo. Como la imagen constituye . . . uno de los principales instrumentos de la cultura europea, la gigantesca empresa de occidentalización que se abatió sobre el continente americano adoptó—al menos en parte—la forma de una guerra de imágenes que se perpetuó durante siglos y que hoy no parece de ninguna manera haber concluido." ["In the sixteenth century, the image played a significant role in the discovery, conquest and colonization of the New World. As the image constituted one of the principal instruments of European culture, the giant enterprise of Westernization that befell the American continent adopted—at least in part—the form of a war of images that was perpetuated for centuries and that does not appear to have concluded even today."][20]

Gruzinski's text explores the mediating role of the visual image both as an instrument of colonization and an object of resistance to that colonization within a multiracial society. If race itself is an essentially visual category that becomes culturally inscribed on the body, then it stands to reason that in a society that, from its inception, is based upon racial violence, visual representation becomes a contested site of struggle for identity. It is in the visual realm that anxieties of the elite minority sector of Mexican society about difference and diversity, and the concomitant quest for a homogenized body politic, are played out.

Workers Parade

Given that *Mexican Folkways* was explicitly engaged in a project that sought to define, control, and contain the diverse indigenous communities that existed within the nation-space, and given that visual material was accorded privileged status within its pages, how can we read Modotti's photograph within this context?

In chapter 4, I suggest that *Workers Parade* is an image that represents the body politic within postrevolutionary Mexican society. The key to grasping the significance of *Workers Parade* lies, however, in a more complex understanding of the body politic, both within the photographic frame and beyond it. In Modotti's photograph, the sombrero racially inscribes the body below it as indigenous. Looking at notions of the body politic that were in the process of being formed beyond the photographic frame in postrevolutionary cultural politics, it is important to establish that the Indian body is the body that challenges the very definition of the coherent and containable *mestizo* body politic. The Indian body is the body that *indigenismo* struggles to draw into a reconfigured definition of the body politic as *mestizo*. The *mestizo* body politic is neither European nor Indian but a synthesis of the two categories. The Indian body, or certain parts of it at least, must therefore be drawn into the *mestizo* body politic.

Workers Parade is a photograph that can be read against the grain of containment and the modernizing thrust of the nation as an image that dramatizes the inverse of the body politic: the abject body. The abject is that which defies boundaries and that which resists delimitation. Its dramatization, in keeping with the notion of troubled boundaries, is played out on a number of levels in *Workers Parade*, both within the photographic frame and beyond it.

In her essay "National Abjects: Julia Kristeva on the Process of Political Self-Identification," Norma Claire Moruzzi offers an account of the formation of national identity by reworking Kristeva's theory of abjection in *Powers of Horror*.[21] Abjection is concerned with liminality, with the borders and boundaries, with where the subject starts and the other ends. In psychoanalytic terms, abjection harks back to the baby's pre-Oedipal (what Kristeva calls "semiotic") experience of both its own and its mother's bodily fluids. In order to become a subject, the baby must learn to distinguish itself from the (m)other. To do so, it must recognize the boundaries and borders of its own body. Bodily fluids and the mother's body, therefore, pose a potential threat to subjectivity, insofar as they have the potential to blur the boundary between the subject and object. The maternal body and bodily fluids are neither subject nor object but instead partake of both categories. In the post-Oedipal phase, the subject starts to harbor a sense of disgust for its own and its mother's bodily fluids, which become the "abject." The abject is therefore both part of the body and not part of it. It is that which threatens the integrity of the subject in that it is something that could potentially blur the boundaries of the self. At the same time, that integrity is predicated on the abject, for the abject delineates those very boundaries.

Moruzzi reformulates Kristeva's theory of abjection in order to address the question of national identity.[22] Moruzzi's formulation provides us with critical insight into the liminal figure of the *mestizo*. Moruzzi argues that the nation-state must delimit and maintain its identity through "encounters with an other, strangers either outside or within its borders." These encounters with the other are absolutely essential to the maintenance of the legitimacy of national identity. For after all, what defines the nation-state other than what it is not? Or as Moruzzi writes: "Historically, the nation-state establishes itself through the convulsions of a body politic which rejects those parts of itself, defined as other or excess, whose rejected alterity engenders the consolidation of a national identity."[23]

Within the arena of Mexican nation formation, abjection allows us to theorize the relationship between the *mestizo* body politic and the Indian body. The *mestizo* body politic, which is both Indian and European (or neither Indian nor European), in the process of self-consolidation seeks to map out its own borders. In this process the Indian body becomes the abject, which "is that which seems to confound the possibility of meaning, its presence threatening a chaos that must be withheld. The self abjects that which is most necessarily inescapable and rejected: the bodily reminders of physical dependence and necessity." Being neither subject nor object in the process of consolidating national identity, the abject "must constantly be ejected or assimilated."[24] Thus the *mestizo* body politic expels those parts of its self defined as abject: the disparate indigenous communities considered to exist in temporal and spatial dislocation. But equally, not being totally other, the abject must also be assimilated into the body politic. The status of the abject Indian body in postrevolutionary Mexico is then that which simultaneously threatens and reinforces the integrity of the nation-state. Thus in *indigenista* policy, what happens is a process of ejection and assimilation. On the one hand, the state seeks to eradicate "backwardness," to eliminate "otherness" through, for example, a series of educational campaigns designed to draw the Indian communities away from their more "primitive" practices and into the twentieth century. On the other, it seeks to salvage a "pristine" notion of Indian folk culture, which it would incorporate into the body politic. This process of ejection and assimilation comes into focus in Toor's first editorial.

> In Mexico there are about ten million [Indians], at least two-thirds of the population, living in the remnants of their ancient civilizations. It is these ten million that President Calles has promised to incorporate into modern life. The task will be a tremendously slow and difficult one, but it would be even slower and more difficult if it were not that through his folkloric expression the Indian has kept alive that something which has prevented him from degenerating into a mere beast of burden, compatible with his mode of living.[25]

The move to instate *mestizo* identity is a double-edged gesture, an act of both rejection and incorporation. *Mestizo* identity is established through the delimitation of boundaries: *mestizo* identity excludes that which is primitive and backward in Indian culture (that which would mean that the Indian would *degenerate* into a beast of burden); it includes that which is "positive" (folkloric expression).

If the abject is that which confounds boundaries, that which potentially disturbs identity, system, and order, then we can read *Workers Parade*, against the thrust of *Mexican Folkways*, as an image that precisely troubles boundaries. First, it is important to note that *Mexican Folkways* was not the only source in which the photograph appeared. Sarah M. Lowe states that the photograph was published in at least five different sources with five different titles. She lists these as *Mexican Folkways* (as *Workers Parade*, 1926), *New Masses (as May Day in Mexico*, 1928); *Creative Art* (as *A Peasants' Manifestation*, 1929) *Transition* (as *Strike Scene*, 1929) and *BFI* (as *Mexique*, 1930). Furthermore, Modotti tended to send her photographs to journals for publication without specifying a title.[26] For whatever reasons Modotti did this, the different contexts in which the image was published and the range of titles under which it was published already signal the potential for multiple readings. That is to say, if titles and the contexts in which images are viewed fix meaning, *Workers Parade* is already framed in a whole variety of discursive situations.

Even as the image cannot be fixed beyond the frame via its title and context, what lies within the frame does not allow easy assimilation into prescribed categories. To a certain degree *Workers Parade* will always offer itself as an image to be read in purely aesthetic, formal terms. If we let our eyes go out of focus while viewing the image, we start to see a rhythm of disklike shapes. However, by losing focus, we lose critical depth and insight. An aesthetic response to the image is predicated on an opposition between pure contemplation on the one hand and, on the other, contingency and circumstance, where the latter are potentially elided by the former. But *Workers Parade* does not allow the viewer to lose focus. The unavoidable, palpable texture of the body below the sombrero insists on restoring substantiality to form. The body below the sombrero urgently reinstates itself into the viewer's field of vision, forcing the viewer to confront racial difference in the contiguity of sombrero and body. I suggest there is a striking parallel between the viewer's encounter with the racially inscribed body in the image and, on a national level, the Mexican state's encounter with the abject indigenous body. By drawing the indigenous subject into the space of visual representation—a space that, with the rise of state-sponsored muralism, was strongly associated with official ideology—the state, while it could never hope to homogenize difference, could, nevertheless, control and contain it. *Mexican Folkways*, with its wealth of visual material and its links to the state through official patronage, was actively engaged in the national project of containment. Thus where the state would assimilate difference through the visualizing discourse of *indigenismo*, in much the same way, the viewer of Modotti's photograph would assimilate difference in a purely aesthetic response to *Workers Parade*. If the photograph would allow such a response, that is. But the fact is the photograph does not. Instead, *Workers Parade* constantly blurs the boundary between aesthetics and difference, between sombrero and body.

Within the photograph itself, the constant slippage between sombrero and body is mirrored in the way in which the photograph sets up internal boundaries only to undermine them. In this way, the photograph shares a formal connection with *Roses*; both images are about framing and excess. *Workers Parade* particularly plays on the viewer's desire to see order and coherence in the image. At first sight, the photograph seems to be bisected, where the sombrero-cum-bodies appear to cut a neat line. Yet on closer inspection, this line dissolves into the irregular masses on either side. The photograph is bereft of a conventional vanishing point. The viewer's gaze is left to slip across the bodies/hats in search of a center. Equally, what initially seems to be a kind of visual rhythm, where rhythm connotes regularity, soon gives way to chaos as the sombreros blur into the bodies below and into one another. This is especially prominent in the top right-hand corner where the sombreros/bodies lose definition altogether, blurring into a white haze before slipping over the frame of the photograph. The viewer's desire to find order and coherence in what is essentially a chaotic image can be linked to the way in which the photograph makes its appeal to that viewer on an aesthetic level. Such a viewing experience is ultimately thwarted in a photograph that constantly disrupts the search for order and coherence.

If *Workers Parade* invites the viewer to read it in aesthetic terms, and to search for order and coherence, then as a photograph, by definition, it also simultaneously invites the viewer to read it as evidence. When viewing a photograph, there is ultimately no avoiding photography's ostensible documentary purchase on the real. Photography has traditionally been associated with super-legibility. It records people, places, and events. It furnishes evidence. *Workers Parade* appears in *Mexican Folkways* alongside an article by Pablo González Casanova entitled "El origen de los cuentos del México indígena" ["The Origins of the Stories of Indian Mexico"]. This juxtaposition of text and image would further seem to indicate that the image will offer the viewer some kind of visual information to complement, or illustrate, the text.

In fact the vast majority of photographic images that appear in *Mexican Folkways* belong to a tradition of photographic representations that do precisely that: claim to provide illustrative information. Most belong to a tradition of anthropological photographic representation. According to Iskander Mydin, this is a practice that "arose in the nineteenth century as a visual parallel of anthropological ideas about culture. This was also the period of the Western forward movement of colonial conquest and consolidation of territories on a worldwide scale. Anthropological photography of non-Western peoples and cultures in these territories therefore emerged at a time of unprecedented social change for non-Western societies as they were incorporated into alien, industrialist-capitalist metropolitan economies."[27] Anthropological photography is bound up in a colonizing project to make the other knowable, to make the other visible. Such photographs in *Mexican Folkways* claim to offer a "true" and "faithful" representation of their subjects.[28] They appear alongside articles that set out to chart in minute detail the customs and rituals of the indigenous groups they portray. Within the context of the national project of *indigenismo*, not until the indigenous other is made visible, and therefore knowable, can that other be assimilated into the body politic.

How, then, are we to understand Modotti's photograph? What information does *Workers Parade* provide the viewer about the other? What relationship does it bear to the text alongside which it appears? If we read text and image together, a set of striking convergences and divergences emerge. Pablo González Casanova's article, as its title suggests, attempts to trace a genealogy of Indian "folk" stories. Its tone is markedly academic as it seeks to offer an analytic overview of "folk" stories from around the world, in order to map out correspondences between these stories. "The story is considered, with reference to its origin and significance, from diverse and even opposite points of view by the different schools. Among these the principal ones are the schools of Mythography and Phylology [*sic*] headed by Grimm and Max Mueller, both philologists of world renown, in whose opinion the stories would be mythical reminiscences of one cosmological pre-Aryan conception, interpretable through the study of words."[29]

Employing precise bibliographic references, González Casanova writes from a position of objective mastery as he surveys the terrain below him. He has at his fingertips examples of folk stories from different geographical locations, which he juxtaposes in order to highlight striking parallels between these locations. The move to synthesize and fix his material means that González Casanova's text is in a number of ways reminiscent of the photographic act. That is, the article deals with the oral tradition; therefore, its subject matter stands in contradistinction to the written tradition to which González Casanova belongs. Just as the article freezes and reifies what is essentially a fluid and mutating form of representation, photographs capture and fix a moment that will implicitly slip away. Similarly, the camera angle of this particular image affords the viewer and photographer a position of objective mastery over the subject matter. Thus the perspective and format of both González Casanova's article and Modotti's photograph qua photograph would seem to share similar concerns that revolve around issues of mastery and categorization.

Yet if *Workers Parade* resists being read in terms of pure form, so too does it resist legibility. Unlike most of the photographs that appear in *Mexican Folkways*, which offer up a wealth of "factual" information, this image does not offer the reader any "knowledge." The photograph's blurred bodies and transgressed boundaries leave the viewer ultimately confounded. Yet maybe this feeling of being confounded is the ultimate "evidence," or knowledge, that *Workers Parade* furnishes. Indeed, *Workers Parade* seems to challenge the basic premise that the other is representable and ultimately knowable. The photograph suggests that it might be possible to engage in a more sophisticated manner not only with the image itself but also with the discourse of postrevolutionary *indigenismo*. If this cultural discourse would, through a process of assimilation and rejection of the abject, ensure the nation's distance and difference from (parts of) the indigenous body, then the dramatization of abjection in *Workers Parade* insists upon a different kind of dynamic. By attending to the complexity of *Workers Parade*, by attending to the constant slippage between sombrero and body, and boundary and body, the viewer can at least avoid fixing an unfocused gaze on the cultural other.

If the theoretical and cultural contexts through which *Workers Parade* has passed represent forms of framing, then my readings of this photograph demonstrate that the photograph is ultimately a cultural product that resists such framing impulses. This resistance to framing discourses takes place on a number of levels, significantly both within and beyond the photographic frame itself. On a compositional level, *Workers Parade*, like *Roses*, is an image that plays on and thereby plays up the whole notion of photographic framing. On a contextual level, the different and often conflicting readings—from body politic to cultural tourist to abject body—that can be generated around the image reveal that this is a photograph that defies the frame that will fix meaning. To defy the frame, however, is also to reinstate its presence. Indeed, photographs, as James C. Faris puts it,

> whether still or moving—are bounded. That is, they are framed. As such they inject another space—the limits, the edges—proscriptions, prohibitions of the image. These cannot be treated as arbitrary nor as artifact of technique. They define what is to be photograph and what is not. They deny (what was not in the photograph). They decide looking from and looking at. What makes these decisions—who frames and who focuses? What discursive authority, what appeal, determines where the space takes place, and what is thereby excluded, marked, made visible?[30]

It is one thing, however, to attend to the way in which photographs are ultimately framed and bounded entities; it is quite another to ignore the limits and edges of the critical discourse that would articulate a notion of the photograph as pure frame. If on one level the photograph is indeed pure frame, then there is a figure that has haunted the limits/edges of my own theoretical and cultural framing of Modotti's photographs without, as yet, having attained articulation: the photographic framing of the female body.

The Matrixial Gaze, or How We Might Look Again at the Female Body

In an article on the work of the Israeli psychoanalyst and artist Bracha Ettinger Lichtenberg, Griselda Pollock argues:

> Feminism has been waging a war on the myths, legends, texts and canons of what it names patriarchal culture. Using post-structuralist theory, such a culture is also defined as phallo-centric, a culture not only ruled by the Name of the Father,

but one semantically organized around the privileged signifier, the Phallus, in whose sovereign and single image being and
meaning are said to be exclusively constituted by a series of
oppositions: self/other, presence/absence, love/hate, incorpo-
ration/rejection. Various feminist theorizations have emerged
over the last twenty-five years of renewed and dedicated feminist intellectual and political activity. . . . However critically
they engage with the culture of the Father, they tend, however, to be caught in the very binary relation that fundamentally underpins that culture. Inversion or regression, valuing the
mother, the pre-Oedipal, the archaic, all these projects are
haunted by their relativity to the dominant phallic terms.[31]

Pollock's line of argument is, as ever, a cogent and committed critique of feminist theory and, at the same time, represents a productive
point of departure for what, within the context of the current study,
represents a return to origins: namely a return to the maternal body.

Having located a key contextual frame within which to read
Modotti's photographs—that is, *Mexican Folkways*—I now explore
what happens when we bring the female body back into view within
it. Modotti published some forty-five photographs in *Mexican
Folkways*, including two from her series of mothers and children.
More specifically, *An Aztec Mother* and *An Aztec Baby*, both made ca.
1926–27, appear alongside an article by the anthropologist Margaret
Park Redfield entitled "Nace un niño en Tepoztlán" ["A Child Is Born
in Tepoztlán"].[32] Mother and child are, in fact, a theme that occupies
a central position in Modotti's photographic work, where, as Mulvey
and Wollen note, the images are framed in such a way so as to
"emphasize not [the mothers'] own form but that of their interaction
with the children."[33] Their notion of the interaction between the
maternal and infant body interests me. However, my focus on this
interaction requires a further theoretical paradigm shift, one that
moves away from a notion of abjection and its attendant problems
toward another kind of conceptualization of the maternal body.

While my reading of *Workers Parade* as a photograph that dramatizes the abject indigenous body can help us understand the logic of the
same on which the formation of Mexican cultural identity is predicated, abjection falls short of the mark when it comes to the question of
reading the maternal body. This is because, following the Freudian/

Lacanian psychoanalytic paradigm to which Kristeva's theory of abjection is indebted, the maternal body is precisely the locus of abjection, it is that from which the subject must mark its distance in order for nonpsychotic subjectivization to take place. In her excellent introduction to Kristeva's work, Elizabeth Grosz has articulated the troubling implications that this work contains for feminist critical theory, arguing that "in her textual analyses, her use of Lacanian and Freudian, as well as Kleinian frameworks, she is uncritical of her sources and affirms their various misogynistic, phallocentric presuppositions. This is particularly problematic in her use of psychoanalytic models, which rely on the correlation of femininity and the maternal with castration."[34] For Kristeva, following Freud and Lacan, the maternal body is the site of fusion, of nondifferentiation between the fetus and (m)other, whose presence, forever after, will threaten to engulf the subject. The maternal body potentially defies identity and order. It is an extremely ambiguous entity and, for the child, the maternal embodies the abject against which it must struggle and in opposition to which it must identify with the father in order to achieve subjectification.

If we were to read Modotti's photographs of mothers and infants—that is to say, images that focus minutely and intricately on the relationship *between* the maternal body and infant body—through the prism of a Kristevan notion of abjection, we would more than likely end up repositioning these images within the "dominant phallic paradigm" that feminist critics such as Grosz and Pollock so deftly expose. Such a reading of the photographs would invariably produce an understanding of the maternal body inscribed within them as the threatening, boundary-defying body. How are we to imagine a different kind of reading of the maternal body? How can we arrive at a reading of this body that, if it were not to replace the phallic paradigm (which would be undesirable), then would at least displace its hegemony? Following the model of my reading of *Workers Parade*, I return these photographs to their material context in *Mexican Folkways* and then set them to work in and against their context. The theoretical paradigm for reading that I adopt here is based on the work of Bracha Lichtenberg Ettinger and on her notion of the matrix, a psychoanalytical concept she invokes as a signifier that coexists alongside the phallus and offers the possibility of a different way of imagining subjectivity.

Modotti's photographs *An Aztec Mother* and *An Aztec Baby* appear alongside Margaret Park Redfield's article "A Child Is Born in

Tepoztlán." Park Redfield's article, as its title suggests, concerns birthing practices in Tepoztlán, Morelos. More specifically, "A Child Is Born" deals with birthing practices within the indigenous community of Tepoztlán, which the author claims are "like folk customs generally, a combination of practical utility and magic developed by the group in order to meet inevitable crises in the lives of the individuals which compose it." We are back in the familiar domain of articles in *Mexican Folkways*, which are generally involved in the documentation of folk "practices" and their containment within the dominant discourse of *indigenismo*. Park Redfield's account of the ritualistic, "primitive" aspects of childbirth within the indigenous community she observes represents classic anthropological testimony. The anthropologist, with privileged access to her subjects, writes from a position both within and without the community she documents. Park Redfield has an informant within the community under observation, whose authority is based on both intimacy and experience and whose testimony Park Redfield faithfully transcribes: "My principal informant in this case was for some months an intimate of our family, a native Tepoztecan who had given birth to nine children and was thus entirely conversant with the 'etiquette' of the occasion, I have set the materials down almost as she gave them to me." At strategic points throughout the text, Park Redfield quotes her informant directly in order to give her own account greater authority. So for example, with reference to childbirth, she says: "The actual birth is assisted by a midwife (partera, Nahuatl, Amantecatl) of whom there are five or more in Tepoztlán. The midwife cuts the umbilical cord with scissors ("not washed"—she states), measuring four fingers length from the child."[35]

"A Child Is Born in Tepoztlán" is clearly caught up in the same dynamic as the González Casanova article on Indian folk stories, which is illustrated by *Workers Parade*. That is, if *Mexican Folkways* is about making the multiple single, of containing and mastering the other within the phallocentric logic of the modernizing nation, then Park Redfield's article can be seen to be mapping out with objective mastery the rituals surrounding birthing practices that she describes. There is, however, more at stake here. This something more resides in the difference between "folkway" as, for example, folk stories, and "folkway" as birthing practices. The birthing practices within the indigenous female communities documented in the article exist in a zone outside the conventional Western male sphere of medicine.

Moreover, they represent radical otherness insofar as these practices are associated with an indigenous community and specifically women within that community. It is only through the quasi-scientific discourse of anthropology that this radical otherness can be contained within an *indigenista* discourse wherein birthing practices are domesticated and put on a par with folk song, dance, and arts and craft. As a piece of anthropological writing located within the specific context of *Mexican Folkways*, Park Redfield's article is a fascinating piece in its own right. However, my interest here is in the relationship between the text and Modotti's photographs that "illustrate" it.

Just as *Workers Parade* is not representative of the kind of anthropological photographs commonly found within the pages of *Mexican Folkways* that are designed to make the other in all its otherness visible and therefore knowable, nor do *An Aztec Baby* and *An Aztec Mother* belong to this photographic tradition. *An Aztec Mother* depicts the head and shoulders of mother and female child and is positioned on the second page of Park Redfield's article. *An Aztec Baby* focuses on the child suckling at her mother's breast and is positioned on the penultimate page of the article and at some three-page distance from *An Aztec Mother*. In this second image, the mother's body is truncated from just above the neck and her body recedes toward the right-hand side of the frame. Despite the truncated heads that would enable us to identify the subjects clearly, the clothing strongly suggests that this is the same mother and child. The pair of images can be seen to work against the all-seeing, masterful photographic gaze, insofar as they are fundamentally fragmented, heads truncated from bodies, and separated by pages of text. Moreover, the photographs' captions fragment their subjects further—*An Aztec Mother, An Aztec Baby*—for they provide incomplete information, in that both images include mother *and* baby. In other words, where the classic anthropological photograph would objectify its subject, would purport to present its subject as a knowable, visible whole, *An Aztec Mother* and *An Aztec Baby* confound the possibility of knowledge in their fragmentation of mother and child.

Such an approach to this pair of images contains a number of questionable assumptions that turn upon the thorny question of the "exemplary," non-objectifying gaze. To suggest that by fragmenting her subjects, Modotti somehow defies the phallocentric logic of mastery is tantamount to claiming, as Mulvey and Wollen do, that "Tina Modotti, whose career had began as a film-actress and a model, redirected the look which had focused on her outwards when she herself became a photographer. . . . Modotti's [art became] one of depiction of others—predominantly women, but seen with an eye quite different from the one that had looked at her."[36] I do not rule this possibility out, but I suggest that the formulation of the question of the feminine gaze requires more complex articulation.

If we are to accept that Modotti, on some level, as a woman photographer enjoyed a special relationship with her subjects by virtue of her dual and problematic position as subject/object of the gaze, upon what phenomena might this relationship be based? And how do we speak (of) the female gaze as it focuses on the female body? I propose that this is where the work of Bracha Lichtenberg Ettinger on the matrix becomes so richly suggestive. A reading of Modotti's photographs that frames them in the light of the concept of the matrix makes it possible to say something about how the female gaze might focus on the female body and at the same time enables us to imagine a different kind of relationship between self and other. Indeed, in her 1992 article "Matrix and Metramorphosis" Lichtenberg Ettinger suggests: "Since the Matrix implies a link between the feminine and unknown others, it is interesting to explore its socio-political meaning and consequences. We might discover for example, that the affinity between women and minority groups is far richer and more complex than a simple identification or solidarity between culture and history's 'underdogs.'"[37]

Bracha Lichtenberg Ettinger's work marks a radical shift in the predominantly Freudian/Lacanian psychoanalytic paradigm with its emphasis on the phallus as the privileged signifier. She proposes the concept of the matrix to describe aspects of subjectivity that have remained foreclosed within the symbolic. Sensitive to the charge of phallocentrism, Lichtenberg Ettinger makes a point of stressing that she does not propose the concept of the matrix as a replacement for the phallus. Instead, she imagines a symbolic order structured by both the matrix and the phallus, where the matrix corresponds to the feminine dimension and is associated with "asymmetrical, plural, and fragmented subjects composed of the known as well as the not-rejected and not-assimilated unknown, and to unconscious processes of change and transgression in borderlines, limits, and thresholds of 'I' and 'not-I' emerging in co-existence."[38] She argues that the process of subjectivization can be traced back not just to the onset of the Oedipus complex, as Freud suggested, but also to the child's prenatal

Chapter Five

Figure 13.

Tina Modotti, *An Aztec Mother*, ca. 1926–27, gelatin-silver print,
7 1/4" × 7 1/2" The Museum of Modern Art, New York. Anonymous gift.
Copy print © 2000 The Museum of Modern Art, New York.

experience in the mother's womb.[39] Where in the Freudian paradigm
the intrauterine experience is imagined as one of fusion, of nondifferentiation between maternal body and infant, in Lichtenberg
Ettinger's work, mother and infant are understood as originally dif-
ferentiated. In Lichtenberg Ettinger's model, subjectivity is a process
of coemergence for both mother and infant whereby "the elements
or the subjects which meet in the Matrix recognize one another without knowing one another."[40] Traces of this prenatal experience—an
experience, it is important to note, that is essentially nonvisual and

moreover tactile—exist in the unconscious and structure, in part, subjectivization.

Lichtenberg Ettinger also proposes the concept of "metramorphosis" to describe the processes of shared encounter between the "I" and the "not-I," which takes place along shifting and intimate boundaries between the two. She argues that "the borderlines between them are surpassed and transformed to become thresholds. When these transformations relate to transformation in the borderlines and in the shared spaces, metramorphosis may occur, creating redistribution in the shared field and a change in common subjectivity." What makes Lichtenberg Ettinger's work so suggestive for feminist cultural theory is that it offers the possibility of accounting for a nonaggressive relationship between self and other. A relationship that, rather than being based upon a phallic model of assimilation or rejection, "deals with the possibility of recognizing the other in his/her otherness, difference, and unknown-ness."[41]

How might the concepts of matrix and metramorphosis relate to cultural production and, more specifically, to Modotti's photographs as located within the context of *Mexican Folkways*? In an essay on Bracha Lichtenberg Ettinger's own artistic practice and psychoanalytic theory, Griselda Pollock argues that the possibility of the matrixial is "something that can be discerned already there in texts, signifiers, legends, paintings, ourselves."[42] I suggest it is possible to read traces of the matrix in Modotti's photographs of women and children, insofar as the focus of these images—both in terms of formal composition and subject matter—finds particular resonance with Lichtenberg Ettinger's work. Modotti's images both play up and play on texture and tactility and place a special emphasis on the relationship between the infant and maternal body that has everything to do with borderlines and boundaries between these bodies. Because they do so, they invite a reading of their representation of the maternal body that focuses on the matrixial.

An Aztec Mother and *An Aztec Baby* appear as a pair of images that, positioned together, can be read against the thrust of Park Redfield's article. On one level, within the context of this particular article, Modotti's photographs highlight the ultimate fragmentation of the gaze that defies visual mastery. As a pair of images they function within an overall structure of antithesis whereby the first, *An Aztec Mother*, serves to accentuate elements in the second, *An Aztec Baby*. That is to say, *An Aztec Mother* stages an encounter between the viewer and the

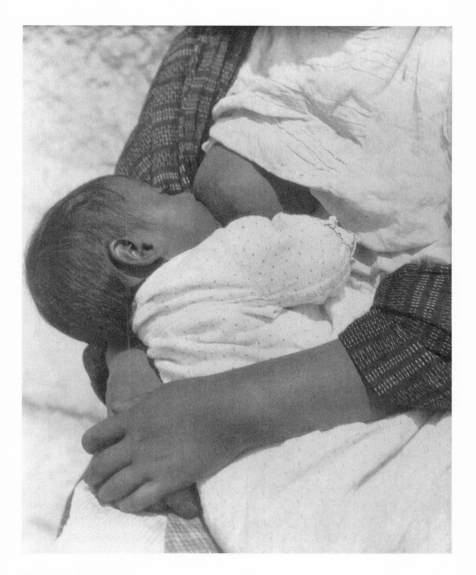

Figure 14.
Tina Modotti, *An Aztec Baby*, ca. 1926–27, gelatin-silver print, 8 1/4" × 7"
Throckmorton Fine Art, New York.

image wholly at the level of the gaze. The head and shoulders of mother and child occupy most of the picture plane. The sharp focus of their heads and the blurred focus of the textured wall behind throw them into sharper relief—almost as if they were superimposed upon their background. The baby's gaze meets the viewer's; the mother's heavily lidded eyes fall below the gaze of the viewer, who struggles to make eye contact with her. If *An Aztec Mother* is all gaze, I suggest that *An Aztec Baby* is all touch.

In *An Aztec Baby* almost the entire picture plane is occupied by the bodies of the mother and child. Only a relatively small segment to the left-hand side of the photograph is taken up by the background wall upon which the subjects' head and shoulders are superimposed in *An Aztec Baby*, and that is even more out of focus. The blurred background serves to place an emphasis on the bodies in the image and, more important, on their interaction. Indeed, I suggest that it is the interaction between the maternal and infant body that is the key concern in this photograph. That this is the case is amply confirmed if we place *An Aztec Baby* alongside other images of mothers and children that Modotti made over a period of three years. In a number of images of the maternal body and infant we find Modotti's gaze transfixed by the relationship between the bodies within the frame. If we look, for example, at *Mother and Child, Tehuantepec*, which Modotti made while on a visit to the Isthmus of Tehuantepec around 1929, we find the same cropping of the mother's head, which serves to focus our gaze on the interaction between the infant's and the mother's heavily pregnant body. Or again, in *Baby Nursing*, which is almost certainly the third image in the Aztec mother and baby series, our attention is focused wholly on the infant at the breast, where the maternal body is reduced to its representation as breast.

In all three images—*An Aztec Baby*, *Baby Nursing*, and *Mother and Child, Tehuantepec*—the background, which would conventionally create an illusion of depth, blurs into insignificance. This is not to say that these are flat images. On the contrary, they are full of depth, but depth is achieved not through an interplay between fore- and backgrounds but through the interacting folds of flesh and fabric that create pockets of depth across the photographs' very surface.

In *An Aztec Baby* and its sister images, depth is also coupled with texture and tonality. Modotti's photograph provides the viewer with a variety of different tactile experiences as her eye ranges across the image. The baby is cradled in the mother's dark arms, which change in tone as light bounces off the lower forearm, whereby her skin texture comes into sharper relief. Further points of textured dark tonality can be found at the mother's breast and the child's head. Our gaze is drawn to the silkiness of the child's hair and brighter points of shiny light within the crevasses of the child's ear. The dark skin tonalities are offset against the mother's dark shawl with its embroidered white stitches, which are in especially sharp focus in the lower right-hand side of the image. The darkness of the shawl frames the bunched textures of the fabric of the mother and child's clothing. The crisper, crumpled folds of the mother's shirt contrast with the softer, fleecier texture of the child's polka-dot shirt.

With its focus on texture, tactility, and depth at the level of the body and its folds, the aim of this reading of *An Aztec Baby* is to give a sense of the way in which the photograph might inscribe traces of Lichtenberg Ettinger's notion of the occluded matrixial experience. This functions on two interrelated levels. First, thanks to photography's privileged purchase on the real, to its ontological link with reality, it is arguably the most emphatically visual form of visual representation; it is that which corresponds most closely to what we imagine to be "natural" vision. If we accept this as the case, and if the matrix deals with the nonvisual, the tactile, in what way might *An Aztec Baby* be considered matrixial? I suggest that this photograph inscribes traces of matrixial experience precisely because it takes visuality to its limits, whereby visuality gives way to tactility. The photograph engages the viewer in the experience of a range of textured and tactile experiences whereby she is drawn out of a visual engagement with the image and momentarily onto another sensual plane: pure touch.

Second, if phallic logic is predicated on the working of metaphor and metonymy where the one stands in for/replaces the other, then

the Matrix is related to processes of metramorphosis on the edge of metaphor and metonymy. Metramorphosis is the process of change in borderlines and thresholds between being and absence, memory and oblivion, *I* and *not-I*, a process of transgression and fading away. The metramorphic consciousness has no center, cannot hold a fixed gaze—or if it has a center, it constantly slides to the borderline, to the margins. Its gaze escapes the margins and returns to the margins.

Figure 15.
Tina Modotti, *Mother and Child, Tehuantepec*, ca. 1929, 8¹⁵/₁₆" × 6¹/₈"
Philadelphia Museum of Art, gift of Mr. and Mrs. Carl Zigrosser.

Through this process the limits, borderlines, and thresholds conceived are continually transgressed or dissolved, thus allowing the creation of new ones.[43]

Following Lichtenberg Ettinger's analysis, we can read *An Aztec Baby* as an image that does have a center. That center is the borderline along which the child's mouth meets the mother's breast. However, the photograph's center finds its echo in the folds and borders between the bodies and fabrics across the image. Above the borderline at which the mouth and breast meet there is the fold of white cloth out of which the breast appears, creating a darker cavernous space just above the child's elbow. Similarly, below the center borderline we find the shadowy line that marks the end of the child's shirt and the beginning of the mother's arm. The effect of this play of borderlines and folds that undulate across the image is to draw the viewer's gaze to the borders of the photographic frame, to its margin, suggesting the possibility of the creation of new boundaries and borders.

To state that *An Aztec Mother* inscribes traces of matrixial experience makes no sense, however, until the photograph is put into context. Lichtenberg Ettinger argues:

> We can recognize an unknown *not-I* in a matrixial way while he/she/it remains different, neither assimilated nor rejected. In other words, the Matrix is a composition of *I* and *not-I's*, of selves and not selves while they are unknown or anonymous. Some selves identify one another as *not-I* without aspiring to assimilate in order to become one, without abolishing differences and making the other a same in order to accept him/her, and without creating a phallic rejection so that only one of them can occupy the physical/mental space. They co-exist and change one another though neither dominates nor submits in a recognized space.[44]

The potential of the matrixial for a reading of *An Aztec Baby* comes into focus when we consider that the general thrust of *Mexican Folkways* is concerned precisely with "abolishing differences and making the other a same." Here is a photograph by a woman photographer who was herself caught up in the dynamic of specularity and the voyeuristic gaze, and yet made photographic images of the maternal/infant interaction in which we can discern the possibility of another kind of gaze. This gaze, with its appeal to another sense, namely, the palpability of touch with its associations with matrixial experience, suggests that it might be possible to see the other differently: that is to say, as different. And within the context of *Mexican Folkways*, which is all about assimilating the other as same, the possibility of a matrixial reading is, of itself, radically different.

Beside

My readings of Modotti's photographs *Workers Parade* and *An Aztec Baby* deal with the specificities of cultural context, by locating them

Figure 16.
Tina Modotti, *Baby Nursing*, ca. 1926–27, gelatin-silver print, 7 1/4" × 9 1/8"
The Museum of Modern Art, New York. Anonymous gift. Copy print
© 2000 The Museum of Modern Art, New York.

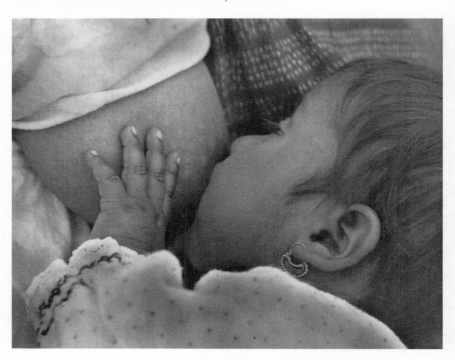

Chapter Five

within *Mexican Folkways*; sexual difference, by reading them as images made by a woman photographer; and the medium of representation, by attending to the particular qualities of photographic images. And this brings the study around full circle, back to the beginning and to the whole question of the feminine gaze and the representation of the female body. Another form of spatial metaphor can also be discerned in the movement of my study. This metaphor resides precisely in a notion of "beside." Bracha Lichtenberg Ettinger is adamant, despite the danger associated with imagining a concept such as the matrix, that "the Symbolic must be penetrated by women even if choosing one name/concept will be considered phallic. In that way, alternative ideas, deviating from the Phallus, may enlarge the text of culture." The matrix, however, is not a concept to replace but one to place "alongside a relativized concept of the phallus in a universe which is plural/partial."[45] I embrace this notion of an "alongside," in that I place a reading of the maternal body—a reading that attempts to offer an approach to difference that exists in a zone previously occluded from view—beside (but not upon) a reading of the abject body of *Workers Parade* that is ultimately predicated on the concept of the phallus. And perhaps ultimately this is a space alongside that we can imagine to exist in that secret offscreen space associated with the active feminine gaze in *Open Doors*.

Notes

Introduction

1. Lesley Cunliffe, "Guns and Roses," *Vogue*, September 1993, 210.

2. Griselda Pollock, "Trouble in the Archives: Introduction," *Differences: A Journal of Feminist Cultural Studies* 4 (1992): iii.

3. Full information about the material listed in this section is to be found in the bibliography.

4. Information in this section is based upon readings of the biographical sources listed in the bibliography. Margaret Hook's biography and Modotti's letters to Edward Weston were particularly useful sources. Where a particular detail is derived from a specific source, this is indicated in the text.

5. Patricia Albers's 1999 biography provides fascinating new information about this period in Modotti's life.

6. Amy Stark, "The Letters from Tina Modotti to Edward Weston," The Archive, Center for Creative Photography, University of Arizona, 22 (1986): 39; Edward Weston, *The Daybooks of Edward Weston*, ed. Nancy Newhall (New York: Aperture, 1961), 1:76.

7. Anita Brenner, *Idols behind Altars* (New York: Brace, 1929); Edward Weston, *The Daybooks of Edward Weston*, ed. Nancy Newhall (New York: Aperture, 1961), 175.

8. Diego Rivera, "Edward Weston y Tina Modotti," *Mexican Folkways* 2 (1926): 27. Translation in the original.

9. Sarah M. Lowe, *Tina Modotti: Photographs* (New York: Abrams, 1995), 18. Nicolas Sacco and Bartolome Vanzetti were Italian radicals who were executed in the United States for their political activity. For a comprehensive guide to the published locations of Modotti's photographs see Lowe, *Tina Modotti*. For an analysis of *El Machete* see Alicia Azuela, *"El Machete* and *Frente a Frente:* Art Committed to Social Justice in Mexico," *Art Journal* 52 (1993): 82–87.

10. Poniatowska, Hooks, and Cacucci all consider the assassination of Mella as the single most significant (and dramatic) event in Modotti's life and accordingly open their accounts with it.

11. Tina Modotti, "On Photography" [Sobre la fotografía], *Mexican Folkways* 5 (1929): 198.

12. Stark, "Letters," 68.

13. Ibid., 66.

14. See Phillipe Cheron, "Tina, Staliníssima," *Vuelta* (September 1983): 46–47.

15. Stark, "Letters," 74.

16. Elena Poniatowska's *Tinísima* (Mexico City: Era, 1992) offers a lively, fictionalized account of this obscure period of Modotti's life.

17. Stark, "Letters," 75.

18. Personal Narratives Group, *Interpreting Women's Lives: Feminist Theory and Personal Narratives* (Bloomington and Indianapolis: Indiana University Press, 1989), 5.

19. Margaret Hooks, *Tina Modotti: Photographer and Revolutionary* (London: Pandora, 1993), x.

20. I have in mind, of course, Barthes's seminal essay, "The Death of the Author," in *Image, Music, Text* (London: Fontana, 1977), 142–49.

21. Lowe, *Tina Modotti*, 10.

22. See Laura Mulvey, "Visual Pleasure and Narrative Cinema," in *Visual and Other Pleasures* (London: Macmillan, 1989), 14–26.

23. I cite this particular painting here as it has received a great deal of traditional art-historical attention and is also the subject of recent feminist revisionist readings. See in particular Griselda Pollock's essay "Modernity and the Spaces of Femininity," in *Vision and Difference: Femininity, Feminism, and the Histories of Art* (London: Routledge, 1988).

24. Martin Jay, "Photo-unrealism: The Contribution of the Camera to the Crisis of Occularcentrism," in *Vision and Textuality*, ed. Stephen Melville and Bill Readings (London: Macmillan, 1995), 345.

25. Roland Barthes, "The Photographic Message," in *Image, Music, Text* (London: Fontana, 1977), 17.

26. Barthes, "The Photographic Message," 69. The classic example of this is the way in which, after the invention of photography, horses' legs were discovered not to move in the splayed-out fashion represented in oil-painting.

27. Jay, "Photo-unrealism," 345.

28. Throughout the book, I have opted to reproduce the photographs' titles in English. As Lowe indicates, Modotti often sent her photographs for publication untitled (Lowe, *Tina Modotti*, 150). As a consequence, many of the images possess multiple titles. The most consistent system of naming is to be found in the English language texts which exist on Modotti. On the whole, I have followed the titles given by Lowe; her excellent art-historical work on Modotti would seem to be the most detailed and accurate.

Chapter One

1. Amy Stark, "The Letters from Tina Modotti to Edward Weston," *The Archive*, Center for Creative Photography, University of Arizona, 22 (1986): 71.

2. Reproduced in Laura Mulvey, "Frida Kahlo and Tina Modotti," in *Visual and Other Pleasures* (London: Macmillan, 1989), 103.

3. Mulvey, *Visual and Other Pleasures*, 19.

4. Ibid., 15.

5. For a critique of "Visual Pleasure and Narrative Cinema" see Mulvey,

"Afterthoughts," in *Visual and Other Pleasures*, and Victor Burgin, "Geometry and Abjection," in *Abjection, Melancholia, and Love: The Work of Julia Kristeva*, ed. by John Fletcher and Andrew Benjamin (London: Routledge, 1990) 104–23.

6. "Centenario de Tina," *Raíces* 2, agusto-septiembre 1996 [no author to text].

7. Lynda Nead underlines the way in which the construction of the nude is overdetermined by the connotations implicit in the male/female binary opposition: "If the male signifies culture, order, geometry . . . , then the female stands for nature and physicality. Woman is both *mater* (mother) and *materia*, biologically determined and potentially wayward. Now, if art is defined as the conversion of matter into form, imagine how much greater the triumph for art if it is the *female* body that is thus transformed—pure nature transmuted, through the forms of art, into pure culture. The female nude, then, is not simply one subject among others, one form among many, it is *the* subject, *the* form." *The Female Nude: Art, Obscenity, and Sexuality* (London: Routledge, 1992), 18.

8. Mariana Figarella Mota, "Edward Weston y Tina Modotti en México: Su inserción dentro de las estrategias estéticas del arte post-revolucionario" (Masters thesis, Universidad Nacional Autónoma de México, 1995; Linda Nochlin, "Why Have There Been No Great Women Artists?" in *Women, Art and Power: and Other Essays* (London: Thames and Hudson, 1989), 145–78; Tina Modotti, "On Photography" [Sobre la fotografía], *Mexican Folkways* 5 (1929): 196–98. It is curious that Modotti's article is abridged, given that it represents a unique insight into her thoughts on photography and also given that it is by no means a long piece.

9. Laura Mulvey and Peter Wollen, *Frida Kahlo and Tina Modotti*, Whitechapel Art Gallery, 26 March–7 November 1982; hereinafter cited as Mulvey and Wollen. All subsequent references are to the original catalog unless otherwise stated.

10. Ibid., 9.

11. Ibid., 10.

12. Ibid., 26.

13. Rozsika Parker and Griselda Pollock, *Framing Feminism: Women, Art, and Ideology* (London: Pandora, 1987), 62.

14. Rosemary Betterton, ed., *Looking On: Images of Femininity in the Visual Arts and Media* (London: Pandora, 1987); Mulvey, *Visual and Other Pleasures*; Francis Frascina and Jonathan Harris, eds., *Art in Modern Culture: An Anthology of Critical Texts* (London: Phaidon, 1992).

15. Mulvey, *Visual and Other Pleasures*, ix.

16. Ibid., vii.

17. Mulvey and Wollen, 12.

18. Amelia Jones, "Modernist Logic in Feminist Histories of Art," *Camera Obscura: A Journal of Feminism and Film Theory* 27 (1992): 155.

19. It is worth mentioning, in anticipation of chapter 2, that the margins themselves, in the wake of feminist theory, have shifted ground and come to signify something altogether different and therefore require other critical approaches.

20. Mulvey and Wollen, 10.

21. Ibid., 26.

22. Ibid., 26.

23. I take up this issue again in chapter 5.

24. Anne Higonnet, "Women, Images, and Representation," in *A History of Women: Towards a Cultural Identity in the Twentieth Century*, ed. Francoise Thébaud (Cambridge, Mass.: Harvard University Press, 1996), 360.

25. Griselda Pollock, *Generations and Geographies in the Visual Arts: Feminist Readings* (London: Routledge, 1996), 285.

26. See for example, Griselda Pollock, "Missing Women: Rethinking Early Thoughts on Images of Women," in *The Critical Image*, ed. Carol Squiers (London: Lawrence and Wishart, 1991), 203.

27. See Roland Barthes, "The Photographic Message," in *Image, Music, Text*, ed. and trans. Stephen Heath (London: Fontana, 1977), 17.

28. This detour serves as an introduction to issues raised in the current chapter; it also provides a cultural framework for understanding Modotti's "Mexican-ization" and her interventions as a photographer into postrevolutionary visual space, issues that will come into focus again in later chapters.

29. For a full account of the revolution, see Alan Knight, *The Mexican Revolution* 2 vols. (Lincoln and London: University of Nebraska Press, 1986). See also Mulvey and Wollen's gloss in the Whitechapel catalog for a brief but surprisingly dense and complex summary of the revolution and cultural renaissance.

30. Knight, *Mexican Revolution*, 1:2.

31. Alan Knight, "Popular Culture and the Revolutionary State in Mexico, 1910–1940," *Hispanic American Historical Review* 74 (1994): 393.

32. Alan Knight, "Racism, Revolution, and Indigenismo: Mexico, 1910–1940," in *The Idea of Race in Latin America, 1870–1940*, ed. Richard Graham (Austin: University of Texas Press, 1990), 86.

33. Knight, "Popular Culture," 405.

34. Ibid., 404.

35. Ricardo Pérez Montfort, "Indigenismo, hispanismo, y panamericanismo en la cultura popular mexicana de 1920 a 1940," in *Cultura e identidad nacional*, ed. Roberto Blancarte (Mexico City: Fondo de Cultura Económica, 1994), 349.

36. Elizabeth Grosz, "Bodies-Cities," in *Space, Time, and Perversion* (London: Routledge, 1995), 109.

37. Ibid., 104.

38. Ben Maddow, *Edward Weston: His Life* (New York: Aperture, 1984), 101.

39. See Karen Cordero Reiman, "Los espacios de Chapingo: apuntes hacia una relectura," in *Arte y espacio* (Mexico City: UNAM, Instituto de Investigaciones Estéticas, 1996), 210.

40. Grosz, "Women, Chora, Dwelling," in *Space, Time, and Perversion*, 123; Cordero Reiman, "Los espacios de Chapingo," 212.

41. Whitechapel, 26.

42. Whitechapel, 12.

43. The section of mural reproduced here is Rivera's *In the Arsenal* from the third floor gallery at the Ministry of Education. To the right are Tina Modotti and Julio Antonio Mella, with Frida Kahlo in the center.

44. Dawn Ades, ed., *Art in Latin America: The Modern Era, 1820–1980* (New Haven: Yale University Press, 1989), 324.

45. Laura Mulvey, "Pandora: Topographies of the Mask and Curiosity," in *Sexuality and Space*, ed. Beatriz Colomina (Princeton: Princeton Papers on Architecture, 1992), 65; Abigail Solomon-Godeau, *Photography at the Dock: Essays on Photographic History, Institutions, and Practices* (Minneapolis: University of Minnesota Press, 1991), 180.

46. Sue Best, "The Boundary Rider: Response to 'Battle Lines,'" in *Rethinking Borders*, ed. John C. Welchman (London: Macmillan, 1996), 69.

47. Griselda Pollock, "The Gaze and the Look: Women with Binoculars—A Question of Difference," in *Dealing with Degas: Representations of Women and the Politics of Vision*, ed. Richard Kendall and Griselda Pollock (London: Pandora, 1992), 130.

Chapter Two

1. *Print Collectors' Newsletter* 22 (1991): 91. The actual price fetched by Modotti's photograph varies according to the source; $165,000 rather than $150,000 seems to be the figure most often quoted. Also, the photograph is most commonly known as *Roses*, not *Roses, Mexico*.

2. Ian Jeffrey, *Photography: A Concise History* (London: Thames and Hudson, 1981), 56; Naomi Rosenblum, *A World History of Photography* (New York: Abbeville Press, 1984). See the introduction to Liz Wells, ed., *Photography: A Critical Introduction* (London: Routledge, 1997) for an account of the historiography of photography.

3. Modotti's status as a "mistress" of photography has recently been confirmed by her inclusion in the Aperture masters of photography series, *Tina Modotti* (New York: Aperture, 1999).

4. In March 1983 the exhibition showed at the Grey Art Gallery in New York and in June-August of the same year it showed at the Museo de Arte Nacional in Mexico City. It is worth noting that the exhibition's trajectory from Europe, via the USA and finally on to Mexico seems to be a common homeward route for Mexican exhibitions, for example the mammoth 1991 exhibition, "Mexico, Splendors of Thirty Centuries" originated in the USA. Having

been legitimated in the northern cultural center, it then traveled back to peripheral Mexico. For a discussion of this particular exhibition's ambassadorial status see Brian Wallis, "Selling Nations: International Exhibitions and Cultural Diplomacy," in *Museum Culture: Histories, Discourses, Spectacles*, ed. Daniel J. Sherman and Irit Rogoff (London: Routledge, 1994), 265–81.

5. Griselda Pollock, "The Power of Feminist Art," *Women's Art Magazine* 62 (1995): 32.

6. The 1993 *Vogue* article by Lesley Cunliffe indicates the package contained a total of thirty photographs.

7. I am reluctant to classify Modotti's photographs into "types" or phases, such as "political" versus "romantic" as it is a boundary I attempt to undermine in chapter 4. However, for the purpose of the current section, the division is strategically important, if only a temporary step in my argument.

8. Peter Wollen, *Raiding the Icebox: Reflections on Twentieth-Century Culture* (London: Verso, 1993), 101.

9. Carol Squiers, "Suzie Tomkins Markets Modotti," *American Photo* 4 (1993): 16.

10. *Sotheby's Photographs*, Sale Catalog, 7–8 April 1995.

11. Esprit public relations, publicity blurb, undated, received June 1995.

12. I have been unable to find any source that lists the photograph's title as *Roses, Mexico* other than in the literature that appeared around the time of the sale.

13. Vasconcelos quoted in Bertram D. Wolfe, *The Fabulous Life of Diego Rivera* (New York: Stein and Day, 1963), 193.

14. Squiers, "Suzie Tomkins," 16.

15. Cathy Schwichtenberg, *The Madonna Connection: Representational Politics, Subcultural Identities, and Cultural Theories* (Oxford: Westview Press, 1993), 10.

16. Sabrina Rubin, "Lucky Star," *Philadelphia*, September 1995, 75.

17. Ibid., 75

18. Janis Bergman-Carton, "Strike a Pose: The Framing of Madonna and Frida Kahlo," *Texas Studies in Literature and Language* 35 (1993): 442. For further discussion of the commodification of Frida Kahlo see Oriana Baddeley, "'Her Dress Hangs Here': Defrocking the Kahlo Cult," *Oxford Art Journal* 14 (1991): 10–17. Baddeley points to the Whitechapel exhibition as instigating the first wave of popular interest in Kahlo.

19. Jean Franco, "'Manhattan Will Be More Exotic This Fall': The Iconization of Frida Kahlo," *Women: A Cultural Review* 2 (1991): 226.

20. Madonna's interest in Latin American women in general was confirmed when she played Eva Perón in Alan Parker's 1996 musical *Evita*.

21. Sotheby's catalog entry. Sale date, 17 April 1991.

22. Diego Rivera, "Edward Weston and Tina Modotti," *Mexican Folkways* 2 (1926): 16–17, 27–28.

23. Wollen, *Raiding the Icebox*, 194.

24. For a fascinating assessment of the relationship between the United States and Mexico, see Mauricio Tenorio Trillo, "The Cosmopolitan Mexican Summer, 1920–1949," *Latin American Research Review* 32 (1997): 224–42.

25. California, New Mexico, Arizona, and Texas were "sold" to the United States in 1848 under the Treaty of Guadalupe Hidalgo.

26. Helen Delpar, *The Enormous Vogue of Things Mexican: Cultural Relations between the U.S. and Mexico, 1920–1935* (Tuscaloosa: University of Alabama Press, 1992), 15.

27. Octavio Paz, "Frida y Tina: Vidas no paralelas," *Vuelta* (September 1983): 48. I discuss Octavio Paz and his status as an art critic more fully in chapter 3.

28. "El que calla otorga," *Vuelta* (September 1983): 48.

29. Amy Stark, "The Letters from Tina Modotti to Edward Weston," *The Archive*, 22 (1986): 68–69.

30. Squiers, "Suzie Tomkins," 16.

31. Cunliffe, "Guns and Roses," 275.

32. Celeste Olalquiaga, "Vulture Culture," in *Rethinking Borders*, ed. John C. Welchman (London: Macmillan, 1996), 86.

33. Abigail Solomon-Godeau, *Photography at the Dock: Essays on Photographic Histories, Institutions, and Practices* (Minneapolis: University of Minnesota Press, 1991), 4.

34. I am not oblivious to my own position as a critic bound up in the whole dynamic of what I have termed "commodity feminism." There is no easy answer to this problem, other than adopting a position of critical awareness.

35. Victor Burgin, *The End of Art Theory: Criticism and Postmodernity* (London: Macmillan, 1986), 72. For an interesting discussion of Barthes's relationship with the (photographic) image see Jean Michel Rabaté, ed., *Writing the Image after Roland Barthes* (Philadelphia: University of Pennsylvania Press, 1997). Roland Barthes, *Mythologies* (London: Paladin, 1973).

36. Dates here refer to original publication in French. Both essays appear in English in Roland Barthes, *Image, Music, Text* (London: Fontana, 1977).

37. Barthes, *Image, Music, Text*, 18–19.

38. Roland Barthes, *Camera Lucida* (London: Flamingo, 1984), 26.

39. Ibid., 117.

40. I develop this notion of the taming/framing of the photographs in chapter 3.

41. Barthes, *Camera Lucida*, 118.

42. Ibid., 119.

43. Griselda Pollock, "The Gaze and the Look: Women with Binoculars—A Question of Difference," in *Dealing with Degas: Representations of Women and the Politics of Vision*, ed. Richard Kendall and Griselda Pollock (London: Pandora, 1992), 130.

44. Rozsika Parker and Griselda Pollock, *Old Mistresses: Women, Art, and Ideology* (London: Pandora, 1981), 51.

45. For detailed discussions of this phenomenon see Parker and Pollock, "God's Little Artist," in *Old Mistresses*, and Linda Nochlin, "Why Have There Been No Great Women Artists?" in *Women, Art and Power: And Other Essays* (London: Thames and Hudson, 1991).

46. M. H. Grant, *Flower Painting through Four Centuries*, (London, 1952), 21, quoted in Parker and Pollock, *Old Mistresses*, 54; Parker and Pollock, *Old Mistresses*, 58.

47. Lindsay Smith, "The Politics of Focus: Feminism and Photography Theory," in *New Feminist Discourses: Critical Essays on Theories and Texts*, ed. Isobel Armstrong (London: Routledge, 1992), 239; Victor Burgin, "Geometry and Abjection," in *Abjection, Melancholia, and Love: The Work of Julia Kristeva*, ed. John Fletcher and Andrew Benjamin (London: Routledge, 1990), 105.

48. Sarah M. Lowe, "The Immutable Still Lifes of Tina Modotti," *History of Photography* 18 (1994): 207.

49. Lynda Nead, *The Female Nude: Art, Obscenity, and Sexuality* (London: Routledge, 1992), 20.

50. Ludmilla Jordanova cited in Laura Mulvey, "Pandora: Topographies of the Mask and Curiosity," in *Sexuality and Space*, ed. Beatriz Colomina (New York: Princeton Papers on Architecture, 1992), 61.

51. Jane Gallop, *Thinking Through the Body* (New York: Columbia University Press, 1988), 151, 153.

52. Ibid., 152.

53. Ibid., 155.

54. Barthes, *Camera Lucida*, 26.

55. Ibid., 117.

56. John Tagg, "A Discourse (with Shape of Reason Missing)," in *Vision and Textuality*, ed. Stephen Melville and Bill Readings (London: Macmillan, 1995), 97.

57. Tetzlaff quoted in Schwichtenberg, *The Madonna Connection*, 248.

Chapter Three

1. Griselda Pollock, "Modernity and the Spaces of Femininity," in *Vision and Difference: Femininity, Feminism, and the Histories of Art* (London: Routledge, 1988), 54.

2. Rosalind Krauss, *The Originality of the Avant-garde and Other Modernist Myths* (Cambridge, Mass.: MIT Press, 1985), 157.

3. I understand "avant-garde" here as a cutting-edge, convention-breaking artistic or literary practice, rather than as the historical avant-garde.

4. Anita Brenner, *Idols behind Altars* (New York: Brace, 1929), 7; Edward Weston, *The Daybooks of Edward Weston*, ed. Nancy Newhall (New York: Aperture, 1961), 1:89, 175.

5. Amy Conger, "Tina Modotti and Edward Weston: A Re-evaluation of their Photography," in *EW100: Centennial Essays in Honor of Edward Weston*, ed. Peter C. Bunnell and David Featherstone (Calif.: Friends of Photography, 1986), 63. The critics cited are Robert d'Attilio and Anita Brenner, respectively.

6. Conger, "Tina Modotti," 70.

7. Ibid., 71.

8. Abigail Solomon-Godeau, *Photography at the Dock: Essays on Photographic History, Institutions, and Practices* (Minneapolis: University of Minnesota Press, 1991), 5, 6.

9. Octavio Paz, "Frida y Tina: Vidas no paralelas," *Vuelta* (September 1983): 48.

10. Bridget Elliott and Jo-Ann Wallace, *Women Artists and Writers: Modernist (im)positionings* (London: Routledge, 1994), 34.

11. I thank Eduardo Alegría for pointing this out to me.

12. Solomon-Godeau, *Photography at the Dock*, 10.

13. Walter Benjamin, "The Work of Art in the Age of Mechanical Reproduction," in *Illuminations*, trans. Harry Zohn (London: Jonathan Cape, 1969), 222.

14. Ibid., 226.

15. For an account of the historical relationship between art and photography see Aaron Scharf, *Art and Photography* (London: Penguin, 1968). See also John Tagg, *The Burden of Representation: Essays on Photographies and Histories* (London: Macmillan, 1988).

16. It is ironic to note that in the wake of recent feminist excavationary work that has showcased Modotti's photographs, Modotti now outsells Weston at auction.

17. I thank John Gash for bringing Morelli to my attention.

18. Carlo Ginzburg, "Morelli, Freud, and Sherlock Holmes: Clues and Scientific Method," trans. Anna Davin, *History Workshop Journal* 9 (1980): 12.

19. See Jane Gallop, *Thinking Through the Body* (New York: Columbia University Press, 1988) for a discussion of Morelli's identity.

20. Solomon-Godeau, *Photography at the Dock*, 128.

21. Claude Gandelman, *Reading Pictures, Viewing Texts* (Bloomington and Indianapolis: Indiana University Press, 1991), 5. For a fascinating discussion of the notion of haptic perception, see Laura U. Marks, "Video Haptics and Erotics," *Screen* 39 (1998): 331–48.

22. John Berger quoted in Jane Collins and Catherine Lutz, "America's Lens on the World: The *National Geographic* in the Twentieth Century," in *Eloquent Obsessions: Writing Cultural Criticism*, ed. Marianna Torgovnick (London: Duke University Press, 1994), 143.

23. It is worth noting that in the painterly tradition, hands are considered one of the most difficult parts of the body to represent graphically. Thus studies of hands frequently form part of the preparatory stages of a painting. For example, Diego Rivera made a sketch of Modotti's hands as part of his preparations for the Chapingo murals.

24. Benjamin, "The Work of Art," 226.

25. Rosalind Krauss, "A Note on Photography and the Simulacral," in *The Critical Image*, ed. Carol Squiers (London, Lawrence and Wishart, 1990), 21.

26. Tina Modotti, "On Photography" [Sobre la fotografía], *Mexican Folkways* 5 (1929): 196. Translation in original article.

27. Pierre Bourdieu, *Photography: A Middle-Brow Art*, with Luc Boltanski et al., trans. Shaun Whiteside (Oxford: Polity Press, 1990).

28. Mildred Constantine, *Tina Modotti: A Fragile Life* (London: Bloomsbury, 1993), 9.

29. For further discussion of the role of these institutions see Pierre Bourdieu, "The Production of Belief: Contribution to an Economy of Symbolic Goods," in *Media, Culture, and Society: A Critical Reader*, trans. Richard Nice, ed. Richard Collins and others (London: Sage, 1986), 131–63.

30. Bourdieu, *Photography*, 96, 98.

31. *El Machete*, 19 January 1929. The nude photographs, which have significantly not survived among Modotti's oeuvre, were used in the court case after Mella's assassination to prove Modotti's "immorality." This is particularly ironic given the artistic status that Weston's nudes of Modotti accorded him.

32. Margaret Hooks, *Tina Modotti: Photographer and Revolutionary* (London: Pandora, 1993), 156.

33. Gandelman, *Reading Pictures, Viewing Texts*, 5.

34. Katherine Adler and Marcia Pointon, eds., *The Body Imaged: The Human Form and Visual Culture since the Renaissance* (Cambridge: Cambridge University Press, 1993), 126.; Krauss, "A Note on Photography," 18.

35. Victor Burgin, "Looking at Photographs," in *Thinking Photography*, ed. Victor Burgin (London: Macmillan, 1982), 144.

36. Solomon-Godeau, *Photography at the Dock*, 110.

37. Elena Poniatowska, *Tinísima* (Mexico: Era, 1992), 42.

38. Although the source of contextual information came from biography in this instance, it is important to stress here that I am not advocating a return to biographical reading. I suggest what contextual reading might be in chapters 4 and 5.

Chapter Four

1. Sarah M. Lowe does address the issue of the context of Modotti's photographs and provides a comprehensive guide to the sources in which they were originally published. However, Lowe's text ultimately ends up following the traditional art-historical path of approaching the photographs through Modotti's biography. Lowe, *Tina Modotti: Photographs* (New York: Abrams, 1995).

2. I thank Ian Macdonald and Alex Hughes for pointing this out to me.

3. Amy Stark, ed., "The Letters of Tina Modotti to Edward Weston," *The Archive* 22 (1986): 71.

4. Raquel Tibol, *Episodios fotográficos* (Mexico City: Libros de Proceso, 1989), 124.

5. Laura Mulvey and Peter Wollen, *Frida Kahlo and Tina Modotti*, Whitechapel Art Gallery, 26 March–7 November 1982, 16; hereinafter cited as Mulvey and Wollen. All subsequent references are to the original catalog unless otherwise stated.

6. Sarah M. Lowe also sets up a notion of Modotti's photographic phases and suggests that *Workers Parade* represents the transitional point between the two phases: "Shortly after her return from California in the spring of 1926 Modotti made *Workers Parade*, which marks the beginning of a new phase in her photographic practice, the point at which she realizes her ambition to marry politics and art in her photography," Lowe, *Tina Modotti*, 32. It must, however, be noted that Lowe does not set up the political and aesthetic as antithetical, proposing instead a "marriage" between the two categories.

7. Mulvey and Wollen, 16, 12. The reference to *Workers Parade* illustrates the way in which Mulvey and Wollen chose to describe rather than to name Modotti's photographs.

8. I discuss the Casasola archive and the iconization of the sombrero in more detail later in this chapter.

9. Elizabeth Grosz, "Bodies-Cities," in *Space, Time, and Perversion* (London: Routledge, 1995), 105.

10. Ibid., 106.

11. Mulvey and Wollen, 23.

12. James D. West, "Aquellos Ojos Verdes," *Third Text* 26 (1994): 35.

13. Grosz, "Bodies-Cities," 106.

14. For an introduction to the Casasola archive see, Flora Lara Klahr's introductory essay to the collection in, *Jefes, héroes, y caudillos: Fondo Casasola* (Mexico City: Fondo de Cultura Económica, 1986), and the *History of Photography* 20 (1996), which, guest-edited by John Mraz, is devoted to Mexican photography. For close readings of two key images in the collection, see Andrea Noble, "Photography and Vision in Porfirian Mexico," *Estudios interdisciplinarios de América Latina y el Caribe* 9 (1998): 121–31, and Noble, "Zapatistas en Sanborns (1914): Women at the Bar," *History of Photography* 22 (1998): 366–70.

15. Flora Lara Klahr, *Jefes, héroes, y caudillos*, 107.

16. John J. Johnson, *Latin America in Caricature* (Austin: University of Texas Press, 1980), 278.

17. Salman Rushdie, *The Jaguar Smile: A Nicaraguan Journey* (London: Picador, 1987), 22. I thank John King for bringing Sandino's hat to my attention.

18. Enrique Krauze, *El amor a la tierra: Emiliano Zapata* (Mexico City: Fondo de Cultura Económica, 1987), 43. For a discussion of the "charro" and other

myths in Mexican cultural history, see also Enrique Florescano, ed., *Mitos mexicanos* (Mexico City: Aguilar, 1995).

19. Alan Knight, "Racism, Revolution, and Indigenismo: Mexico, 1910–1940," in *The Idea of Race in Latin America, 1870–1940*, ed. Richard Graham (Austin: University of Texas Press, 1990), 72–113, 77.

20. Ibid., 74.

21. In chapter 5, I look in detail at the debates around *indigenismo* that emerged in the aftermath of the revolution in order to determine the relationship between Modotti's *Workers Parade* and the discourse of indigenismo.

22. Carlos Monsiváis, "Notas sobre la historia de la fotografía en México," *Revista de la Universidad de México* 35 (1980).

23. Ibid., my italics; Susan Sontag, *On Photography* (London: Penguin, 1977), 20, my italics.

24. Terry Eagleton, *The Ideology of the Aesthetic* (Oxford: Blackwell, 1990), 13.

25. Michael C. Meyer and William L. Sherman, *The Course of Mexican History* (Oxford: Oxford University Press, 1987), 49.

26. The sombrero as a cultural stereotype is also employed by Mexican cultural producers. For a discussion of cultural stereotypes, see Ricardo Pérez Montfort, "Indigenismo, hispanismo, y panamericanismo en la cultura popular mexicana de 1920 a 1940," in *Cultura e identidad nacional*, ed. Roberto Blancarte (Mexico City: Fondo de Cultura Económica, 1994), 343–83. A television advertisement on Mexican television in September 1997 to celebrate "el mes de la patria" featured the sombrero as a unique marker of "Mexicanness" in its reminder to the nation of its cultural and patriotic identity.

   As I write there is an advertising campaign for payment by "Switchcards" that features a "Mexican," recognizable by his sombrero and moustache, sitting with his checkbook. The caption below reads "Not so speedy González."

27. Griselda Pollock, *Generations and Geographies in the Visual Arts: Feminist Readings* (London: Routledge, 1996), 279.

28. Homi K. Bhabha, "The Other Question: Stereotype, Discrimination, and the Discourse of Colonialism," in *The Location of Culture* (London: Routledge, 1994), 67.

Chapter Five

1. Amy Stark, ed., "The Letters from Tina Modotti to Edward Weston," *The Archive*, Center for Creative Photography, University of Arizona Research Series 22 (1986): 67.

2. Sarah M. Lowe, *Tina Modotti: Photographs* (New York: Abrams, 1995), 149.

3. Mieke Bal, "The Construction of Gender in 'Rembrandt,'" in *Vision and Textuality*, ed. Stephen Melville and Bill Readings (London: Macmillan, 1995), 148.

4. Laura Mulvey and Peter Wollen, *Frida Kahlo and Tina Modotti*, Whitechapel Art Gallery, 26 March–7 November 1982, 11; hereinafter cited as Mulvey and Wollen. All subsequent references are to the original catalog unless otherwise stated.

5. Alan Knight, "Racism, Revolution, and Indigenismo: Mexico, 1910–1940," in *The Idea of Race in Latin America, 1870–1940*, ed. Richard Graham (Austin: University of Texas Press, 1990), 75, 76, 85; David A. Brading, "Manuel Gamio and Official Indigenismo in Mexico," *Bulletin of Latin American Research* 7 (1988): 85.

6. Francisco Reyes Palma, "La educación artística postrevolucionaria (1920–1934)," *Historia del arte mexicano* 13 (1982): 1932.

7. *Mexican Folkways* was read by Mexicans and North Americans alike. Here, I limit myself to an analysis of the magazine as an intervention within Mexican cultural politics. For an account of the overlap between U.S. and Mexican cultural policy of this period see Helen Delpar, *The Enormous Vogue of Things Mexican: Cultural Relations between the United States and Mexico, 1920–1935* (Tuscaloosa: University of Alabama Press, 1992).

   For a detailed overview of the contents of the magazine see Ralph Steele Boggs, "Una bibliografía completa, clasificada, y comentada, de los artículos de *Mexican Folkways* (MF), con índice," *Boletín de antropología americana*, Instituto Panamericano de Geografía e Historia, 1946. See also, Margarito Sandoval Pérez, "Lo cotidiano público y lo cotidiano privado en el arte mexicano según la revista *Mexican Folkways*, 1925–1937," *El arte y la vida cotidiana* (Mexico City: UNAM, Instituto de Investigaciones Estéticas, 1995), 253–66.

8. Manuel Gamio (1883–1960), an archaeologist and anthropologist, was responsible for the excavation work that took place at Teotihuacán, part of the wide-scale and unprecedented national project to unearth Mexico's indigenous heritage. For a discussion of Gamio's role in *indigenismo* see David A. Brading, "Manuel Gamio and Official Indigenismo in Mexico," *Bulletin of Latin American Research* 7 (1988): 75–89. Alfonso Caso, (1896–1970), also an archaeologist and *indigenista*, excavated the Mayan site at Monte Albán, Oaxaca; he held a number of prestigious posts throughout his career, including director of the Museo Nacional, la Escuela Nacional Preparatoria, and Instituto Nacional de Antropología e Historia.

9. Barbara Braun, *Pre-Columbian Art and the Post-Columbian World: Ancient American Sources of Modern Art* (New York: Abrams, 1993), 187, 188.

10. Toor's history of *Mexican Folkways* was originally written for *Southwest Review* in 1932 and was then translated and reprinted in *Mexican Folkways* 7 (1932): 205–11. Throughout this chapter I quote in English in order to avoid lengthy translations into Spanish. However, when appropriate, I make reference to the Spanish text.

11. Toor, "Mexican Folkways," 209.

12. Ibid., 205.

13. Ironically, the Spanish version reads: the Revolution "ha sido, tal vez, *necesaria-mente* lenta en su obra." ["has been, possibly, necessarily slow in its reconstruction work."]

14. Susan Ritchie, "Ventriloquist Folklore: Who Speaks for Representation?" *Western Folklore* 52 (1993): 368.

15. Manuel Gamio, "El aspecto utilitario del folklore" [The Utilitarian Aspect of Folklore] *Mexican Folkways* 1 (1925): 7.

16. Ibid., 7.

17. James C. Faris, "A Political Primer on Anthropology/Photography," in *Anthropology and Photography 1860–1920*, ed. Elizabeth Edwards (London: Yale University Press, 1992), 254; Knight, "Racism, Revolution, and Indigenismo," 82.

18. Modotti became a member in the spring of 1927.

19. Toor, "Mexican Folkways," 206.

20. Serge Gruzinski, *La guerra de las imágenes: De Cristóbal Colón a "Blade Runner"* (1492–2019), (Mexico City: Fondo de Cultura Económica, 1994), 14.

21. Norma Claire Moruzzi, "National Abjects: Julia Kristeva on the Process of Political Self-Identification," in *Ethics, Politics, and Difference in Julia Kristeva's Writing*, ed. Kelly Oliver (London: Routledge, 1993), 135–49; Julia Kristeva, *Powers of Horror: An Essay on Abjection* (New York: Columbia University Press, 1982).

22. Moruzzi's text specifically addresses the issue of French national identity in the face of Islamic immigrants from North Africa whose presence within the French community raise a series of issues around national formation and stability.

23. Moruzzi, "National Abjects," 142, 143.

24. Ibid., 143, 145.

25. Toor, "Mexican Folkways," 3.

26. *Mexican Folkways* was published in Mexico City; *BFI*, in Paris; the others, in New York. See Lowe, *Tina Modotti*, 34. Since the publication of Lowe's study new research findings mean that the title of *Workers Parade* has changed to *Mexican Peasants*. For the sake of consistency, I have opted to retain Lowe's title. Significantly, in *Tina Modotti: vivir y morir*, Antonio Saborit (Mexico City: Conaculta/INAH, 1999) chooses to reproduce Modotti's photographs without titles in order to avoid the "laberinto de nombres que se ha creado artificial-mente en los últimos años" ["labyrinth of names that has been created artificially in recent years"], 32.

27. Iskander Mydin, "Historical Images—Changing Audiences," *Anthropology and Photography, 1860–1920*, ed. Elizabeth Edwards (New Haven: Yale University Press, 1992), 249.

28. See, for example, the photographs that appear alongside an article by Carlos Basauri entitled "Creencias y prácticas de los tarahumaras" [Beliefs and Practices of the Tarahumaras], *Mexican Folkways* 3 (1927): 218–34.

Notes

29. Pablo González Casanova, "El orígen de los cuentos del México indígena" [The Origins of the Stories of Indian Mexico] *Mexican Folkways* 3 (1926): 12–22.

30. Faris, "A Political Primer," 255.

31. Griselda Pollock, "Gleaning in History or Coming After/Behind the Reapers," in *Generations and Geographies in the Visual Arts: Feminist Readings* (London: Routledge, 1996), 267–68.

32. *Mexican Folkways* 4 (1928): 102–9.

33. Mulvey and Wollen, 26.

34. Elizabeth Grosz, *Sexual Subversions: Three French Feminists* (St. Leonards: Allen and Unwin, 1989), 63.

35. Margaret Park Redfield, "Nace un niño en Tepoztlán" [A Child Is Born in Tepoztlán], *Mexican Folkways* 4 (1928): 102.

36. Mulvey and Wollen, 26.

37. Bracha Lichtenberg Ettinger, "Matrix and Metramorphosis," *Differences: A Journal of Feminist Cultural Studies* 4 (1992): 176–207.

38. Ibid., 176.

39. In "Metramorphic Borderlinks and Matrixial Borderspace," in *Rethinking Borders*, ed. John C. Welchman (London: Macmillan, 1996), Lichtenberg Ettinger makes it clear that her notion of the Matrix in no way contradicts political debates concerning a woman's right to abortion: "As I speak of the pre-natal 'I or non-I' as a partial subject only at the last stage of pregnancy when the infant is already post-mature," 155.

40. Lichtenberg Ettinger, "Matrix and Metramorphosis," 199.

41. Ibid., 200.

42. Pollock, *Generations and Geographies in the Visual Arts: Feminist Readings*, 268.

43. Lichtenberg Ettinger, "Matrix and Metramorphosis," 201.

44. Ibid., 200.

45. Ibid., 196, 206.

Notes

Bibliography

Adams, Parveen. *The Emptiness of the Image: Psychoanalysis and Sexual Difference*. London: Routledge, 1996.

Ades, Dawn, ed. *Art in Latin America: The Modern Era, 1820–1980*. New Haven: Yale University Press, 1989.

Adler, Kathleen, and Marcia Pointon, eds. *The Body Imaged: The Human Form and Visual Culture since the Renaissance*. Cambridge: Cambridge University Press, 1993.

Albers, Patricia. *Shadows, Fire, Snow: The Life of Tina Modotti*. New York: Clarkson Potter, 1999.

Arias, Ana Lilia. "Sexo sin método: Entrevista con Eli de Gotari." *La jornada semanal* (9 September 1990).

Azuela, Alicia. "*El Machete* and *Frente a Frente*: Art Committed to Social Justice in Mexico." *Art Journal* 52 (1993): 82–87.

Baddeley, Oriana. "'Her Dress Hangs Here': Defrocking the Kahlo Cult." *Oxford Art Journal* 14 (1991): 10–17.

Baddeley, Oriana, and Valerie Fraser. *Drawing the Line: Art and Cultural Identity in Contemporary Latin America*. London: Verso, 1989.

Bal, Mieke. "The Construction of Gender in 'Rembrandt.'" In *Vision and Textuality*, ed. Stephen Melville and Bill Readings, 147–73. London: Macmillan, 1995.

Baldwin, Gordon. *Looking at Photographs: A Guide to Technical Terms*. London: Paul Getty Museum–British Museum Publications, 1991.

Barckhausen-Canale, Christiane. *Verdad y Leyenda de Tina Modotti*. Mexico City: Diana, 1992.

Barthes, Roland. *Camera Lucida*. Trans. Richard Howard. London: Flamingo, 1984.

———. *Image, Music, Text*. Ed. and trans. Stephen Heath. London: Fontana, 1977.

———. *Mythologies*. London: Paladin, 1973.

Basauri, Carlos. "Creencias y prácticas de los tarahumaras." *Mexican Folkways* 3 (1927): 218–34.

Battersby, Christine. *Gender and Genius: Towards a Feminist Aesthetics*. Bloomington and Indianapolis: Indiana University Press, 1989.

Benjamin, Walter. "The Work of Art in the Age of Mechanical Reproduction." In *Illuminations*, trans. Harry Zohn, 219–53. London: Jonathan Cape, 1969.

Berger, John. *Ways of Seeing*. London: Penguin, 1972.

Bergman-Carton, Janis. "Strike a Pose: The Framing of Madonna and Frida Kahlo." *Texas Studies in Literature and Language* 35 (1993): 440–52.

Bernier, Rosamund. "Photography: An Eye of Passion." *Vogue* (USA), September 1995, 362–64.

Best, Sue. "The Boundary Rider: Response to 'Battle Lines.'" In *Rethinking Borders*, ed. John C. Welchman, 65–70. London: Macmillan, 1996.

Betterton, Rosemary, ed. *Looking On: Images of Femininity in the Visual Arts and Media*. London: Pandora, 1987.

Bhabha, Homi K. "The Other Question: Stereotype, Discrimination, and the Discourse of Colonialism." In *The Location of Culture*, 66–84. London: Routledge, 1994.

Bolton, Richard, ed. *The Contest of Meaning: Critical Histories of Photography*. Cambridge, Mass.: MIT Press, 1992.

Bourdieu, Pierre. *Photography: A Middle-Brow Art*. With Luc Boltanski et al., trans. Shaun Whiteside. Oxford: Polity Press, 1990.

———. "The Production of Belief: Contribution to an Economy of Symbolic Goods." In *Media, Culture, and Society: A Critical Reader*, trans. Richard Nice, ed. Richard Collins and others, 131–63. London: Sage, 1986.

Brading, David, A. "Manuel Gamio and Official Indigenismo in Mexico." *Bulletin of Latin American Research* 7 (1988): 75–89.

Bradu, Fabienne. *Antonieta*. Mexico City: Fondo de Cultura Económica, 1991.

———. "Tina." *Vuelta* (December 1993): 43–45.

———. "Una mujer sin país." *Vuelta* (July 1992): 49–50.

Braun, Barbara. *Pre-Columbian Art and the Post-Columbian World: Ancient American Sources of Modern Art*. New York: Abrams, 1993.

Brenner, Anita. *Idols behind Altars*. New York: Brace, 1929.

Brettle, Jane, and Sally Rice, eds. *Public Bodies, Private Selves: New Perspectives on Photography, Representation, and Gender*. Manchester: Manchester University Press, 1994.

Bryson, Norman. *Vision and Painting: The Logic of the Gaze*. London: Macmillan, 1983.

Burgin, Victor. *The End of Art Theory: Criticism and Postmodernity*. London: Macmillan, 1986.

———. "Geometry and Abjection." In *Abjection, Melancholia, and Love: The Work of Julia Kristeva*, ed. John Fletcher and Andrew Benjamin, 104–23. London: Routledge, 1990.

———. *Thinking Photography*. London: Macmillan, 1982.

Cacucci, Pino. *Tina Modotti*. Barcelona: Circe, 1992.

Casanova-Olivier Debroise, Rosa. *Sobre la superficie bruñida de un espejo: Fotógrafos del siglo XIX*. Mexico City: Fondo de Cultura Económica, 1989.

Chadwick, Whitney. *Women, Art, and Society*. London: Thames and Hudson, 1990.

Chadwick, Whitney, and Isabelle de Courtivron, eds. *Significant Others: Creativity and Intimate Partnership*. London: Thames and Hudson, 1993.

Cheron, Phillipe. "Tina, Staliníssima." *Vuelta* (September 1983).

Collins, Jane, and Catherine Lutz. "America's Lens on the World: The *National Geographic* in the Twentieth Century." In *Eloquent Obsessions: Writing Cultural Criticism*, ed. Marianna Torgovnick, 128–57. Durham, N.C.: Duke University Press, 1994.

Colomina, Beatriz, ed. *Sexuality and Space*. New York: Princeton Papers on Architecture, 1992.

Conger, Amy. "Edward Weston and Tina Modotti: A Re-evaluation of their Photography." In *EW100: Centennial Essays in Honor of Edward Weston*, ed. Peter C. Bunnell and David Featherstone, 63–79. Carmel, Calif.: Friends of Photography, 1986.

———. *Edward Weston in Mexico: 1923–1926*. Albuquerque: University of New Mexico Press, 1983.

Conger, Amy, and Elena Poniatowska. *Compañeras de México: Women Photograph Women*. Riverside: University of California Press, 1990.

Constantine, Mildred. *Tina Modotti: A Fragile Life*. London: Bloomsbury, 1993.

Cordero Reiman, Karen. "Los espacios de Chapingo: Apuntes hacia una reflectura." In *Arte y espacio*, 209–16. Mexico City: UNAM, Instituto de Investigaciones estéticas, 1996.

Cunliffe, Lesley. "Guns and Roses." *Vogue* [British edition], September 1993.

de Lauretis, Teresa, ed. *Feminist Studies/Critical Studies*. London: Macmillan, 1986.

Delpar, Helen. *The Enormous Vogue of Things Mexican: Cultural Relations between the United States and Mexico, 1920–1935*. Tuscaloosa: University of Alabama Press, 1992.

Eagleton, Terry. *The Ideology of the Aesthetic*. Oxford: Blackwell, 1990.

Edwards, Elizabeth, ed. *Anthropology and Photography, 1860–1920*. New Haven: Yale University Press, 1992.

Ehrlich, Richard. "Exquisite Textures, Noble Forms: Still Lifes and Nudes." *Creative Camera* 10 (1986): 26–28.

"El que calla otorga." *Vuelta* (September 1983): 48.

Elliott, Bridget, and Jo-Ann Wallace. *Women Artists and Writers: Modernist (im)positionings*. London: Routledge, 1994.

Esprit public relations. Publicity blurb, undated. Received June 1995.

Faris, James C. Faris. "A Political Primer on Anthropology/Photography." In *Anthropology and Photography 1860–1920*, ed. Elizabeth Edwards, 253–61. London: Yale University Press, 1992.

Ferguson, Russell, Martha Gever, and Trinh T. Minh-ha, eds. *Out There: Marginalization and Contemporary Cultures*. Cambridge, Mass.: MIT Press, 1990.

Ferré, Rosario. "Tina y Elena: El ojo y el oído de México." *Nexos* (February 1986).

Figarella Mota, Mariana. "Edward Weston y Tina Modotti en México: Su inserción dentro de las estrategias estéticas del arte post-revolucionario." Masters thesis, Universidad Nacional Autónoma de México, 1995.

Figueroa, Julio. "Tina Modotti, la mirada en el deseo." *El Nacional Dominical* (27 October 1992): 36–37.

Florence, Penny, and Dee Reynolds, eds. *Feminist Subjects, Multi-media Cultural Methodologies*. Manchester: Manchester University Press, 1995.

Florescano, Enrique, ed. *Mitos mexicanos*. Mexico City: Aguilar, 1995.

Foucault, Michel. *The History of Sexuality*. Vol. 1. London: Penguin, 1979.

Franco, Jean. "'Manhattan Will Be More Exotic This Fall': The Iconization of Frida Kahlo." *Women: A Cultural Review* 2 (1991) 220–27.

———. *The Modern Culture of Latin America: Society and the Artist*. London: Pall Mall, 1967.

———. *Plotting Women: Gender and Representation in Mexico*. London: Verso, 1989.

Frascina, Francis, and Jonathan Harris, eds. *Art in Modern Culture: An Anthology of Critical Texts*. London: Phaidon, 1992.

Gallop, Jane. *Thinking Through the Body*. New York: Columbia University Press, 1988.

Gamio, Manuel. "El aspecto utilitario del folklore" [The Utilitarian Aspect of Folklore]. *Mexican Folkways* 1 (1925): 7–8.

Gandelman, Claude. *Reading Pictures, Viewing Texts*. Bloomington and Indianapolis: Indiana University Press, 1991.

Gibson, Margaret. *Memories of the Future: The Daybooks of Tina Modotti*. Baton Rouge: Louisiana State University Press, 1986.

Ginzburg, Carlo. "Morelli, Freud, and Sherlock Holmes: Clues and Scientific Method." Trans. Anna Davin. *History Workshop Journal* 9 (1980): 5–36.

González Casanova, Pablo. "El orígen de los cuentos del México indígena." *Mexican Folkways* 3 (1926): 12–22.

Graham, Richard. *The Idea of Race in Latin America, 1870–1940*. Austin: University of Texas Press, 1990.

Grosz, Elizabeth. *Sexual Subversions: Three French Feminists*. St. Leonards: Allen and Unwin, 1989.

———. *Space, Time, and Perversion*. London: Routledge, 1995.

Gruzinski, Serge. *La guerra de las imágenes: De Cristobal Colón a "Blade Runner."* Mexico City: Fondo de Cultura Económica, 1994.

Heilbrun, Carolyn G. *Hamlet's Mother and Other Women: Feminist Essays on Literature*. London: Women's Press, 1990.

Henessy, Alistair. "The Muralists and the Revolution." In *Los Intelectuales y el Poder en México*, ed. Roderic A. Camp and others. Mexico: Centro de Estudios Históricos, El Colegio de Mexico, 1991.

Higgins, Gary. "Tina and Edward." *Creative Camera* 314 (1992): 20–23.

Higonnet, Anne. "Women, Images, and Representation." In *A History of Women: Towards a Cultural Identity in the Twentieth Century*, ed. Francoise Thébaud, 342–96. Cambridge, Mass.: Harvard University Press, 1996.

History of Photography 20 (1996).

Hooks, Margaret. "Assignment, Mexico: The Mystery of the Missing Modottis." *Afterimage* 19 (1991): 10–11.

———. *Tina Modotti: Photographer and Revolutionary*. London: Pandora, 1993.

Iversen, Margaret. "What Is a Photograph?" *Art History* 17 (1994): 450–64.

Jay, Martin. "Photo-unrealism: The Contribution of the Camera to the Crisis of Occularcentrism." In *Vision and Textuality*, ed. Stephen Melville and Bill Readings, 344–60. London: Macmillan, 1995.

Jeffrey, Ian. *Photography: A Concise History*. London: Thames and Hudson, 1981.

Johnson, John J. *Latin America in Caricature*. Austin: University of Texas Press, 1980.

Johnson, M. K. "Reframing the Photograph." *Word and Image: A Journal of Verbal and Visual Enquiry* 9 (1993): 245–51.

Jones, Amelia. "Modernist Logic in Feminist Histories of Art." *Camera Obscura: A Journal of Feminism and Film Theory* 27 (1992): 149–65.

Jones, Kathleen B. *Compassionate Authority: Democracy and the Representation of Women*. London: Routledge, 1993.

Kendall, Richard, and Griselda Pollock, eds. *Dealing with Degas*. London: Pandora, 1992.

Kimmelman, Michael. "A Legacy That Mingles Myth with Politics," *New York Times*, 8 October 1995.

Klahr, Flora Lara. *Jefes, héroes, y caudillos: Fondo Casasola*. Mexico City: Fondo de Cultura Económica, 1986.

Knight, Alan. *The Mexican Revolution*. 2 vols. Lincoln and London: University of Nebraska Press, 1986.

———. "Popular Culture and the Revolutionary State in Mexico, 1910–1940." *Hispanic American Historical Review* 74 (1994): 393–444.

———. "Racism, Revolution, and Indigenismo: Mexico, 1910–1940." In *The Idea of Race in Latin America, 1870–1940*, ed. Richard Graham, 72–113. Austin: University of Texas Press, 1990.

Krauss, Rosalind E. "A Note on Photography and the Simulacral." in *The Critical Image*, ed. Carol Squiers, 15–27. London, Lawrence and Wishart, 1990.

———. *The Originality of the Avant-Garde and Other Modernist Myths*. Cambridge, Mass.: MIT Press, 1985.

Krauze, Enrique. *El amor a la tierra: Emiliano Zapata*. Mexico City: Fondo de Cultura Económica, 1987.

Kristeva, Julia. *Powers of Horror: An Essay on Abjection*. New York: Columbia University Press, 1982.

Laplanche, J., and J.-B. Pontalis. *The Language of Psychoanalysis*. London: Karnac Books, 1988.

Lichtenberg Ettinger, Bracha. "Metramorphic Borderlinks and Matrixial Borderspace." In *Rethinking Borders*, ed. John C. Welchman, 125–60. London: Macmillan, 1996.

———. "Matrix and Metramorphosis." *Differences: A Journal of Feminist Cultural Studies* 4 (1992): 176–207.

Lowe, Sarah M. "The Immutable Still Lifes of Tina Modotti." *History of Photography* 18 (1994): 205–10.

———. *Tina Modotti: Photographs*. New York: Abrams, 1995.

Maddow, Ben. *Edward Weston: His Life*. New York: Aperture, 1984.

Marks, Laura U. "Video Haptics and Erotics." *Screen* 39 (1998): 331–48.

McNay, Lois. *Foucault and Feminism*. London: Routledge, 1993.

Melinkoff, Ellen. "Who Was Tina Modotti?" *Art and Antiques* 9 (1992): 58–63.

Melville, Stephen, and Bill Readings. *Vision and Textuality*. London: Macmillan, 1995.

Meyer, Michael C., and William L. Sherman. *The Course of Mexican History*. Oxford: Oxford University Press, 1987.

Miller, Nancy K. *Getting Personal: Feminist Occasions and Other Autobiographical Acts*. London: Routledge, 1991.

Mirzoeff, Nicholas. *Bodyscape: Art, Modernity, and the Ideal Figure*. London: Routledge, 1995.

———. ed. *The Visual Culture Reader*. London: Routledge, 1998.

Mitchell, W. J. T. *Picture Theory: Essays on Verbal and Visual Representation*. Chicago: University of Chicago Press, 1994.

Modotti, Tina. "On Photography" [Sobre la fotografía]. *Mexican Folkways* 5 (1929): 196–98.

Moi, Toril. *Sexual/Textual Politics: Feminist Literary Theory*. London: Routledge, 1985.

Monsiváis, Carlos. "Notas sobre la historia de la fotografía en México." *Revista de la Universidad de México* 35 (1980).

Moruzzi, Norma Claire. "National Abjects: Julia Kristeva on the Process of Political Self-Identification." In *Ethics, Politics, and Difference in Julia Kristeva's Writing*, ed. Kelly Oliver, 135–49. London: Routledge, 1993.

Mulvey, Laura. "Pandora: Topographies of the Mask and Curiosity." In *Sexuality and Space*, ed. Beatriz Colomina, 53–73. Princeton: Princeton Papers on Architecture, 1992.

———. *Visual and Other Pleasures*. London: Macmillan, 1989.

Mulvey, Laura, and Peter Wollen. *Frida Kahlo and Tina Modotti.* Whitechapel Art Gallery, 26 March–7 November 1982.

Mydin, Iskander. "Historical Images—Changing Audiences." *Anthropology and Photography, 1860–1920,* ed. Elizabeth Edwards, 249–52. New Haven: Yale University Press, 1992.

Nead, Lynda. *The Female Nude: Art, Obscenity, and Sexuality.* London: Routledge, 1992.

Noble, Andrea. "Framing the Mexican Body." In *The Legacy of Colonialism,* ed. Máire ní Fhlathúin, 195–208. Galway: University of Galway Press, 1998.

———. "Photography and Vision in Porfirian Mexico." *Estudios interdisciplinarios de América Latina y el Caribe* 9 (1998): 121–31.

———. "Tina Modotti and the Politics of Signature." *Women: A Cultural Review* 6 (1995): 287–95.

———. "Zapatistas en Sanborns (1914): Women at the Bar." *History of Photography* 22 (1998): 366–70.

Nochlin, Linda. *The Politics of Vision: Essays on Nineteenth-Century Art and Society.* London: Thames and Hudson, 1989.

———. *Women, Art and Power: And Other Essays.* London: Thames and Hudson, 1991.

Olalquiaga, Celeste. "Vulture Culture." In *Rethinking Borders,* ed. John C. Welchman, 85–100. London: Macmillan, 1996.

Park Redfield, Margaret. "Nace un niño en Tepoztlán" [A Child Is Born in Tepoztlán]. *Mexican Folkways* 4 (1928): 102–9

Parker, Rozsika, and Griselda Pollock. *Framing Feminism: Women, Art, and Ideology.* London: Pandora, 1987.

———. *Old Mistresses: Women, Art, and Ideology.* London: Pandora Press, 1981.

Paz, Octavio. "Frida y Tina: Vidas no paralelas." *Vuelta* (September 1983): 48.

Pérez Montfort, Ricardo. "Indigenismo, hispanismo, y panamericanismo en la cultura popular mexicana de 1920 a 1940." In *Cultura e identidad nacional,* ed. Roberto Blancarte, 343–83. Mexico City: Fondo de Cultura Económica, 1994.

Personal Narratives Group. *Interpreting Women's Lives: Feminist Theory and Personal Narratives.* Bloomington and Indianapolis: Indiana University Press, 1989.

Plagens, Peter. "What a Life She Red." *Newsweek,* 2 October 1995.

Pollock, Griselda. "The Gaze and the Look: Women with Binoculars—A Question of Difference." In *Dealing with Degas: Representations of Women and the Politics of Vision,* ed. Richard Kendall and Griselda Pollock, 106–30. London: Pandora, 1992.

———. *Generations and Geographies in the Visual Arts: Feminist Readings.* London: Routledge, 1996.

———. "Missing Women: Rethinking Early Thoughts on Images of Women." In *The Critical Image,* ed. Carol Squiers, 202–19. London: Lawrence and Wishart, 1991.

———. "The Power of Feminist Art." *Women's Art Magazine* 62 (1995): 32.

———. "Trouble in the Archives: Introduction." *Differences: A Journal of Feminist Cultural Studies* 4 (1992): iii–xiv.

———. *Vision and Difference: Femininity, Feminism, and the Histories of Art*. London: Routledge, 1988.

Poniatowska, Elena. *Tinísima*. Mexico City: Era, 1992.

Print Collectors' Newsletter 22 (1991).

Pultz, John. *Photography and the Body*. London: Everyman, 1995.

Rabaté, Jean-Michel, ed. *Writing the Image after Roland Barthes*. Philadelphia: University of Pennsylvania Press, 1997.

Rascón, Víctor Hugo. *Tina Modotti y otras obras*. Mexico City: SEP, 1986.

Reyes Palma, Francisco. "La educación artística postrevolucionaria (1920–1934)." *Historia del arte mexicano* 13 (1982): 1929–49.

Ritchie, Susan. "Ventriloquist Folklore: Who Speaks for Representation?" *Western Folklore* 52 (1993): 365–78.

Rivera, Diego. "Edward Weston y Tina Modotti." *Mexican Folkways* 2 (1926).

Rose, Jaqueline. *Sexuality in the Field of Vision*. London: Verso, 1986.

Rosenblum, Naomi. *A World History of Photography*. New York: Abbeville Press, 1984.

Rubin, Sabrina. "Lucky Star." *Philadelphia*, September 1995, 75–77.

Rushdie, Salman. *The Jaguar Smile: A Nicaraguan Journey*. London: Picador, 1987.

Saborit, Antonio. *Una mujer sin país: Las cartas de Tina Modotti a Edward Weston, 1921–1931*. Mexico City: Cal y Arena, 1992.

———. *Tina Modotti: vivir y morir*. (Mexico City: Conaculta/INAH, 1999), 32.

Said, Edward. *Orientalism*. London: Routledge, 1978.

Sandoval Pérez, Margarito. "Lo cotidiano público y lo cotidiano privado en el arte mexicano según la revista *Mexican Folkways*, 1925–1937." *El arte y la vida cotidiana*. Mexico City: UNAM, Instituto de Investigaciones Estéticas, 1995, 253–66.

Scharf, Aaron. *Art and Photography*. London: Penguin, 1968.

Schultz, Reinhard, ed. *Tina Modotti: Photographien und Dokumente*. Berlin: Socialarchiv, 1989.

Schwichtenberg, Cathy, ed. *The Madonna Connection: Representational Politics, Subcultural Identities, and Cultural Theories*. Oxford: Westview Press, 1993.

Sherman, J., and Irit Rogoff, eds. *Museum Culture: Histories, Discourses, Spectacles*. London: Routledge, 1994.

Smith, Lindsay. "The Politics of Focus: Feminism and Photography Theory." In *New Feminist Discourses: Critical Essays on Theories and Texts*, ed. Isobel Armstrong, 238–62. London: Routledge, 1992.

Solomon-Godeau, Abigail. *Photography at the Dock: Essays on Photographic History, Institutions, and Practices*. Minneapolis: University of Minnesota Press, 1991.

Bibliography

Sontag, Susan. *On Photography*. London: Penguin, 1977.

Sotheby's Photographs. Sale Catalog, 7–8 April 1995.

Spence, Jo, and Patricia Holland. *Family Snaps: The Meanings of Domestic Photography*. London: Virago, 1991.

Squiers, Carol. "Suzie Tomkins Markets Modotti." *American Photo* 4 (1993): 16.

———. *The Critical Image: Essays on Contemporary Photography*. London: Lawrence and Wishart, 1991.

Stark, Amy, ed. "The Letters from Tina Modotti to Edward Weston." *The Archive*, Center for Creative Photography, University of Arizona Research Series 22 (1986).

Steele Boggs, Ralph. "Una bibliografía completa, clasificada, y comentada, de los artículos de Mexican Folkways (MF), con índice." *Boletín de antropología americana*, Instituto Panamericano de Geografía e Historia, 1946.

Sullivan, Edward. *Women in Mexico*. National Academy of Design, 27 September–2 December 1990.

Tagg, John. *The Burden of Representation: Essays on Photographies and Histories*. London: Macmillan, 1988.

———. "A Discourse (with Shape of Reason Missing)." In *Vision and Textuality*, ed. Stephen Melville and Bill Readings, 90–114. London: Macmillan, 1995.

———. *Grounds of Dispute: Art History, Cultural Politics, and the Discursive Field*. London: Macmillan, 1992.

Tenorio Trillo, Mauricio. "The Cosmopolitan Mexican Summer, 1920–1949." *Latin American Research Review* 32 (1997): 224–42.

Tibol, Raquel. *Episodios fotográficos*. Mexico City: Libros de Proceso, 1989.

———. *Julio Antonio Mella en "El Machete."* Mexico City: Fondo de Cultura Económica, 1986.

Tina Modotti. (New York: Aperture, 1999).

Toffoletti, Ricardo. *Tina Modotti: Perché non muore el fuoco*. Udine: Arti Grafiche Friulane, 1992.

Toor, Frances. "Mexican Folkways." *Mexican Folkways* 7 (1932): 205–11.

Torgovnick, Marianna. *Eloquent Obsessions: Writing Cultural Criticism*. London: Duke University Press, 1994.

Trueba Lara, José Luis. "Cámara, camarada: Tinísima, la imagen del cuerpo." *El Nacional* (24 October 1992): 187–88.

Vidali, Vitorrio. *Fotografa e Rivoluzionaria*. Milan: Idea Editions, 1979.

Wallis, Brian. "Selling Nations: International Exhibitions and Cultural Diplomacy." In *Museum Culture: Histories, Discourses, Spectacles*, ed. Daniel J. Sherman and Irit Rogoff, 265–81. London: Routledge, 1994.

Welchman, John C. *Rethinking Borders*. London: Macmillan, 1996.

Wells, Liz, ed. *Photography: A Critical Introduction*. London: Routledge, 1997.

West, James D. "Aquellos Ojos Verdes." *Third Text* 26 (1994): 33–43.

Weston, Edward. *The Daybooks of Edward Weston. Vol 1.* Ed. Nancy Newhall. New York: Aperture, 1961.

Wolfe, Bertram D. *The Fabulous Life of Diego Rivera.* New York: Stein and Day, 1963.

Wollen, Peter. *Raiding the Icebox: Reflections on Twentieth-Century Culture.* London: Verso, 1993.

———. *Readings and Writings.* London: Verso, 1982.

Wright, Elizabeth. *Feminism and Psychoanalysis: A Critical Dictionary.* Oxford: Blackwell, 1992.

Index

Index

fashion industry, 57; see also Tomkins, Susie

female attributes, as dangerous secrets, 54

female body: as erotic spectacle, 2; as mappable terrain, 19; maternal, 125–38; sale of Roses image, 29; visual representation, 7

female nudes: binary oppositions, 142n7; xiv, 35–36, 52, 53, 54, 149n31

feminism: described, 4; market forces, 29; political, formulation of, 92; radical chic, 38

feminist aesthetics, 91

feminist iconoclasm, 2, 4–13

feminist theory: art history, ix–x; body and state, 94; cone-of-vision metaphor, 51; critical work on Modotti, 87; interrogating vision, xxii; negative aesthetics, 107; phallic terms, influence, 125–26; political, 91–92; of vision, 3, 4; vision, 11

feminization, of flower painting, 49

Flor de manita (1925), 72

flower painting, 48–50

folk, as qualifier, 115

folk culture: birthing practices, 128–29; "pristine" Indian, 120

folklore, study of, 115

folk stories, 123–24

Foucault, Michel, 7

frame: awareness of viewer, 25; defying, 125; discourse of, 50; discursive, in Roses, 56; of flower painting, 50; lack represented, 56; notion of, 23; Open Doors, 24; photograph as pure, 125; transgressed frames within frames, 50; *Workers Parade* (1926), 105–6

framing: discourses, containment in, 47; framing/taming, 48; psychic anxieties, 54; scandal and danger, 58; sexual difference, 48; *The Tiger's Coat*, 12–13; *Workers Parade*, 122–25

France, xviii, 153n22

French influences, 14

Freud, Sigmund, 126–27, 131

Gamio, Manuel, 112–13, 115–16, 152n8

gaze: aggressive look of, 55; *An Aztec Mother*, 134; control by (male) revolutionary action, 20; exemplary female, 4, 10; female, with curiosity and agency, 26, 139; female, qualities transcending, 26–27; female, status of, 21, 139; haptic, 70–71, 72, 81; matrixial, 125–38; metramorphic consciousness, 135, 137; Mexican Folkways, 137–38; Modotti as object, xxiii; Modotti's, on female subjects, 109, 130; Modotti-the-actress, 2; phallic regime of sexual difference, 3; problems attendant on practice of, 10; psychic investments, 25; Weston on, 7; Weston snapshot, 60; women as passive objects, xx, xxii

gender: at Sotheby sale, 33–34; body politic, 94–96; selling images, 34; space and, 21–22

gender and marginality theme, 44, 58; over-emphasis, 97; Paz rejecting, 64; *Workers Parade*, 93, 96

genitalia, female, 54, 56

genitals, body politic, 94

geometral perspective, 50–51

Germany, xvi–xvii

Gómez Robelo, Ricardo, xii

González Casanova, Pablo, 122–24

Guerrero, Xavier, xiv–xv

gyno-images, 33, 56

hands: Modotti photographs, 69–73; Morelli method, 68–70; as motif, 72; painterly tradition, 149n23

Hands Holding Tool, notion of signature, 61

Hands Resting on Tool: 70, fig., 71, 73, 76–77; challenge to signature notion, 77

mestizos, 14–15; backwardness and poverty, 114; body politic, 118, 120; Gamio on, 115–16; identity as rejection and incorporation, 120–21; as liminal figures, 119; Mexican Revolution, 102; national identity, 110

metramorphosis, 132, 135–36

mexicandidad, 102, 151n26

Mexican Folkways, 111–17; anthropological photography, 123; audience, 152n7; functions, 122, 137; gaze, 137–38; as material context, xxiv; maternal subject matter, 126; Modotti's photographic exposure, 108; state policy, 112–13

Mexican hats. see sombrero

Mexicanization, 16, 35, 143n28

Mexican Revolution: aestheticization, 103; background, 13–14; Casasola photographic archive, 102; charro-style sombrero, 101; effects, 92–93; indigenismo, 110; indigenous peoples, 113–14; photojournalism, 98–99

Mexico: arrival in, xii; art affinity, 117; body as Mexican object, 35–36; California as gateway, 39; Madonna's interest in feisty women, 38; Modotti-Mexico nexus, xxii; return from Europe, xviii

Mexico City, 13–17

middlebrow culture, 74, 77

Modotti, Assunta Adelaide Liugia (Tina): article by, xv, 73, 142n8; attribution of photographs, 61–62; beauty, 1–2; biographical entries, 28; biography, xi–xviii ; deportation from Mexico, xvi, 89–90; feminist aesthetics, 91; Madonna's admiration, 37, 145n20; Mexican Folkways, 117; as model and muse, 4, 35; Paz on, 40–41; on photography, xv, 73; on politics, xii; politics and men, 40; return from Europe, xviii; Rivera on, xiii–xiv; two peri-

ods of photography, 90–91, 145n7, 150n6

Monsiváis, Carlos, 102–3, 106

Morelli, Giovanni, 58–70

Morelli method, 68–70

Mother and Child, Tehuantepec (ca. 1929), 134; fig., 136

motion picture standard, 2

movie career, xii, 2

muralism, 16; indigenismo expressed, 116–17; Modotti as photographer, 18; Rivera's use of space, 20–21; viewing as intensely bodily experience, 22

mural painting, frame, 23

Museo Nacional, xvi, 41–42

name, failure to, 9–10

national identity, 110, 119, 153n22

nation-state, 119

negative, 72

negative aesthetics, 11–12, 19, 107

Nicaragua, 100

nuance, concept of, 88

nudes of Modotti, xiv, 35–36, 52, 53

objectification, 35–36, 51

obra [oeuvre], 65, 66

obscenity concept, 52

occluded matrixial experience, 135

oeuvre: aura of work of art, 66; meaning, 65, 66

Open Doors (ca. 1925): fig., 19; space body frame, 20–26

oral tradition, 124

original, photography, invention of, 66

originality, multiplicity vis-à-vis, 73

originality theme: avant-garde as site of struggle, 60, 64–65; introduced, 59

Orozco, José Clemente, 16, 112

other: exotic, 29; national identity, 119; nonaggressive relationship, 132; *Workers Parade*, 123

otherness, Rivera, 39

packaging of Modotti, x, xx, 1–2
painting: hands, 149n23; history of
    flower, 48–50; photography's trou-
    bled relationship, 66
Palacio Nacional, 16, 17
Palm Trunk, Cuernavaca, 33
Pandora myth, 24
parallelism, 94
Park Redfield, Margaret, 127–29
Partido Comunista Mexicano, xiv, 41
patriarchal culture, 125
Paz, Octavio, 40–41, 64–65, 66,
    67–68, 76, 85
Personal Narratives Group, xviii–xix
phallocentric, 125; paradigm, 126,
    127; visual economy, 25–26
photographic meaning, Barthes essays,
    45
photographs, systems for titles,
    141n28
photograph-within-the-photograph,
    82
photography: as academic study, xx;
    arriviste mentality, 66; considera-
    tions, xx–xxi; culture legitimacy,
    74–75, 76; as liminal culture activity,
    75; as "mad" or "tame," 48; as mes-
    sage with a code, xxi; name, failure
    to, 9–10; photograph as pure frame,
    125; politics of, 78, 80; repro-
    ducibility, 72; seriality, 72; social
    value of, xv–xvi; status as art, 61
photography theory, relationship to
    reality, 12–13
point of view, 25
political photography, 89–91
political themes, in Modotti's photog-
    raphy, 31
politics: Communist, 78; of photogra-
    phy, 78, 80
politics of context, 77–86
Porfiriato, 13–14, 15
pornography, 30–31, 32
positive aesthetics, 12
power, framing *Workers Parade* (1926),
    105–6

power and authority, xx
prenatal experience, 130–32
productivity of the image, x
psychic anxieties, 54–55
psychoanalytic models, 119, 127
Puig Casauranc, J.M., 112, 113
punctum, 46–47, 55–56
purchase on the real, 45, 122–23, 135

race: Mexican cultural politics, 101–2;
    national identity, 110–11; sombrero
    symbolism, xxiv; visual representa-
    tion, 117; *Workers Parade*, 121
racial difference: sombrero, 97, 99;
    Zapata, 101
radical chic, 29, 35, 42, 57; feminism,
    38; monetary value, 44
radical politics: signature and, 33; xii,
    xiv, xvi
reading: Modotti's photographic
    images, xx; the photographic image,
    82, 83–84; as re-wrapping, ix
reality: xxi; "intractable," of *Roses*, 30;
    photography theory and, 12–13,
    135
reciprocity, tropes of, 81
reportage tradition, 67
representation, photographic: xx–xxi;
    Barthes on, 45
representation of the body,
    Whitechapel exhibition, 7
Richey, Roubaix de l'Abrie ("Robo"),
    xi–xii, xiv, 52, 54
Rivaud Valdés, Jean, 41
Rivera, Diego: celebrity endorsements,
    39; essence of Modotti's work,
    38–39; Mexican Folkways, 112,
    117; Modotti on his expulsion, 41;
    Modotti's hands sketched, 149n23;
    muralist leader, 16; otherness, 39;
    radical ideas, 40; use of space,
    21–22; xiii–xiv
Roses (1924): artist-celebrity validation
    code, 37–38; auction prices, 28;
    commodity value, 35; culture sig-
    nificance of rose, 51–52; discursive

frames, 56; fig., 34; intractable reality, 30; investment in iconic body,
42; roses, as memento mori, 51, 52;
as scandalous, 57; viewer's positionality, 51
Ruíz, María del Carmen (pseud.), xviii
rural images, 17
rural/urban dynamic, 17, 18
Rushdie, Salman, 100

Sacco, Nicolas, 140n9
Sáenz, Moisés, 112, 113
Sandino, Augusto César, 100
scandalous nature of images, 57, 58
seepage, 55, 56
self-referentiality, 81
semiology, 45
seriality, of photographs, 72–73
sexual difference: framing, 48; male as
locus of active gaze and woman as
spectacle, 25; sombrero, 94;
Whitechapel exhibition, 6–7
signatural style, issue of, 61, 87
signature: auterist boundaries, 73;
authority overturned, 66; connoisseurship, 68; dubious status, 84;
erasure of, 42–43
signature, Modotti's: McCarthyism,
32; as radical chic, 35; symbolic
associations, 33; Tomkins's investment in, 36
signature: Octavio Paz, 65; original
versus copy, 59–60; on *Roses*, 29;
theme introduced, xxiii–xxiv; three
signatures of *Mella's Typewriter*,
85–86; Weston on, 61; Weston's
snapshot, 60
Siqueiros, David Alfaro: Mexican
Folkways, 112; Modotti lecture, xv;
muralist leader, 16
skull image, 54
Snapshot (Weston, 1924), 59–61, fig.,
60, 75
social class, 76; Mexican Revolution,
110

sombrero, 87, 93–95; *La calle de
Plateros*, 103–5; Casasola archive,
99; charro, 101; cultural significance, xxiv; as culture icon, 99;
indigenous body, 118; as Latin
American symbol, 99; as Mexican
symbol, 99; as Nicaraguan symbol,
100; racial difference, 97, 99;
site/sight, 89; as stereotype, 106,
151n26; as symbol, 93; Emiliano
Zapata, 101
Sotheby's sale of *Roses*, xxiii, 144n1
space: clearing space, 26; feminine and
active look, 25; Mexico as mythical
and exotic, 39
space-body relationship, 17, 21; Open
Doors, 20–26
spaces: official, 24; public, 24
Spain, xviii
spatiality, *The Tiger's Coat*, 12–13
Sphere of the Arbitrary, 47, 75
Sphere of Legitimacy, 74, 75, 76
Sphere of the Legitimizable, 74
stereotypes, 106–7, 151n26
still-life painting, 49
studium, 46, 55
subjectivity, as process of coemergence, 131
subjectivization process, 130–31
subject-object relationship, 25
suffering, images of, 103

tactility: *Mella's Typewriter*, 80; mother-
child photography, 132, 134; notion
of, 70–72
taming, fashion industry, 57
taming photographs, 30; Barthes on,
47–48
technological changes in photography,
67
Temptation (1920), 52, fig., 53, 54–55
text, intertextuality, 83–84
texts, 84
texture, 72; *Mella's Typewriter*, 80;
mother-child photography, 132,
134–35